Business Coaching

Wisdom and Practice

Business Coaching

Wisdom and Practice

Unlocking the Secrets of Business Coaching

Second Edition

by

Sunny Stout-Rostron

with contributing author

Marti Janse van Rensburg

kr publishing

2012

First published in 2009
Second updated print in 2012

ISBN: 978-1-86922-191-1

Published by Knowres Publishing (Pty) Ltd
P O Box 3954
Randburg
2125
Republic of South Africa

Tel: (011) 706-6009
Fax: (011) 706-1127
E-mail: orders@knowres.co.za
Website: www.kr.co.za

Project management: Cia Joubert, cia@knowres.co.za
Typesetting, layout and design: Cia Joubert, cia@knowres.co.za
Cover design: Carike Meiring, webmaster@scribbleandsplot.co.za
Editing and proofreading: Nick Wilkins

Endorsements

"The world of business coaching can rejoice – the book we have been wanting and needing is here. This book harnesses the vast and complex world of excellence in coaching and offers it to us digestibly, delectably and with impressively accessible scholarship. I want every coach and soon-to-be coach to read this book. The inner world of coaching, cogently, warmly, thoroughly presented is a *tour de force* and a gift to us all. There are many kinds of bibles in the world - this will be one of them."

– Nancy Kline, President of Time To Think, Inc., and author of *Time To Think: Listening To Ignite The Human Mind* and *More Time To Think: A Way Of Being In The World*.

"Finally a coaching 'Whole Earth Catalogue' in the form of a user-friendly book has emerged that addresses the needs of practising coaches *vs.* someone's theory about coaching. What comes through loud and clear is that Stout-Rostron and Janse van Rensburg are the voice of the coach - they are in the marketplace and they have tested what works and what does not.

This is a masterful work that enables anyone who wishes to coach, whether they are a peer coach or an executive, to find guidelines as well as skills, tools, attitudes and behaviours that become developmental building blocks in any good coaching process. This is a must-read, essential for anyone wishing to help others in any corporate, educational or group setting. Very inspiring to read."

– Mark R. Rittenberg EDd., Guest Professor, Executive Education Division, Kellogg School of Management, Northwestern University in Illinois, and President of Corporate Scenes, Inc., in California.

"You simply must read this book if you are serious about being a top-notch business coach. It is an excellent guide to best practices based on clear theory, experience and business wisdom."

– Carol Kauffman PhD ABPP PCC, co-founder and Director of the Coaching and Positive Psychology Initiative at Harvard Medical School, and Co-Editor-in-Chief of *Coaching: An International Journal of Theory Research and Practice*.

"This is an extraordinarily thorough book. It covers a great range of practical guidance on matters that will concern the new coach, and it also addresses the current issues for those concerned with coaching worldwide, including the deliberations of the Global Convention on Coaching. It is clearly written and very widely referenced. It addresses a wide range of approaches to coaching while remaining firmly embedded in an experiential learning tradition."

– David Megginson, Professor of Human Resource Development, Sheffield Hallam University, UK.

"A book that will further advance your appreciation for and understanding of the powerful intervention known as business coaching."

– Wendy Johnson, President and CEO, Worldwide Association of Business Coaches (WABC)

"A magnificent book. Not only does it cover all the aspects, ideas, theories, considerations, dilemmas of the prospective coach and the field of coaching, but I believe it will become the quintessential guide to anyone who wants to know anything quickly about coaching and will become the handbook to reference for scholars and business people alike."

I also believe that this work will become the cornerstone reference guide for other works that may expand on aspects of the book. It is equally applicable to the HR manager requiring a deeper understanding of what coaching is and how to contemplate coaching in their business, as it is to the prospective coach as a guidebook examining the nuances of coaching. I believe it answers the questions 'what is coaching, who can be a coach and what does it take to become one?' – simply put, it professionalises the field."

– Shani Naidoo, HR Director, Foschini Group

"To stay abreast, I tend to read every book on coaching I can lay my hands on – this one is by far the best: comprehensive, practical and clearly filled with years of experience and insights shared. I felt that the book makes deep connections with the reader. I felt as if I was in the presence of my coach, being supported and learning from the best and being inspired to rise to greater levels. The book supports business leaders and the 'lay-coach' needing to know more about coaching and coaching styles. It also captures the pure joy of being a coach! This book is so great, it doesn't need to be just 'in South Africa'."

– Jenny Hoggarth, Business Coach, Purple Pineapple Consulting

Table of Contents

List of tables

List of figures

Preface

This book aims to provide an overview of a wide spectrum of coaching theory and practice. It is structured as a practical, easy-to-access guide to the most important aspects of business coaching. This is not the publication of my own personal executive coaching model, but aspires to offer practitioners a general handbook or encyclopaedia of the very best theoretical models, current practice and thinking in business coaching.

Coaching is a new, dynamic and emerging profession, and this book was written to fill a gap in the South African marketplace. Marti and I have tried to accommodate all learning styles in the book, and we want you to dip in and find the chapters most relevant to you.

The aim has been to offer a wide perspective of differing approaches and models that practitioners would find immediately useable and applicable to their business coaching practice.

Designed to provide a professional, clear and accessible overview of business coaching practice in South Africa, the book is also linked with the foundation-stones of business coaching internationally.

This book is dedicated to all coach practitioners in the hope that this helps take our emerging profession forward to a new and exciting chapter.

Sunny Stout-Rostron

Foreword by Nick Binedell

Most of what we learn about our work as leaders we learn by doing. We learn from the sweet taste of success and from its bitter sister, failure. We learn from the daily grind, the sheer hard work, from the moments of inspiration and the particular insights and moments of truth that a fast-changing world provides us.

This hard-earned knowledge comes from years of constant effort and practice, and finally and hopefully, becomes a body of knowledge resident in our heads and hands, that we put to daily use and to good effect. We also learn from observing others. We observe and learn from our colleagues, from those who lead us and those who follow – and of course, we learn by watching our competitors, our suppliers, our customers, and those whom we have euphemistically come to call our stakeholders.

The power of coaching, the primary aim of which is to facilitate the development of the client's own wisdom and competence through a process of experiential learning, has become a very important part of a curriculum aimed at improving our personal and organisational performance.

This book integrates and develops a broad discourse about the "why", the "what" and the "how" of coaching in a way that makes the coaching process accessible to the spectrum of all those involved in this new and developing profession: from the master practitioner to those just starting out who wish to be abreast of the very latest and most up-to-date coaching theory and practice.

Both authors are experienced and well-known business coaches. With this book, they have found another way to coach, this time through the written word.

Nick Binedell

Nick Binedell is the founding director and Sasol Chair of Strategic Management at the Gordon Institute of Business Science of the University of Pretoria. Nick has spent the past 20 years focusing on business education. His academic qualifications include a PhD from the University of Washington in Seattle, an MBA from the University of Cape Town, and a Bachelor of Commerce degree from Rhodes University. His area of expertise is business strategy formulation, and his academic and consulting work, although predominantly in South Africa, includes work in the USA, Europe and Australia.

The Gordon Institute of Business Science has established itself as a leading business school in South Africa with a strong focus on partnering with corporates and providing a high level of local and international business education. It was recently ranked by the London Financial Times *as one of the top 40 global executive education providers.*

About the Authors

SUNNY STOUT-ROSTRON, DPROF, MA

Sunny coaches at senior executive and board level, and has a wide range of experience in leadership development and business strategy. With over 20 years' international experience as an executive coach, Sunny believes there is a strong link between emotional intelligence and business results – she works with executive leaders and their teams to help them achieve individual, team and organisational goals.

Director of Sunny Stout-Rostron Associates, she is a Research Mentor for the Institute of Coaching at Harvard/McLean Medical School, and a non-executive director with Resolve Encounter Consulting in Johannesburg. As Founding President of the professional association Coaches and Mentors of South Africa (COMENSA), Sunny is passionate about the development of leaders and leadership coaches in South Africa. She completed her Doctoral research into Executive Coaching with Middlesex University London, and is currently involved in developing international standards for business coaches with the Worldwide Association of Business Coaches (WABC). She frequently speaks at conferences in the USA, UK, South Africa and Australia, and is a founding faculty member of the Thinking Environment® (developed by Nancy Kline) in South Africa.

Sunny manages an executive coaching practice, while continuing to develop new leadership and executive coaching programmes within the corporate, legal and education sectors worldwide. She has played a leading role in building the emerging profession of coaching, and her passion is to develop the knowledge base for coaching through research and the critical reflective practice of dedicated coach practitioners.

As an author, Sunny's books include: *Business Coaching International: Transforming Individuals and Organizations* (Karnac, 2009); *Business Coaching Wisdom and Practice: Unlocking the Secrets of Business Coaching* (Knowres, 2009); *Accelerating Performance: Powerful New Techniques to Develop People* (Kogan Page, 2002), and *Managing Training* (Kogan Page, 1993). She is a contributing author to Passmore, J. *et al.*, *The Wiley-Blackwell Handbook of the Psychology of Coaching and Mentoring* (Wiley-Blackwell, 2011); *Positive Psychology as Social Change* (Springer, 2010); *Sharing the Passion: Conversations with Coaches* (Advanced Human Technologies, 2006); *The Sage Handbook of Coaching* (Sage, 2009); and *Trends in Developing Human Capital* (Knowres, 2010).

MARTI JANSE VAN RENSBURG, MBA (Contributing author)

Marti Janse van Rensburg has an extensive and varied business background that she brings to her successful coaching practice. This broad experience, ranging from scientific research to corporate management, gives her invaluable, hands-on knowledge and insights, both of which provide a critical key to understanding clients and coaching in the corporate world.

Marti's clients range from Woolworths, Johnnic Publishing, Standard Bank, Eskom, Sasol, Discovery, Liberty, IS, McKinsey & Company, AngloGold Ashanti, to the US Centre for Leadership and Public Values (a joint venture with the University of Cape Town and Duke University). Marti coached and facilitated the ALDP (Accelerated Leadership Programme) at Sasol through the Gordon Institute of Business Science (GIBS).

In addition to one-on-one coaching, Marti facilitates team coaching and leadership development for clients such as the Eskom CEO Programme. She designed a countrywide training programme for Standard Bank managers on how to give and receive feedback. She also designed a Performance Coaching programme for Standard Bank in conjunction with their Leadership Development Team, and started their Leader-as-Coach Programme at the Global Leadership Centre (GLC).

In 2003, Marti was involved in the ground-breaking Action Reflection Learning (ARL) programme at the MIL Institute in Sweden. Marti was a founding director of the professional association Coaches and Mentors of South Africa (COMENSA), and is a member of the WABC (Worldwide Association of Business Coaches). She took part in the Global Convention on Coaching (GCC) Working Group on a Research Agenda for Development of the Field, 2007–8.

In her previous career, Marti was a researcher at the CSIR before moving into the high fashion industry where she worked as a designer and owner of a training facility for designers. She taught and consulted for 10 years in fashion retail, which gave her business experience in Asia. Marti has a degree in Chemical Engineering from the University of Pretoria, and an MBA from the Gordon Institute of Business Science (GIBS) with a focus on executive coaching. Her coaching and leadership development career over the past 10 years has introduced her to a range of international coaches, consultants and clients in Africa, the UK, Europe and the USA.

Authors' Acknowledgements

The purpose of this book is to share our research, teaching and practice in order to contribute to the growing expertise and developing knowledge about our emerging profession of coaching. In the preparation of this book, we owe a large debt of gratitude to Nick Wilkins, for his astute advice on editing issues.

From Sunny: appreciation is extended to our earliest readers, in particular to Helena Dolny, Director of the GLC Coaching and Mentoring Unit at Standard Bank, Paddy Pampallis Paisley, Head of Faculty at The Integral Coaching Centre, Cape Town, and Creina Schneier who is a lecturer and facilitator at The Integral Coaching Centre.

From Marti: a special thank you to Kerry and Caroline, for their help and professional guidance, and to Kitty, my sister, who helpfully critiqued and cajoled – as always – both as a sister and from her knowledge of psychology. Further, I relish and appreciate the opportunity to be part of the creation of this book.

We would both like to record our special appreciation to Nick Binedell, head of the Gordon Institute of Business Science (GIBS). He took time out of a hectic schedule to read our early drafts and, in his Foreword, we reap the rich benefit of Nick's characteristically shrewd and elegant analysis.

Sunny thanks Marti for her collaborative work in designing the concept and framework for the book, and for her two important contributing chapters: "Chapter 6: Diversity, personality and culture", and "Chapter 7: Competences in business coaching".

The core concept underpinning this book is experiential learning. We constantly returned to how we work with clients: reflecting, observing and sharing – knowing that, as a result, our coaching practice and teaching will be the stronger for it. We hope yours will be enriched too.

1

About This Book

WHAT'S DIFFERENT ABOUT THIS BOOK?

Everything! This book is about the essential "practice" and "practices" of a business coach. The authors speak from their experience, with practical examples, analysing the complexities of the **coaching conversation** – the basic tool of the business and executive coach. They believe that business coaching can make a huge contribution to leadership competence inside organisations and, in this book, comprehensively integrate their practical experience as business coaches with their own research and teaching.

Business Coaching Wisdom and Practice takes an in-depth, dynamic and integrative look at the coaching process, question frameworks, how to use current coaching models, and examines key coach/client concerns such as ethics, contracting, supervision and the "relationship" between coach and client. The book also focuses on the hub of the coaching conversation – learning from experience. The authors believe this is crucial for individual and organisational transformation.

This book also explores:
- the diversity of the South African marketplace and how the business coach needs to adapt accordingly;
- how to handle existential issues that affect meaning and purpose for the over-stretched executive;

- where emotional intelligence fits into the matrix of core competences for the business coach; and
- the core theoretical underpinnings of business coaching that will transform your business coaching practice.

Although there are many excellent studies available about coaching, this book is specifically targeted to the diverse and multifaceted South African marketplace. Whereas the majority of publications look at coaching as a recipe, ours takes a deeper look at what it takes to become an effective business or executive coach.

Business Coaching Wisdom and Practice investigates the significance, meaning and structure of the coaching intervention within the coach-client conversation, and takes a look at what, how and who you need to be to coach. At the heart of the business coaching process, irrespective of the model or approach, is "the relationship". This means that business coaching is not necessarily about "doing" for the client, but more about "being" – creating a safe thinking environment: a space where thinking, feeling, insight and creative decision-making can take place. Applying the knowledge and techniques within this book will deepen your practice.

Some of the tools and processes explored in this book will help you to coach your executive clients in:

1. Business issues such as leading a team, thinking strategically, managing people, processes and tasks, maintaining relationships, promoting, networking, succession planning and continuing professional development.
2. Emotional intelligence (EQ) issues such as developing self-awareness, managing oneself in the workplace, becoming aware of relationships, values and culture at work, and managing relationships in a complex and diverse environment.
3. Relationship issues, which dominate if executives do not lead a healthy lifestyle, thus diminishing their effectiveness at work. The anxiety of not coping, either at home or in the office, impacts on the other half of their life.
4. Body, mind and stress issues such as maintaining health and fitness, a balanced diet and getting enough sleep.

Each chapter is designed to be a world unto itself. What we suggest to make it fun, useful and intriguing for yourself is to read the first chapter, then read those chapters most relevant to you right now. Immediately you can begin to apply new thinking that will help build the rigour of your own business coaching practice – whether you oversee a stable of business coaches or run your own individual practice.

Both authors coach and consult internationally, and although we have written this book specifically for South African coaches and coaching consultants, the tools, techniques, case studies and applications are relevant to any business coach anywhere. We share with you from our personal experiences as executive coaches – both of us having worked in organisations for nearly 30 years, much of that time engaged in coaching senior managers and executives at the highest level. We also share our various learning and research findings from coaching inside organisations in South Africa, the UK, Europe and the USA. Both of us have been involved in the Working Group on a Research Agenda for Development of the Field of the Global Convention on Coaching (GCC), looking at the development of the coaching profession worldwide. In this book, we explore several international developments that may have an impact on the supervision and regulation of coaching in South Africa.

WHERE DOES COACHING FIT INTO THE BUSINESS?

Whether you are an external coaching consultant, head of Human Resources (HR) or Organisational Development (OD) within your organisation, it is important that coaching is aligned to both the business and the talent strategies. Within most organisations there tends to be a unique combination of **internal coach** programmes combined with training to develop the "manager as coach", or the "leader as coach", as well as group coaching programmes for "team coaching" – in addition to some kind of programme to recruit and bring in **external coaches** for senior executives. There is some confusion between "team coaching" and "group facilitation". It is imperative for anyone coaching teams or groups to be skilled not just in facilitating group-learning processes, but also in teaching coaching skills and competences.

What we recommend is that both internal and external coaching programmes are in alignment with each other, and with the organisation's business and talent development strategies. It is crucial to be able to measure the efficacy of internal and external coaching programmes, and we would encourage some qualitative or quantitative measurement of all coaching that takes place in the organisation. One of the ways to measure success is to have feedback sessions with the coaches two or three times a year, with the coaches giving feedback on what is working and not working within the system, and on that which impedes or supports the coaching and/or mentoring processes. Secondly, ensure that there is a process in place to adequately supervise internal and external coaches, and build a systemic coaching programme that is fully integrated with the company's talent management systems and processes to create a feedback loop to senior management and line managers as well as internal and external coaches.

Also crucial is some kind of qualitative and quantitative measurement of the coaching process, identifying the return on investment (ROI) for the organisation. We recommend clearly specifying the aims and objectives of the coaching process, both internal and external. This requires the development of criteria for external coaches that you recruit, as well as building a bespoke training programme for internal coaches to cover the basics: the coaching process, an understanding of coaching models and question frameworks, the theoretical and psychological underpinnings of coaching, as well as the competences required for the coach.

These competences range from attention, active and deep listening, intervention skills such as questions, reframing and giving feedback and experiential learning techniques, to an understanding of ethics and confidentiality as well as psychological processes. Equally important are the ability to understand management and/or personality profiles, an understanding of and ability to work with diversity and cultural competence, and the requirements of continuing professional development.

WHO SHOULD READ THIS BOOK?

If you are a business coach working within a business, entrepreneurial, organisational or corporate environment, then this book is for you. If you are a practising business coach hired externally into organisations, an internal organisational coach working with junior, senior and executive managers, a managerial leader who uses coaching to develop your team, an HR manager/director setting up an internal coaching programme, or if you are facilitating coach-training programmes within an organisation – then this book is definitely for you.

No manager or executive leaves their personal life behind when they walk into work. It is simply another role or function that frames who they are. So it follows that business coaching cannot be effective without looking at clients holistically. Even if business coaches primarily help clients to identify their core purpose, strategies, developmental objectives, strengths, weaknesses and obstacles to be overcome, business coaching also takes in all aspects of an executive's life, from the meaning and purpose of the work that they are doing, to managing people, processes and systems, as well as creating a balance between work and personal life.

This book is for you if you are:

- a master business or executive coach with an existing successful practice wishing to deepen your competence, knowledge and skills because you believe in your own continuous improvement;

- a practising business or executive coach with varying levels of expertise;
- a business coach new to the field keen to develop your expertise;
- a business coach who wishes to expand and improve your skills and competence in the coaching process with a deeper understanding of the coaching conversation and its impact in the workplace;
- a coach who wants to understand the coaching process within the coaching conversation more fully, as well as the entire coaching intervention over a period of time;
- an HR professional responsible for setting up the coaching interventions within the organisation, and often find yourself in a coaching role;
- a senior managerial leader who wants to understand the principles of business coaching because you are experiencing coaching or considering it as a profession;
- a senior leader who needs to understand the role of the business coach because you are responsible for leading, managing and coaching your team or organisation;
- an experienced external and/or internal business coach actively engaged in business coaching;
- a coach actively engaged in business coaching-related matters, for example, one-on-one coach training or leadership/management development programmes;
- a coach who has one or more years of business coaching and who needs an in-depth understanding of the coaching process and coaching models;
- someone at the beginning stages of coaching in business, with over five years' business and organisational experience; or
- a coach practitioner who has delivered coaching services to small, medium and large organisations, including public and private institutions.

We hope the following chapters will give you a broader perspective on your practice and the challenges that you face when coaching individuals and teams. This is a growing field built on the cumulative experience of business coaches, and we firmly believe that our most powerful learning comes from experience. As a business coach, you are helping your clients to learn from and interpret their own experiences, and to understand the complexity of the environment in which they work. We hope that our learning will make a substantial contribution to your competence and practice.

It is critical that the coaching strategy is in alignment with both the business and the talent strategies. Often the HR department is not in alignment with the Coaching and

Mentoring unit, and often neither is in alignment with Organisational Development. Only when these are all working together in an integrated way will you be able to develop a successful internal and external coaching programme and process with sustainable and measurable outcomes.

CHAPTER CONTENTS

Chapter 2: The business coaching process

In Chapter 2, we take a brief look at the origins and foundation-stones of business coaching worldwide. We examine the core theoretical and psychological underpinnings of coaching, and describe the current reality for business coaching as it is emerging in South Africa and in the international marketplace. We outline modern management theory from the 1970s to the twenty-first century, from transformational leadership to the learning organisation, managing complexity and talent development – and the way it influenced the beginnings of corporate coaching.

Business coaches encourage their clients to think for themselves and to develop an awareness of their own conscious and unconscious behaviours, which may influence performance in the workplace. Business coaching is essentially about the results experienced through the dynamic relationship between coach and client, and how those results impact on individual, team and organisational performance.

In this chapter, we address the influence of adult learning and experiential learning on the business coaching process, where coach and client probe the essence of an experience to understand its significance and the learning that can be gained from it. However, ultimately, business coaching needs to be aligned with all the leadership and management development initiatives within the organisation.

Chapter 3: The coaching conversation

This chapter explores the purpose and focus of the conversation and the competences useful to the business coach. The "coaching conversation" is the face-to-face or telephone interaction between coach and client. It is a "thinking partnership" (Kline, 1999/2004) where coach and client reflect on the client's experience, transforming it into potential for learning and action. How the client takes responsibility for change can emerge from the coaching conversation.

The focus of a coaching conversation is to help the client work towards achieving their desired outcomes. The coach primarily explores with each client what it is that is holding back or stopping the client from achieving their goals. One example would be to identify and replace disempowering assumptions and paradigms with empowering ones.

Chapter 4: Working with question frameworks

This chapter explores the range of coaching question frameworks available in the marketplace, e.g. those of John Whitmore, Nancy Kline and Jinny Ditzler. We describe how to use two-, three-, four-, five-, six-, eight- and ten-stage frameworks, including neuro-linguistic programming (NLP) and the Kline Thinking Environment® processes, with examples for understanding. This chapter is designed to have you look specifically at how you can develop your own questioning process.

One of the most difficult paradigms for a coach to understand, as opposed to being a teacher or a therapist, is to not provide answers or solve the client's problems for them. The greatest gift you can offer is to help the client "consider ideas, approaches, strategies, behaviours, and other approaches and actions" not previously considered (Ting and Scisco, 2006:51). Although technically coaches do not offer advice, clients sometimes ask for an opinion, information or advice; it is important that the coach give the required support or guidance without telling the client what to do.

Chapter 5: Understanding and exploring coaching models

Today coaches are trained in an eclectic range of coaching models. This chapter explores a cross-section of coaching models, which influence the work of business and executive coaches worldwide.

Models help us to develop flexibility as coach practitioners. They offer structure and an outline for both the coaching conversation and the overall coaching journey. However, although models create a system within which coach and client work, it is essential that they are not experienced as prescriptive or rigid.

Coaching models help us to understand the coaching intervention from a systems perspective, and the "structure" of the interaction between coach and client. This chapter takes a practical look at how coaching models are constructed, and how they can help you to flexibly structure the overall coaching journey as well as the individual coaching conversation with your business client.

Chapter 6: Diversity, personality and culture

The importance of acknowledging diversity is increasingly recognised in our globalised world. Yet in South Africa many coach practitioners continue to find they still work in a very "white" world. Here Sunny Stout-Rostron introduces the subject of diversity and power relations, looking at how assumptions limit individuals and groups – while Marti Janse van Rensburg comprehensively explores race, cultural and gender issues, personality traits, learning and thinking styles.

Power relations not only have deep roots in our cultural matrix – our shared ways of doing things, of making sense of the world – but can often also inform our personal views, choices, and actions. Any form of power exacerbates difference, and influences how we perceive and react to behaviour. This is true in any area of life, and nowhere more so than in the business context, specifically due to the hierarchical nature of organisational systems.

In the business environment, the coach needs to become aware of, and to manage, their own responses to questions of diversity, before they can begin to coach a client on similar issues. This chapter focuses on raising the business coach's awareness of these crucial diversity issues both within themselves and within their individual and organisational clients.

Chapter 7: Competences in business coaching

This chapter reviews the required skills and competences defined for general coach practitioners and business coaches by professional bodies, including the International Coach Federation (ICF), the Worldwide Association of Business Coaches (WABC), the European Mentoring and Coaching Council (EMCC), and Coaches and Mentors of South Africa (COMENSA).

These national and international bodies represent a valuable spectrum of international standards and requirements for business coaches today. There is considerable consistency amongst the professional bodies with respect to the skills and competences required for a coach. We recommend specific core competences to build your capacity as a business coach.

Chapter 8: Existential and experiential learning issues

Existential philosophy regards human existence as unexplainable, and stresses freedom of choice and taking responsibility for one's acts. Within the business coaching context, the coach helps the client to articulate existential concerns such as freedom, purpose, choice and anxiety, and to identify and replace limiting paradigms with empowering paradigms, thus leading to positive change.

These existential issues are relevant to the coach too. For example, if you look at purpose – the coach might be tempted to confuse their own individual purpose with that of the client, and in the process be seduced to use their position or power to influence the client. In existential terms, the meaning of individual experience is not a given; it is subject to interpretation. In this chapter, we explore existential and experiential learning issues that confront the coach and client at every stage during their coaching conversation.

Chapter 9: Supervision, contracting and ethical concerns

Coaching supervision is in its infancy, worldwide – and is influenced by the role supervision plays for psychologists, who are required to be in supervision throughout their training and years of practice. This chapter examines how supervision is defined and practised worldwide. COMENSA (2010:1), for example, defines the importance of supervision as follows: "Accountability, effectiveness and professionalism are core values for coaches and mentors. Supervision serves to help the coach/mentor manage high levels of complexity, have a mechanism for ensuring accountability and ethical practice and maintain continued professional development."

This chapter explores how you should go about being supervised and/or playing the role of supervisor. We look at the role ethics plays in business coaching, and detail ethical codes that have been developed in recent years through professional bodies such as the WABC, EMCC, ICF and COMENSA. Ethical dilemmas are as important as the professional codes themselves, and the authors explore some of the potential dilemmas that can arise during a coaching intervention. A third corporate governance issue for business coaches is the standard contract they draw up for the client. This chapter makes recommendations for key aspects to incorporate into a coaching contract.

Chapter 10: Building a body of knowledge – coaching research

One of the emerging disciplines in coaching is research. Another way to describe it is to see it as an ongoing "critical appraisal" of your own coaching practice. In this chapter, we discuss current global thinking in terms of coaching research, stressing the importance of writing up your findings as you work within the business environment. This requires more than just being coached yourself and participation in supervision.

In this chapter, we have sought to broaden the definition of research, and have identified possible contributing roles for coach practitioners, academic researchers and coaching psychologists. We believe that collaboration provides a dynamic and realistic way forward, meeting the needs of all coaching stakeholders in order to cultivate the sustainability of practice through a growing body of knowledge.

Chapter 11: Integration and synthesis

How can you move to the next level in your practice? If we talk about "adult stages of development", coaching as an emerging profession is currently journeying from adolescence into its adult phase. A danger is that it becomes a fashion to call oneself a coach, or to be a coach in training. In other words, rather than a respected profession, coaching becomes a passing bandwagon.

The authors see coaching today in terms of its life curve, both in South Africa and globally, more in adolescence than in maturity, with "hormones racing up and down". Right now, coaching needs direction and the continual building of a knowledge base in order to begin to define its move towards professional practice.

COACH'S LIBRARY

The Coach's Library at the end of each chapter is an abbreviated list of useful resources to include in your library for that topic. A full bibliography is listed at the end of the book.

Coaches and Mentors of South Africa (COMENSA). (2010). *Coach/Mentor Supervision Policy*. Available at: www.comensa.org.za.

Lane, D.A. and Corrie, S. (2006). *The modern scientist-practitioner: A guide to practice in psychology*. Hove: Routledge.

Stout-Rostron, S. (2006c). *Interventions in the coaching conversation: Thinking, feeling and behaviour*. Published DProf dissertation. London: Middlesex University.

Ting, S. and Scisco, P. (2006). *The CCL handbook of coaching: A Guide for the leader coach*. San Francisco, CA: Jossey-Bass.

Worldwide Association of Business Coaches (WABC). (2008a). *Code of Business Coaching Ethics and Integrity*. Available at: www.wabccoaches.com.

2

The Business Coaching Process

In Chapter 2, we take a brief look at the origins and foundation-stones of business coaching worldwide. We examine the core theoretical and psychological underpinnings of coaching, and describe the current reality for business coaching as it is emerging in South Africa and in the international marketplace. We outline modern management theory from the 1970s to the twenty-first century, from transformational leadership to the learning organisation, managing complexity and talent development – and how it influenced the beginnings of corporate coaching.

Business coaches encourage their clients to think for themselves and to develop an awareness of their own conscious and unconscious behaviours which may impact on performance in the workplace. Business coaching is essentially about the results experienced through the dynamic relationship between coach and client, and the way such results impact on individual, team and organisational performance.

In this chapter, we address the influence of adult and experiential learning on the business coaching process, where coach and client probe the essence of an experience to understand its significance and the learning which can be gained from it. However, ultimately, business coaching needs to be aligned with all the leadership, management and talent development initiatives within the organisation.

Chapter outline

- What is business coaching?
- Coaching and mentoring
- Foundation-stones of business coaching
  - the Socratic method
  - modern management theory
  - managing complexity

- Guidelines therapy offers business coaching
  - the impact of psychological theory on business coaching
  - behaviour, goals and performance
  - motivation and goal setting
  - adult learning
  - experiential learning
- Business coaching in South Africa
- The future of business coaching worldwide
- Coach's library
- Endnotes to Chapter 2

WHAT IS BUSINESS COACHING?

Research shows that one of the fastest emerging disciplines in the field of coaching is business coaching (WABC, 2008b). Business coaches work with managers, leaders and senior executives to improve their performance. One aim is to achieve long-term results: to manage people, communication, conflict, projects and systems more effectively. Business coaches also help their clients to manage the stresses which arise from balancing work and personal life in the midst of a highly competitive and challenging work environment.

The Worldwide Association of Business Coaches (WABC, 2008b) defines business coaching as:

> Business coaching is the process of engaging in regular, structured conversation with a 'client': an individual or team who is within a business, profit or non-profit organisation, institution or government and who is the recipient of business coaching. The goal is to enhance the client's awareness and behaviour so as to achieve business objectives for both the client and their organisation.

> Business coaching enables the client to understand their role in achieving business success, and to enhance that role in ways that are measurable and sustainable. The coaching process may take different forms (e.g. individual or team coaching) and involve

different goals (e.g. problem solving, career and succession planning, leadership/executive development, creation of high-performing teams), but throughout there is a clear focus on the business objectives of both the client and the organisation.

Business coaching, as comprehensively defined by the WABC, is essentially about the results experienced through the dynamic relationship between coach and client, and how such results impact on individual, team and organisational performance. Business coaching focuses on an effective, sustainable and measurable way of developing managerial leaders and their teams. I view "managerial leadership" similarly to the way Jaques and Clement (1991:4–6) describe it in their book *Effective Leadership*; I see leadership as a process and an accountable function of management, rather than as a role in itself.

One of the reasons why business coaching has become increasingly popular is because organisations understand the importance of getting the best out of talented people. It is now widely accepted that the best way to do this is by investing in people's professional development and encouraging them to participate in decision-making processes. It follows, therefore, that a key component of business coaching is a focus on **executive** coaching – on the development of senior managers and executives to improve their individual performance, and by doing so to optimise organisational results.

A broad study by the American Management Association (AMA) underlines that most coaching is provided to high-performing middle managers and junior managers on the fast track, while executive coaching targets high potentials, problem employees, executives and ex-patriates (AMA, 2008:20).

Although our modern-day use of the term "coaching" originated from the world of professional sport, business coaching is a distinct, unique, emerging profession – differentiated from teaching, training, counselling or mentoring. Particularly in South Africa, where sport is such a passion, many executives perceive themselves to be more akin to high-performing athletes, developing competence and achieving results through professional coaching, rather than dealing with "personal problems" as in therapy or counselling.[1]

COACHING AND MENTORING

Coaching may share some ancient roots with the discipline of "mentoring". The word "mentor" is often attributed to Homer's *Odyssey* where Mentor is referred to as an advisor to Odysseus' son, Telemachus. It has been argued that the French writer, Fenelon, in his seventeenth-century *Adventures of Telemachus*, created the modern-day mentor who embodies the attributes of teacher, guide and counsellor – a definition that has entered contemporary organisational jargon.[2]

Whatever its origins, mentoring takes place in conversations with clients, as does coaching – but while the coach uses question frameworks and coaching models to help the client work out solutions to specific issues, the mentor simply acts as an adviser, directly sharing their experience, expertise, advice and wisdom with the mentee.

Not surprisingly, there is currently a great debate amongst experienced business coaches as to whether being "directive" and "giving advice" is a mentoring rather than a coaching activity, possibly encouraging the client to be too reliant on the coach.

FOUNDATION-STONES OF BUSINESS COACHING[3]

The Socratic method

The first great coach is often considered to be Socrates (469–399 BCE), who massively influenced modern thought. His greatest contribution to modern-day coaching is the Socratic method, characterised by persistent questioning and self-analysis. The philosophical statement "the unexamined life is not worth living" is attributed to Socrates, and although he encouraged individuals to think for themselves, he never called himself a teacher or published any of his thoughts. Perceived to be a threat by the established Greek governing powers of the time, Socrates was tried and found guilty of subverting the good order of Athens. In other words, he encouraged his followers to think, ask questions and to challenge the traditional "common wisdom" and assumptions of his epoch.

Today, best-practice business coaching uses a structured yet flexible question framework to help clients think for themselves without interference. Business coaches encourage their clients to think for themselves and to develop an awareness of their own conscious and unconscious behaviours which may impact on performance in the workplace. The coach thus acts more as a "thinking partner" than as a mentor, enabling the executive to operate at the top of their game and to maintain the cutting edge of business innovation.

A great thinker of our own day, Nancy Kline, in her book *Time to Think*, says that "one of the most valuable things we can offer each other is the framework in which to think for ourselves", and that "as the thinker, knowing you will not be interrupted frees you to truly think for yourself" (Kline, 1999/2004). In Chapter 4, we examine question frameworks used by business coaches today in order to tease out the issues and concerns in which their clients are struggling to take decisions.

Modern management theory

1970s – A mental approach to performance excellence

In the early 1970s, a seminal work by Timothy Gallwey (1974), *The Inner Game of Tennis*, advocated that "learning how to learn" led to a mental approach which would result in greater success than any mere perfection of technique ever could. His approach initiated a trend within organisations worldwide, developing a deeper awareness for executives: that in order to improve individual and organisational performance they first needed to access their own internal resources. This "mental" approach to performance excellence was later perfected by the neuro-linguistic, cognitive-behavioural approach to coaching which advocated "using the brain for a change" (Bandler, 1985).

1980s – Corporate coaching for transformational leadership

Building on this mental approach to managerial performance, the development of corporate leadership became big business in its own right – and the advent of corporate coaching was a logical extension of this movement. There are a variety of opinions as to when the discipline of executive coaching began its ascent. Morris and Tarpley (2000:144) suggest that it was in the late 1980s when a huge gap became increasingly evident between what managers were competently trained to do and what they were actually being asked to achieve.

At the same time, the popularity of organisational gurus such as Peter Senge and Stephen Covey encouraged the growth of the self-help and pop psychology sections of bookshops. Today many executives won't be seen dead without their copy of the latest, most fashionable manual on organisational thinking.

Covey advocated that individuals need to be the first to change if any organisational transformation was to be sustainable. His work signalled the beginning of the shift in the late 1980s towards corporate coaching. He advocated that the critical element of trust be built up within the organisation, and he insisted that leadership began with the individual executive.

1990s – The learning organisation and executive leadership

The 1990s gave birth to the management concept of the "learning organisation". This stressed that, in the face of complexity and uncertainty, individuals and organisations needed to adapt capably and continuously to changing work and social environments. The learning organisation provided a fresh perspective on how "learning" provided a key to more democratic organisational structures and flexible processes.

In other words, the capacity to learn reinforced the ability to make choices. Peter Senge's *The Fifth Discipline* (1990) emphasised systems thinking and the importance of organisational learning. According to Senge (1990:14), a learning organisation is "an organisation that is continually expanding its capacity to create its future". Senge (1990:376) also identified five critical practices within the learning organisation: personal mastery, mental models, shared vision, team learning and systems thinking.

Traditionally, the development of organisations and corporations supported business and performance development models, but ignored the importance of values to individuals and teams. This crucial lack therefore laid the foundation for the development of coaching – not just for leaders and senior executives, but for individuals at all levels in the workforce looking to enhance their personal and professional lives.

At the same time, facilitating successful corporate leadership succession became a critically important need. As a result, corporate consultants began to work in organisations with senior managers and executives, and by the late 1990s the emergence of corporate coaches contributed to the perception that "visionary leadership training" (Hudson, 1998:3) was the way forward, in alignment with executive coaching programmes.

Managing complexity

Today, in the twenty-first century, Shaw and Linnecar suggest dispensing with the "compelling" myth of the "super-executive" that has been built up since the early 1990s. They maintain that "leadership cannot be mythical because we see it in action around us every day" (Shaw and Linnecar, 2007:xiii). Perhaps one of the reasons that the myth of the super-executive continues, apart from media hype, is due to the complexity that executives have to manage daily. This complexity comprises the number and ambiguity of variables operating within the organisation, including the rate and scale of change, and the environment in which people and systems attempt to work together effectively.

Jaques and Clement (1991:xiv–xv) define the qualities that they believe managerial leaders need to acquire as being

> ... the necessary level of cognitive complexity to carry the level of task complexity; a strong sense of value for the particular managerial work, and for the leadership of others; the appropriate knowledge, and skills, plus experienced practice in both; the necessary wisdom about people and things; and the absence of abnormal temperamental or emotional characteristics that disrupt the ability to work with others.

The growing complexity of the twenty-first-century organisation puts great pressure on postgraduate business schools to develop competent, experienced coaches who are able to walk alongside managerial leaders learning to juggle enormous levels of cognitive, emotional and organisational complexity. Every business leader needs to balance the corporate mission, vision, culture, values, organisational targets, as well as guide transformational development of resources and systems, as part of the complexity of the organisational context. In addition, the business coach has a responsibility to be a thinking partner to the managerial leader, and to keep a clear vision of yet another complex system – that of client, coach and organisation, sometimes referred to as client, coach and sponsor.

Leadership and talent development

Standard Bank is an example of an organisation in South Africa, which built a Global Leadership Centre (GLC) to develop cognitive, behavioural and emotional competence for their managerial leaders. Executives were able to make their own choice of external coach from a suite, which was the outcome of a rigorous screening process. "Conducted behind closed doors, the executive coaching relationship is private. Coaching is an unregulated industry; the benefit of the screening process is greater confidence in terms of the fit between the coach and what the company is trying to achieve."

Helena Dolny, then Director of the GLC's Coaching and Mentoring Unit, said that the focus was on providing a range of coaching programmes for different purposes: performance coaching skills for all line managers, peer coaching and team coaching, as well as the flagship executive coaching programme. "The issues we constantly address are about clarifying the difference between coaching approaches and varying purpose, and secondly peoples' concerns about the sustained value of coaching and return on investment. Getting data to support measurability is a major challenge." Dolny believed that a systemic implementation of coaching and mentoring programmes is the key to developing talent and supporting transformation in the changing financial marketplace of a fledgling democracy.

GUIDELINES THERAPY OFFERS BUSINESS COACHING

In this chapter, I refer to various psychologists and psychotherapists whose practice and research has made a substantial impact on the development of coaching: Irvin Yalom, an existential psychotherapist at Stanford University, California; Dr Ernesto Spinelli, former existential professor of psychology at Regent's College London; Carl Rogers, psychologist and author of the client-focused approach; and Bruce Peltier, psychologist and executive coach based in San Francisco, and author of *The Psychology of Executive Coaching*. The core skills of the Rogerian client-centred approach – i.e. active listening, respecting clients and adopting their internal frame of reference – is in alignment with the central aim of achieving results within the coaching conversation.

Because coaching is currently a service industry and an "emerging profession", it does not yet meet the requirements for a "true profession". It is here that psychology and psychotherapy research offer much insight into the complexity of human behaviour and organisational systems for the business coach. For example, it is crucial for the business coach always to refer pathology appropriately and to keep coaching and therapy separate.

As defined by Grant and Cavanagh (2006:3), the key criteria to becoming a profession are:

- creating significant barriers to entry;
- a shared common body of knowledge;
- formal qualifications at university level;
- regulatory bodies with the power to admit, discipline and meaningfully sanction members;
- an enforceable code of ethics; and
- some form of state-sanctioned licensing or regulation.

Once a more rigorous and empirical body of academic and practitioner research is available for the business coach, we will see the emergence of professional coaches, both internal and external to the organisation. As a result of the International Coaching Research Forum (ICRF) which was sponsored by the Foundation of Coaching in September 2008 at Harvard University, a community of coaching researchers has developed a range of research proposal outlines to advance the emerging profession. The Foundation of Coaching, now the Institute of Coaching at Harvard/McLean Medical School, is backing the initiative with grants for academic and organisational grants for coaching research worldwide. In South Africa, in the meantime, it is essential that practising business coaches are encouraged to reflect the rigour of their work in reflective practice, evidence-based research or peer-reviewed journals. It is for this reason that I encourage an awareness of a scientist-practitioner model of coaching aligned to the development of a common body of "empirically tested knowledge" (Grant and Cavanagh, 2006:2).

Historically, the models of therapy have shifted over the years. The first model of the therapist-patient relationship was the "blank screen" where the therapist stayed neutral hoping the patient would project onto this "blank screen major transference distortions". The second model was the therapist as archaeologist digging through the past to understand "the original trauma" (Yalom, 2001:75). Although Freud often enquired into the personal lives of his patients, Carl Rogers in his early years advocated non-directive therapy with minimal direction to the client. He later abandoned this for a more participative, interactive style.

Harry Stack Sullivan defined psychotherapy as "a discussion of personal issues between two people, one of them more anxious than the other" (Yalom, 2001:108). Although the coach is not dealing with the neuroses of their clients, there is a great deal of anxiety that arises in the professional working life of clients that needs to be addressed. Therapy focuses on healing, and the therapist gives feedback on the client/patient relationship as it occurs; coaching focuses on learning, and the feedback is more focused on relationships the client experiences out in the workplace.

This is where the coach needs to have a great deal of awareness in order not to become part of the "client's system". Sometimes it is useful to observe what is happening between coach and client and how this mirrors blind spots or areas of difficulty for the client. This requires the coach to be able to ask questions, make candid observations – or challenge the client's perspective or view of a situation – when this would be helpful to remove limiting assumptions or lead to a more positive result. A key difference is that therapists interpret behaviour; coaches challenge and make observations about client behaviour.

Observing client behaviour

One of the senior executives with whom I work would periodically "explode" about an emotional event that had occurred between him and another at work. It took me a few months to help my client understand that this "explosive" behaviour indicated a certain lack of self-awareness on his part. The client's own behaviour, in fact, was triggering a strong emotional reaction in others. Once we began to discuss the types of reactions that were occurring and to help the client see what role he played in the interactions, he became aware of his own defensiveness.

As his self-awareness grew regarding the impact of his behaviour on others, we started to discuss how to build alliances and heal a few broken relationships in a proactive and positive way. His insight into his own behaviour produced gradual change that, over a period of a year, began to result in a more positive response towards him by subordinates and colleagues. Eventually trust and respect developed into strong support for the work he was initiating in the organisation. To this day, however, he still has to work on his own self-defensive tendencies. Nevertheless, he has developed greater self-awareness and his gradual behavioural change has given more authenticity to his transformational projects – which, in turn, are beginning to impact positively on the organisation. He continues to grow the trust that is now being placed in his abilities.

According to Peltier (2001: xxx), the positive themes to be gained from therapy and which impact the coaching intervention are insight, awareness of the goal, self-examination, intra-personal understanding, talking about things (i.e. making things explicit), rapport building, and special relationship feedback from an impartial party in a confidential relationship.

Therapists can offer insight into the dynamics and motivations of others, adult development, effective listening skills (restatement, summarising, physically listening), resistance, and co-operation. According to Peltier (2001), the basic ingredients of the executive coaching relationship are based on a few common themes from the psychology literature. I have paraphrased and reordered these themes:

- active listening;
- adopting the client's internal frame of reference;
- being a confidante, listener, personal advisor;
- being engaging and responsive;
- building trust and understanding;
- coaching for skill, performance, development, and the executive's agenda;
- directing the client toward a desired outcome;
- empathy;
- equal working partnership;

- forging the partnership;
- listening skills;
- providing challenge and support;
- understanding the dynamics of human behaviour;
- offering an active partnership;
- offering two-way feedback;
- patience;
- respecting clients;
- being an objective, trustworthy source of feedback; and
- wanting to empower others by helping them to take responsibility for change.

In terms of the coaching intervention, Rogerian principles also lead to success for the business coach (Rogers, 1961:61-63):

- creating a genuine, authentic, one-on-one relationship with the client;
- achieving accurate empathy through unconscious positive regard and acceptance;
- by really hearing the client and fully accepting them as they currently are; and
- reflecting what you hear back to the client so that they can fully appreciate their situation as it is.

The impact of psychological theory on business coaching

South Africa, like many other countries around the world, is in a period of rapid transformation – socially, politically and economically. Individuals must learn to adapt to and manage constant change, multi-cultural diversity, educational and linguistic differences. They also have to confront major economic and life transitions within the workplace. To be successful, business coaches require an understanding of organisational systems and complexity, as well as an informed "hands-on" familiarity with psychological theory.

In grappling with the development of managerial leaders, it is critical that business coaches understand the intrapersonal and interpersonal realms. Psychology and psychotherapy have well-established traditions of specialised fields of study, ethics, supervision and published research that are highly relevant to our fast-changing, complex organisational and societal systems. I am **not** saying that business coaches need to be psychologists; simply that they need a practical grounding or "literacy" in psychological theory.

Business coaches work with executive behaviour and performance – and behaviour is determined by the individual's perception of their social situation. Peltier, in *The Psychology of Executive Coaching*, says that contemporary psychotherapy literature is relevant and invaluable for executive coaches because it is systems-oriented, drawing from models of humanistic, existential, behavioural and psychodynamic psychology. This helps executives to develop themselves and become more effective (Peltier, 2001:ix–xx).

Cognitive psychology focuses on current perceptions and on subjective reality, and is the study of the mind, its ways and patterns. Cognitive therapy helps people to begin to notice, and change, their own thought patterns with powerful emotional and behavioural benefits (Peltier, 2001:82). Neuro-Linguistic Programming (NLP) is based on cognitive behavioural psychology, and involves an understanding of the mental and cognitive processes behind behaviour – hence providing vital coaching tools for the development of communication and for the process of change.

Third-position thinking

Third-position thinking is an NLP coaching technique to help the client work with a situation involving another party (with whom the client is having difficulty); the other party is not actually physically present in the coaching conversation. The coach helps the client to think through a situation from three positions (first position/the client's own; second position/the other's position; third position/the coach). This is a technique the coach uses to help the client physically stand in first position (their own position); second position (the other's position); and third position (client adopts a meta position or that of the "coach") in order to resolve a conflict or to see the other person's point of view. I use this frequently when the client has an issue or difficulty with another party and needs to hear, see and feel perspectives from all points of view. Because coach and client enact it, and the client actually verbalises what they, as well as the other person, are thinking and feeling – it helps the client to understand the bigger picture and to determine what needs to change in their own behaviour in order to effect change in the other.

Behaviour, goals and performance

To help clients improve their behaviour and performance, it is useful for business coaches to understand the psychology behind adult behaviour, goals and motivation. Sigmund Freud's five stages of psycho-development (oral, anal, phallic, latency, genital) have remained a benchmark for the interpretation and study of psychotherapy. According to Freud, the early years of infancy and childhood establish the strengths, weaknesses and dynamics that continue into adult life (Freud, 1974).

Alfred Adler, who worked with Freud for 10 years, reasoned that adult behaviour is purposeful and goal-directed, and that life goals provide individual motivation. He focused on personal values, beliefs, attitudes, goals and interests. Adler recommended that adults engage in the therapeutic process using goal setting and reinventing their future, using techniques such as "acting as if", role-playing and goal setting – all tools utilised and recognised by well-qualified business coaches.

Carl Jung diverged from Freudian thinking, viewing the adult years of an individual's life as the phase where true identity emerges in a process he called "individuation". The terms "individuation", "archetype", "extraversion" and "introversion" are based on the psychological model of the relations between conscious and unconscious minds. Jung suggested that individuals carry the world in microcosm, and that the personal psyche is embedded in the archetypal psyche (Stevens, 1994). In his pioneering work, *Psychological Types*, Jung (1977) suggested that people have different preferences, which give them alternative perspectives on situations. These varying perspectives and "attitudes" are now seen as highly relevant to understanding organisational and cultural requirements and the needs of people in relation to motivation and leadership (Stout-Rostron, 2006a). In Chapter 6 we look at personality characteristics and profiles useful to business coaches.

Erik Eriksson, who influenced the NLP movement, further investigated the adult phases of development. To become a normal, healthy person, Eriksson viewed development as a lifelong process where each individual must resolve a series of polarities, which may be stimulated by crises or turning points (Stout-Rostron, 2006a:25). Hudson's renewal cycle helps us to understand an adult's experience of life and change.

Abraham Maslow, like many other psychologists, believed that we need to resolve certain issues before we can move on to the next ones that need resolution (from physiological needs, to safety needs, to social needs, to esteem and self-actualisation needs). Maslow broke the mould of exploring pathology to understand human nature. He looked at motivation and at motivators, believing that "individuals naturally actualise themselves unless circumstances in their development are so adverse that they must strive for safety rather than for growth" (Yalom, 1980:280).

It is nevertheless important that the business coach be able to discern pathology. As Jaques and Clement so succinctly put it, it is important to discern "abnormal temperamental or emotional characteristics that disrupt the ability to work with others" (Jaques and Clement, 1991:xiv–xv). The coach must be able to distinguish when the client should be referred to a registered psychotherapist for such pathologies to be explored and resolved.

John Whitmore in *Coaching for Performance* (2002) highlights the mind as the source of self-motivation, and insists that for people to perform they must be self-motivated. Maslow said that all we have to do is to overcome "our inner blocks to our development and maturity" (Whitmore, 2002:110). The highest state in Maslow's hierarchy of human needs was the self-actualising person who emerges when "esteem needs are satisfied and the individual is no longer driven by the need to prove themselves, either to themselves or to anyone else" (Whitmore, 2002:111). Maslow saw this as a never-ending journey.

Associated with self-actualising is the need to develop meaning and purpose. Clients "want their work, their activities and their existence to have some value, to be a contribution to others"; this relates to motivation because "people seek to engage in those activities that help them to meet their needs" (Whitmore, 2002:112). Through my work with coaching clients, I have come to believe that coaches are responsible for helping both themselves and their clients become aware of their own unconscious thinking processes and how these impact on their behaviour in the world. To understand their own behaviour, clients need to understand their own intrinsic drivers at a conscious level.

Motivation and goal setting

Motivational theories primarily focus on the individual's needs and motivations. I have typically worked with coaching clients to help them understand more fully their intrinsic motivators (internal drivers such as values, beliefs and feelings) and how to use extrinsic motivators (external drivers such as relationships, bonuses, environment, titles) to motivate their team. An important part of my research, therefore, has been to develop an understanding of limiting assumptions which create anxiety and prevent the client from making decisions – or which may interfere with self-belief, self-esteem, self-management and social, interpersonal management and, even, understanding how to work effectively within a system (such as the work environment).

The exercise below frequently forms part of an initial coaching session with a client. This is often where I start a coaching intervention, to determine what are the core values, beliefs and feelings that guide or drive this particular client. It is a powerful experience for a client to come to grips with their own intrinsic drivers, providing you, as the coach, with a tool to begin to understand your client's inner world. I recommend doing this exercise with another coach before using it with a client.

Client exercise: Intrinsic motivators

This involves asking two questions. But write down all the answers to the first question before asking the second question.

1) What is important to you professionally? (anything else?), and

2) What is important to you personally? (anything else?).

Write down the answers in the client's own words, exactly as they say them. What I mean by "important" are the intangibles, the unmeasurables, such as making a difference, collaboration, integrity, leadership, professionalism, balance between work and personal life, family, friends, health.

These intrinsic drivers are values, beliefs and feelings, which are not to be confused with goals. Goals are measurable, often quantifiable and tangible. Values are intangible and unmeasurable.

Finally, ask:

3)   What else is important? (anything else?)

This is to check that nothing has been missed. Once clients have answered all the questions, have them integrate their list of personal and professional drivers, eliminating any duplicates. Ask if there is any one that is most important, or which supersedes the others. Then rank the rest in order of importance.

Aligning intrinsic drivers with goals

Use this list to examine any goals to be set for this individual. An individual's goals always need to be in alignment with their own internal, intrinsic drivers, otherwise there will be difficulties for them in trying to achieve those goals. Intrinsic drivers and motivators need to be in alignment with all goals set.

An example of a conflict between goals or job responsibilities and personal intrinsic drivers was a client who had given up smoking; her top driver had become "health". This executive's job was to edit an international journal for tobacco regulations worldwide. Part of her role entailed translating regulations from various countries into English; she herself was a qualified linguist speaking 15 languages. Every day she was translating "smoking can damage your health" over and over again. Eventually her health began to be affected as her key job responsibilities and targets were in direct conflict with her new core intrinsic driver – health. Her personal coach helped her begin to think about the need to look for a new job.

Personal versus business goals

Another approach to this exercise, particularly if your client has a tendency to view personal and business goals holistically, is to identify business goals as short-term, medium-term and long-term. A clear indication, when asked the question: "What are your goals?" or "Where do you want to be in a year's time?" is that the client often responds with business goals. The next question would then be: "What would you like people to say about you at your funeral?" In a country where, for many clients, "praise singing" at a funeral is *de rigueur*, this is a relevant question. Typically, the answers here are different. The conversation can then proceed to the difference between personal and business goals with a further question as to the appropriate timeframe to achieve personal goals.

An example is a client who lists short- and medium-term business goals as "moving up the corporate ladder to a senior position" and a long-term goal as "owning my own business". The same client responded to the "funeral" question that he would like to be seen as adding value to his community, being loving and kind and always available for people who matter to him. Often the drive to achieve business goals is in alignment with the drive to achieve personal goals.

Adult learning

The goal of adult learning is to achieve balance and transition between new learning, skills development, and the cycles of adult life. Frederick Hudson (1998:106) researched four phases in which individuals and organisations experience change. Hudson's four stages of change (**go for it; doldrums; cocooning; getting ready**) are useful in order to understand cycles of change, and the continuous process of growth throughout adult life. In Chapter 5, we look at how to use Frederick Hudson and David Kolb's learning models as a process for your coaching conversation.

Adult learning theory has influenced coaching from the start. Because the world is in constant flux, the goal of adult learning is to achieve a balance between work and personal life. Although training was the methodology used in the 1980s and 1990s to develop managers, today training is preferred as a methodology for skills transfer. Coaching is thought to be a more powerful method to develop a managerial leader's ability to learn from experience and to develop professional competence. Recent coaching research shows that leadership development is often viewed as the purpose of most coaching assignments (Underhill *et al.*, 2007 cited in AMA, 2008:2).

The coaching conversation is an excellent adult learning and developmental space. Most business coach-client relationships involve an integration of personal and systems work. Personal work is intended to help the client develop the mental, physical, emotional and spiritual competence to achieve their desired goals; systems work may be found within a partnership, marriage, family, organisational team or matrix structure. Business coaching is holistic and encompasses the systems of which the individual client finds themselves a part.

Experiential learning

A powerful influence on coaching, experiential learning is an active process where coach and client probe the essence of an experience to understand its significance and the learning which can be gained from it. Experiential learning is directly influenced by the seminal works of John Dewey, Kurt Lewin, Jean Piaget, David Boud and David Kolb.

The importance of experiential learning is that it emphasises a client's individual, subjective experience. In existential terms, the meaning of experience is not a given; it is subject to interpretation. Coach and client use the business coaching conversation to actively reconstruct the client's experience, with a focus on setting goals that are aligned to the client's intrinsic drivers, i.e. values, beliefs and feelings.

How clients construct their experience is what Boud, Cohen and Walker, in *Using Experience for Learning*, term the individual's "personal foundation of knowledge" (Boud, Cohen and Walker, 1996:11). Coaches need to be aware that more is often lost than gained by ignoring the uniqueness of each person's history and ways of experiencing the world. This is why many coaches will begin their first conversation with a client by asking to hear their life story.

Boud, Cohen and Walker have defined the differences between cognitive, affective and conative (i.e. expressing endeavour or effort) learning. Cognitive learning is more concerned with **thinking**, where affective learning is concerned with **values and feelings**, and conative or psychomotor learning is concerned with **action and doing**. If learning at work is cognitive, affective and psychomotor, then it involves feelings and emotions (affective), the intellectual and cerebral processes (cognitive) and action (conative) (Boud, Cohen and Walker, 1996:46–58).

We now know that not only is learning socially and culturally constructed, but it does not occur in isolation from social and cultural norms and values. Clients will reconstruct their own experience within the context of a particular social setting and range of cultural values. In other words, coach and client do not exist independently from their environment. The client's experience impacts on their own cultural competence, which we explore in Chapter 6 when looking at issues of diversity, personality and culture in coaching.

Other considerations may be language, social class, gender, ethnic background, and the individual's style of learning. In learning from experience, it is useful to understand which barriers prevent the client from learning. Often it is a matter of developing self-reflective skills as much as self-management skills. What clients learn from their experience can transform their perceptions, their limiting and liberating assumptions, their way of interpreting the world – and their ability to achieve results.

BUSINESS COACHING IN SOUTH AFRICA

In the early 1990s, professional coaching was in its formative years in the developed world, while South Africa was in its final years of transformation from an apartheid racial tyranny to a democracy. Leadership succession was of paramount importance in both spheres, leading to greater involvement with individual executives by corporate consultants and coaches.

The emergence of business coaching in South Africa is therefore related to an explosion of talent development as the nation fast-tracks its managers into executive positions in every field of industry, government and education. Like much else in South Africa, coaching was isolated from mainstream professional development due to international restrictions during the years of apartheid. Only within the last five to ten years has coaching sprung to the forefront of managerial leadership development in South Africa, whereas in the global marketplace coaching is beginning to mature.

Coaching became more visible and accessible in South Africa at the turn of the twenty-first century, as new coach training schools sprang up, and graduate business schools accommodated "leader as coach" programmes. Since 2005, Organisational Development (OD) and Human Resources (HR) departments have been training "internal" coaches, and designing assessment programmes to bring external coach consultants into the organisational "suite" of coaches needed for their top executives.

In parallel with the new era of democracy in South Africa, coaching as a new leadership discipline is fresh and vibrant – yet with theoretical roots that are deep and strong. Underpinning the field of coaching are the various disciplines of psychology, the relatively new disciplines of adult and experiential learning, organisational development and systems thinking. Coaching, as a young and developing profession, has integrated a number of mental models from existing professions: psychological, systemic and organisational.

Some confusion between psychology and coaching has arisen among prospective clients because, although coaching is not psychotherapy, it is developmental, and involves a similar format of "conversation" with the client. Influenced by a diverse range of disciplines, academics and practitioners alike view business coaching as related to organisational development, management consulting, leadership development, and human resources management.

Although important academic and practitioner research into the successes and failures of business coaching is currently underway in South Africa, much more is needed. A growing number of master's and doctoral students are in the process of completing research projects with their papers beginning to be circulated worldwide. In addition, new coach-training programmes are springing up in university graduate schools of business at practitioner, master's and doctoral level.

Some of the difficulties in the South African marketplace stem from there being too small a pool of diverse, qualified and experienced business coaches to satisfy the growing needs of small, medium and large organisations. Companies who employ internal and external coaches are beginning to be more demanding of quantifiable and measurable results, value for money, as well as distinguished accreditation, membership of a recognised professional body with a clear ethical code, and an assurance of continuing professional development (CPD), aligned to published or organisational standards of competence.

In response to this, an important development in South Africa has been the founding of the professional association Coaches and Mentors of South Africa (COMENSA). COMENSA's overriding brief is to provide for the regulation of coaching and mentoring, to develop the credibility of coaching as a profession, and to align national standards of professional competence to international standards. One of the crucial, continuing roles of COMENSA is to build relationships and alliances between the organisational buyers and the individual and small-company providers of coaching services.

As the demand for business and executive coaching continues to expand exponentially, there is another area of development inside organisations. Individual corporations are in the process of defining their own standards of assessment to regulate the employment of internal and external coaches. A key prerequisite for the future will be that business coaches conform to organisational demands with the specific ethics, supervisory framework, standards and competences of those organisations. Business coaches are beginning to collaborate and form alliances in order to offer coaching services to corporate executives and their teams.

Business coaching is the trend of the moment. If it continues to develop at its current rate, conforming to internationally acceptable standards, it will make a significant difference in developing the competence and performance of individuals, managerial leaders, their teams and their organisations. More importantly, the role of business coaching will assist South Africa's transition into a democratic future with the very best of inclusive and transformational business practices (Stout-Rostron, 2006b). However, coaching on its own is not a guarantee of success for senior executives in the organisation; it is a critical component that needs to be aligned with all the other leadership and management development initiatives for managers, leaders and executives within a company.

Business coaching should be aligned strategically with the values and objectives of an organisation overall. A question is then raised for executives: if goals are to be motivationally achieved, are they also aligned to the individual's values, beliefs and feelings? Often organisations merely pay lip service to organisational values, and don't necessarily create them as a synthesis of the core individual values which make up the culture of the organisation. Ethical dilemmas can arise during the coaching process if the executive needs to make difficult choices that are incompatible with their own value system.

Ethical challenges among executives are fairly universal. When coaching in the USA, Europe or the UK, for example, one hears stories that are almost identical to the situations faced by clients in other countries and continents, including South Africa. Let me tell you the story of Jim.

Executive dilemmas

Jim[4] is a senior dispensing pharmacist who manages a major pharmaceutical retail chain in southern California. He grappled with a personal and professional dilemma, having been asked to lay off highly qualified and experienced staff in order to increase bottom-line profits for shareholders – not an uncommon position for business executives today. His inner turmoil was highlighted by the fact that the families of his pharmacists would be economically affected by the loss of one family member's income with no guarantee of replacing it, plus the loss of quality service to loyal customers. This was balanced against the short-term profits to be made by shareholders, including himself as the owner of a recently inherited share portfolio.

Jim also faced the problem of having to employ less qualified, less experienced and therefore less expensive dispensers, who would be unable to provide the quality service for which the pharmacy was reputed. One of Jim's concerns was that, although larger profits would be made for the retail organisation's shareholders, these would be at the expense of a seriously reduced quality of expertise offered to a trusting public. A second unease was that all of his experienced staff already worked extensive hours; the enforced cuts to qualified staff would mean even more gruelling working hours for those still gainfully employed, with no seeming concern for the public on the part of shareholders.

"It's a moral dilemma for me, not only because I am faced with laying off people who are providing an expert quality service, but the staff who remain will be asked to take even greater strain, working longer hours yet providing an inferior service.

My heart absolutely goes out to the people who are being sacrificed for short-term profits, as well as those who will step into their shoes.

The guy in the boardroom in LA who looks only at the figures, and never has to look people in the eye like I do, is only interested in immediate gains. By the time those top executives have departed the company in a few years, with large bonuses and share options in return for their quick-buck strategy, my dispensing pharmacists who meet the public will be facing the serious frustration of the people we serve. Our customers will be experiencing a steady decline in the service they have become accustomed to. This may produce financial results for a few years, but the real business decision would be a far-sighted chairman who leaves a business that will flourish for 50 years. This shortsightedness for easy gains is, fundamentally, not good business sense.

On the other hand, I must admit that a couple of years ago my pharmacist father left me a very solid portfolio of shares, on which I need to make good financial returns as part of my retirement planning. In the end, my decision has been to implement what I know to be a fundamentally unfair, unbusinesslike, yet profit-driven decision. It is not business-driven in the long term, because having built up our customer base on loyalty and good service, we will now sacrifice quality of service and expertise for immediate cash returns – but in the end I fear our customers will drift away to our rivals."

This is one of the most common dilemmas faced by executives today all over the world. It is a direct result of intense "bottom-line" pressure, and is a repeated theme expressed to us by many clients worldwide. Critically important is that coaching helps the client to think through such issues and dilemmas, asking questions, making observations and challenging the client's thinking – rather than offering advice on how they should manage them.

THE FUTURE OF BUSINESS COACHING WORLDWIDE

Currently, there is an emergent collaboration amongst coaching industry bodies who are working together to develop ethical codes, supervisory recommendations, professional standards of competence, and regulations for coaching certification. The professional association, Coaches and Mentors of South Africa (COMENSA), is involved with the Global Community of Coaches (GCC), which continues to facilitate regional dialogues to understand the needs of coaching consumers, practitioners and educators, in order to develop commonly agreed understandings, guidelines and frameworks for the practice and training of coaches worldwide.

Also working at a global level to develop coaching as a profession are bodies such as the Worldwide Association of Business Coaches (WABC), the International Coach Federation (ICF), the European Mentoring and Coaching Council (EMCC), the UK Chartered Institute of Personnel and Development (CIPD), and the Association of Coaches (AC).

Business coaching has been defined in many different ways, but is essentially a one-on-one collaborative partnership to develop the client's performance and potential, personally and professionally, in alignment with the goals and values of the organisation. In its formative stages as a profession, coaching sits at an interesting juncture worldwide – and business coaching, which is viewed as the primary way to develop managerial leaders, is at the very cutting edge of the way forward for this new, dynamic discipline.

COACH'S LIBRARY

Boud, D., Cohen, R. and Walker, D. (eds). (1996). *Using experience for learning*. Buckingham: SRHE and Open University Press.

Burger, A.P. (ed.). (1996). *Ubuntu: Cradles of peace and development*. Pretoria: Kagiso.

Freud, S. (1974). *Introductory lectures on psychoanalysis*. Harmondsworth: Penguin.

Hudson, F. (1998). *The handbook of coaching: A resource guide to effective coaching with individuals and organisations*. Santa Barbara, CA: Hudson Institute.

Jaques, E. and Clement, S.D. (1991). *Effective leadership: A practical guide to managing complexity*. Oxford: Blackwell.

Kline, N. (1999/2004). *Time to think: Listening with the human mind*. London: Ward Lock.

Peltier, B. (2001). *The psychology of executive coaching: Theory and application*, New York, NY: Brunner-Routledge.

Shaw, P. and Linnecar, R. (2007). *Business coaching: Achieving practical results through effective engagement*. London: Capstone.

Stern, L. (2008). *Executive coaching: building and managing your professional practice*. Hoboken, NJ: Wiley.

Stout-Rostron, S. (2006a). The history of coaching, in M. McLoughlin (ed.), *Sharing the passion: Conversations with coaches*. Cape Town: Advanced Human Technologies.

Stout-Rostron, S. (2006b). Business coaching in South Africa. *WABC e-zine*, 2(2):7–10. Available at: www.wabccoaches.com.

Whitmore, J. (2002). *Coaching for performance: Growing people, performance and purpose*. Third edition. London: Nicholas Brealey.

Yalom, I.D. (1980). *Existential psychotherapy*. New York, NY: Basic Books.

ENDNOTES TO CHAPTER 2

1.   The origin of the word "coach" is from the French *coche*. It derives from the Hungarian town, Kòcs, where the first coach/wagon was built in the sixteenth century. As a verb, "to coach" was to convey a valued person from where they were to where they wanted to be. At the end of the nineteenth century, American college students had coaches to support them in achieving their best; this is true for executive coaching today (Stout-Rostron, 2006a).

2.   In 1699, *Les Aventures de Telemaque* was published by François de Salignac de la Mothe-Fenelon (1651-1715), a French writer and educator, whose reinterpretation of Homer's *Odyssey* was apparently intended to idealise his own role as tutor to the Dauphin. In Homer's original work, Mentor acted as more of a caretaker than a mentor (Stout-Rostron, 2006a).

3.   This section is an adapted excerpt from Stout-Rostron (2006a).

4.   For confidentiality purposes, this and all executives' names in this book have been changed.

3

The Coaching Conversation

The coaching conversation provides a thinking environment where business professionals are able to develop self-awareness and a depth of understanding of themselves and others – embedding newly acquired skills, competences and attitudes which subsequently impact the actions they take, and visibly demonstrate new behaviours (Sunny Stout-Rostron, 2006c).

Chapter outline

- The coaching conversation as a thinking partnership

- Deepening your understanding of the business coaching process

- Listening, equality and the genuine encounter

- Learning from experience

- Purpose of the coaching conversation

- Measuring results

- Value of positive regard, empathy and appreciation

- Goals and the coach/client relationship

- In conclusion

- Coach's library

- Endnotes to Chapter 3

THE COACHING CONVERSATION AS A THINKING PARTNERSHIP

This chapter explores the purpose and focus of the conversation and the competences useful to the business coach. The "coaching conversation" is the face-to-face or telephone interaction between coach and client. It is a "thinking partnership" (Kline, 1999/2004) where coach and client reflect on the client's experience, transforming it into potential for learning and action. How the client takes responsibility for change can emerge from the coaching conversation.

The focus of a coaching conversation is to help the client work towards achieving their desired outcomes. The coach primarily explores with each client what it is that is holding back or stopping the client from achieving their goals, for example by identifying and replacing disempowering assumptions and paradigms with empowering ones.

DEEPENING YOUR UNDERSTANDING OF THE BUSINESS COACHING PROCESS

I define coaching as "a process that creates sustained shifts in thinking, feeling and behaviour – and ultimately in performance. By asking the right questions, coaches help clients find their own solutions". Tony Grant (2000) defines coaching as a "solution-focused, results-oriented systematic process in which the coach facilitates the enhancement of performance, self-directed learning and personal growth of other individuals". The AMA/Institute for Corporate Productivity define coaching as: "a short- to medium-term relationship between a manager or senior leader, and a consultant (internal or external) with the purpose of improving work performance" (Douglas and McCauley, 1999; cited in AMA, 2008:8).

I see the business coaching process as one that helps business executives and leaders to develop a clear understanding of their roles and responsibilities. Business coaching, like sports coaching, is about high performance. Business coaching, ultimately, is about sustained behavioural change and breakthrough performance.

Some practitioners have had a difficult time differentiating coaching from other areas of practice or approaches by virtue of its supposed lack of "unique characteristics" (GCC, 2008a). One of the reasons for this kind of rationale is that some coaching providers see themselves as business consultants with their coaching services structured around the coaching process. It has been challenging to find one authoritative definition of coaching in the marketplace, not just because every professional body has its own slant on the coaching process, but because there is no agreed global definition available.

So what do business coaches do? The core value of business coaching is to help the individual executive to think clearly about the core issues that present challenges to them in their job, career and daily working life. Coaching is unique, helping individuals to systematise their conscious thoughts about the immediate actions needed to address specific practical issues, and to understand the unconscious processes that may be sabotaging their success.

Mentors focus on the development of the learner, and convey knowledge of organisational values and routines, plus the managerial system, thus helping the learner to navigate the organisation's political system. Mentoring is personalised, domain-specific and creates an atmosphere to acknowledge and recognise people. On the other hand, counselling is more personal and is aimed at specific personal problems. Counsellors and psychologists bring to coaching powerful, interpersonal change skills. The skills highly relevant to the coaching world, which come to us from psychotherapy literature, are:

- active listening;
- empathy;
- self-awareness;
- process observation;
- giving and getting feedback;
- assertive communication;
- conflict resolution;
- cognitive restructuring;
- systems theory; and
- learned optimism.

Robert Hargrove (2003) in *Masterful Coaching* suggests that "Coaching is having both the toughness and the compassion to skilfully intervene in people's learning processes, and that a successful coaching relationship is always a story of transformation, not just of higher levels of performance". John Whitmore (2002:8) in *Coaching for Performance* says, "Coaching is unlocking a person's potential to maximise their own performance; it is helping them to learn rather than teaching them".

These definitions suggest that learning is the key. This indicates that helping your clients grow, develop and become who they want to be, requires asking for their best thinking, rather than sharing yours. Your asking of incisive questions to open up the thinking of your client is "a powerful alliance designed to forward and enhance the lifelong process of human learning, effectiveness and fulfilment" (Whitworth, Kimsey-House and Sandahl, 1998).

The three levels of coaching intervention with which we are working are interconnected (Weiss, 2004):

1. Doing: **What** tasks and goals need to be accomplished?
2. Learning: **How** will you develop the competences needed?
3. Being and becoming: **Who** are you as you grow, develop and transform?

The coach needs to ask: what does the client need to learn to perform better? And which skills and competences do they need to develop to "do the doing" better? Then, as they develop new skills and competences in the workplace, how does that impact on how they "be who they are"; and who is it that they want to become? When we look at coaching models in Chapter 5, we will explore the various levels of the coaching intervention that impact on the learning, growth and development of the client.

LISTENING, EQUALITY AND THE GENUINE ENCOUNTER

The structure of the coaching intervention needs to be framed by the coach's ability to listen, and to actively intervene only when needed. Listening, asking questions and silence are core skills for the business coach – as they help to create safety for clients within the external physical environment, as well as enhancing the client's internal thinking environment.

A competence is simply a set of skills, and I include as part of the competence active listening: listening for feelings, asking relevant questions, giving feedback on clients' listening skills, giving feedback on the impression the client makes on you, paraphrasing, physical listening, reflection, restatement, and summarising.

It is also important that the coach/client relationship be based on an assumption of equality. This is different to the therapist/patient relationship, which is often not considered an equal relationship. In a coaching relationship, neither coach nor client is superior to the other; both are travellers on the client's journey, and each brings in their own professional expertise. A "safe thinking environment" is built through the development of the relationship, and research shows that the relationship is what can help with the onset of change.

Equality also means being willing to be influenced by the client. I see this as a very important aspect of coaching. It is important that coach and client change as the relationship grows. Yalom (2001:26–27), well known for his work with existential individual and group coaching, urges us to let our clients matter to us, "to let them enter your mind, influence you, change you – and not to conceal this from them".

For example, I recently learned a useful, amusing lesson from one of my clients. Both client and coach are raising teenage girls, and the thought from the client was "join them rather than fighting them" – in other words take out a page in Facebook as a way to communicate at the level so desired by teenagers! This was quite a valuable lesson to me as coach – I was willing to listen to how my client related to her teenagers on the web forum as a different way to keep the lines of communication open.

Coaching is an egalitarian relationship, even if the focus is that of the coach on the client. Both individuals bring their experience, expertise and wisdom to the relationship. In coaching, the coach will adapt their style according to their model, but if the major presupposition of the coaching interaction is one of equality, it would be difficult to imagine a coach adopting the road of "minimal direction" or interaction. More important is the development of the relationship through the client/coach interactions.

Thus, I think it is important to share certain facets of yourself as they relate to the situation at hand, or are related to the topic of conversation. This brings you into the conversation as a human being. For example, I have shared with clients if there has been a particularly stressful or emotional event in the life of our families, sad or joyful (such as matric exam results, a wedding anniversary or even the loss of a loved one).

It is critical that the coach should not dwell on their own personal issues, positive or negative – but only to comment if relevant to the conversation in developing rapport and trust. After all, the purpose of the conversation is about "them". For example, one of my clients was undergoing a divorce and was grateful that I had experienced the turbulent emotions of divorce myself. She trusted me to help her articulate her feelings and to think about the benefit of counselling for herself and her children. Yalom (2001:92) talks about the "genuine encounter", and asks the difficult question: "How can one have a genuine encounter with another person while remaining so opaque?"

LEARNING FROM EXPERIENCE

Learning, and particularly learning from experience, seems to be one of the major components of the coaching conversation. Learning from experience implies an understanding of the language and content of the client's story, with the coach helping the client to reconstruct their own reality by searching for meaning through dialogue.

In the context of the coaching conversation, when the client talks about their experience, they are actually creating a narrative or story. This type of storytelling constructs meaning in a different way from merely describing an experience. There is so much power in language and content that the significance of the client's story comes from both the structure of the telling as well as the interpretation and significance given. In South Africa, oral history and storytelling remain very important methods of passing on ritual, tradition and customs. The coaching conversation can literally be seen as an extension of "telling one's story" and looking for meaning and significance in the telling.

As humans, we are "meaning-seeking creatures" and we have been "thrown into a world devoid of intrinsic meaning" (Yalom, 2001:133). It is not uncommon in the coaching conversation for a client to ask the coach to help them figure out the "meaning of their life". Once trust has been established, these important philosophical questions arise as business clients come to terms with the complexities, stresses and ambiguities of the corporate environment.

In therapy, the essential first step is for individuals to recognise their role in resolving their own life predicament; it is similar in the coaching context. The reason is simply that the client is the one with the power to change their situation.

One of the roles of the coach is often to help the client identify where they have control, and where they do not. An example would be when the client's stress is due to focusing on the behaviour of others, over which they have little if any control. On the other hand, the client has control over their own behaviour.

Learning, change and growth are the key principles of the coaching environment. Experiential learning in education is common to Kolb, Jung and Freire, with an emphasis on developing a self-directed, purposeful life (Freire, 1973:65).[1] With this as a precedent, we can look at the "coaching conversation" not just as experiential learning, but as experiential education: learning from one's own life experiences.

The coaching intervention ranges from questions which explore feelings, motivations, perceptions, assumptions and attitudes to reflected statements, reframed questions, role-plays, structured question frameworks, observation or silence. Boud, Cohen and Walker's *Using Experience in Learning* (1996) had a profound effect on my thinking about the coaching conversation, and the space it opens up for coaches to help clients to learn from their own personal experience.

PURPOSE OF THE COACHING CONVERSATION

What is the objective of the coaching conversation? Are you in the process of creating a personal learning or professional development plan with your client (Harri-Augstein and Thomas, 1991:24,38)? What is your overall strategy for working together? What resources are available to support you and the client at work (e.g. regular meetings with the client's line manager, or the Human Resources or Organisational Development departmental heads)? Development plans should contain the overall aims for the entire coaching journey, the strategy of how to achieve them, developmental objectives, and the "learning tactics" and core tasks that will enable the client to achieve and implement their plan.

Case study: Draft management development plan

Below is an example of a draft Leadership Development Plan for one of my clients. The purpose and developmental objectives are continually reviewed, and the actions change with each coaching conversation. The Leadership Development Plan is an organic, evolving document that is shared with the Line Manager. Rather than sharing the content of the coaching conversation, client and coach can share the development plan and results achieved with other stakeholders in the coaching process. This protects client confidentiality.

Purpose:

1. To strategically position my professional career development within the organisation and consistently deliver results that exceed expectations.

2. To motivate and empower my senior management team to acquire specific competences to drive results and performance.

Developmental objectives:

1. Collaboration and team work – Building an effective team that champions best practices, and puts the interests of the organisation first, as well as building strong, productive relationships across the organisation.

2. Organisation and talent development – Demonstrating the ability to motivate and empower the team to achieve targeted results, while putting the right people in the right jobs and giving constructive, candid feedback to develop them.

3. Self-awareness and adaptability – Asserting personal ideas and opinions through productive influence, and maintaining an awareness of how my actions and behaviours impact on others.

Strategy:

1. To develop leadership and management competence by working with my coach, and developing the strategic management skills of my team.

2. To develop self-awareness and adaptability by being willing to listen to diverse points of view, developing some patience, and being flexible and adaptable as and when required.

3. Being focused on career path development for my team, and for myself in terms of succession planning.

Monthly actions:

Obstacles to achievement:

Results achieved:
Overall learning from the coaching journey:

MEASURING RESULTS

There is no point in simply developing a leadership plan in isolation from the rest of the business processes. If the coaching intervention is to be successful in organisations, it is critical to develop a systemic, fully integrated coaching strategy that is in alignment with both the business and the talent strategies for the organisation. Two key factors will be to identify the efficacy of internal and external coaching interventions, and the use of group or team coaching to develop key leaders (Peterson and Little, 2008). I would add to this the complementary mentoring programmes that are often aligned with business coaching inside organisations as a way to develop talent at subordinate levels.

Moreover, although I agree with Shaw and Linnecar (2007) that, in the business context, results are often measured in three specific areas: behavioural change, improved performance, and the individual's personal and professional development (Ting and Scisco, 2006:58–9), I define these categories a bit differently.

1. Visible behavioural change

It is essential that any changes in self-awareness and relationship awareness show up visibly in the workplace through the client's behaviour; otherwise, it is difficult to measure what has changed as a result of the coaching. Coaching is a complex process with both qualitative and quantitative goals set. Your job as a business coach is to develop the core competences of the managerial leader. The development of those competences needs to show up visibly in work-related and behavioural changes. The client's work often starts with growing self-awareness, increased emotional maturity and improved inter-personal skills and competence.

2. *Improved performance and business results*

Performance improvement should have a direct effect on business results. Although it is not always possible to quantify how coaching has directly impacted performance, it is one of the key criteria linked to business coaching. This may require a systemic and developmental approach on the part of coach and client, integrated with an understanding of the complexities of the client's working context, market environment and level of competence. In Chapter 6, we look at the issues of diversity, personality and culture, and examine the impact these may have on the individual coaching client, the context within which they work, and the developmental needs of certain leaders due to their individual perspectives, culture, gender, ethnicity and experience of isolation.

3. *Personal and professional development*

The personal development plan you create with your client relates directly to the areas where it is perceived that they need to work. Their plan will be linked to individual management assessment profiles, 360° feedback surveys, and shadow coaching which help you to identify emotional, behavioural, cognitive and performance-related issues. One of the essentials in creating this personal development plan is to identify the skills and competences that will impact each area, creating medium-term and long-term plans. This includes the client's learning journey, the importance of identifying their learning style, and how they will be able to develop themselves personally and professionally when they have ceased to work with an external coach or internal organisational coach.

Missing a cue

Sometimes the coach misses a cue. One senior coach, working on a contract with a successful multimedia agency in South Africa, was tasked to help a bright young star, Marcus*, to improve his communication skills with his team. Considered one of the most brilliant up-and-coming directors in the advertising industry, Marcus' intellectual capabilities over-shadowed his "perceived" ability to delegate, communicate his vision to his team, and to motivate all those who worked alongside him. His ideas often stayed in his head and, although he was adored by clients, his team were sometimes confused as to their brief.

The coach and Marcus regularly enjoyed an intellectual, if perhaps less goal-directed or action-oriented conversation. The result, after six months of coaching, was a very frustrated senior board, which did not see behavioural or performance change as a result of the coaching. The objective had been to improve Marcus' leadership and communication competence and, although Marcus had matured emotionally and definitely increased his awareness of himself and others, he had not translated his learning into visible behavioural change.

* Not his real name

Insight leads to change. The business coach's job is to facilitate insight, which leads to observable behavioural change impacting on performance. This is because organisations expect to see clear, effective deliverables. The AMA's 2008 research study into the reason why organisations use coaching revealed that 79 per cent wished to improve individual performance/productivity; 63 per cent to address leadership development succession planning; 60 per cent to increase worker skill levels; and 56 per cent to improve organisational performance (AMA, 2008:11).

VALUE OF POSITIVE REGARD, EMPATHY AND APPRECIATION

A vital aspect of the coaching intervention is to be positively supportive of the client. Carl Rogers called it "unconditional positive regard". Rogers identified three essential characteristics for an effective therapist/patient relationship that are useful to us in a business coaching environment: unconditional positive regard, genuineness and accurate empathy (Rogers, 1961:47-49).

The business coach both models and communicates empathy in each present moment of the coaching conversation. Not only do empathy and positive regard build trust in the relationship, but this may be one of the few places where the client is unconditionally supported in their personal and professional life. This does not mean that the coach never challenges the client. It does mean, however, that the client and coach work in a context that is safe for the client to discuss weaknesses, failures, limiting thinking and obstacles to achievement – and yet to feel neither threatened nor judged.

Empathy and positive regard are aligned with the fourth component of Nancy Kline's coaching process, appreciation. Kline's (1999/2004:62) definition of appreciation is "practising a 5 to 1 (5:1) ratio of appreciation to criticism". The most important feature of appreciation is that it needs to be a genuine appreciation of a particular quality in the client, and it needs to be communicated authentically. Appreciation may include positive comments about a particular action or behaviour, or a quality the coach has recently noticed in the client.

The quality of your appreciation for the client will come not only through your words, but also from your body language: your tone of voice, facial expression, the look in your eyes … and, finally, by the enthusiasm and sincerity of your appreciation. Furthermore, and most importantly, the human mind seems to work best with a full picture of reality, and that realistic picture is completed with the positive, appreciative comments of the coach as listener.

What is interesting about the concept of appreciation is that we usually expect to hear "bad news" from others. It is rare that human beings really truly appreciate each other on a regular basis. We are used to hearing where we have failed, messed up, created chaos or uncertainty. In other words, it is not our personal accomplishments for which we often gain recognition, but for our mistakes or where things have gone wrong. For some reason it is the negative side of life that seems to be considered to be reality – especially in the more aggressive corporate environment.

Appreciation highlights the importance of empathy, which is a core component of emotional competence. When the client feels they are being understood, it can contribute not just to their thinking, but also to their ability to make difficult decisions, transitioning through difficult stages of personal learning and development. Empathy is critical for the coach's competence in giving direct feedback, handling uncomfortable feelings and encouraging self-awareness on the part of the client. The emotional competences I refer to here are the underlying skills of Goleman's (2002:39) model: self-awareness, self-management, social awareness, and social management.

The coach's emotional competence has a direct impact on their ability to offer support to their client. Giving support means a willingness to "model" the giving of support. This modelling of excellence is a key role for the business coach. However, it does not take away from the importance of the coach being able to challenge, make observations and ask questions about behaviour or performance that is not appropriate or going well.

Case study: An example of appreciation

I have noticed that it is extremely difficult for people in the business environment to be appreciative of each other; this is because being appreciative of another acknowledges the essence of the other's "being". It was wonderful to receive a message from the CEO of an organisation that I worked with recently that she has started to include "appreciations" into her "blue hat" meetings (meetings where facts only are discussed). These appreciations allow people's emotions or feelings to come to the fore in a safe environment and in a business-like manner.

This CEO indicated that the appreciations would take the form of acknowledgement for deadlines met, projects completed even with a lack of resources, the "up-skilling" of new staff, the reaching of a target for the first time, as well as the recognition of qualities that enabled the different individuals to meet stringent requirements on a project, or to make it through a particularly difficult training, or to handle a difficult client or customer. This client, operating as "leader coach" with her team, has begun to create an environment in meetings where achievements are recognised alongside the difficulties posed by the fast pace of the working environment, the lack of resources or the lack of staff to follow up once a project has been completed.

Research shows that appreciations help us to think better. Experience has shown that appreciation is the one component when coaching in a thinking environment that people feel most fiercely about. They either defend or support the need for appreciations, or fight against the need for them.

Appreciation offsets the thinking of individuals in the team that they are not focused enough, not thinking critically enough, not strong enough, skilled enough – just not good enough. Appreciation also demonstrates a commitment on the part of team members to their own quality of thinking and decision-making – and the value they place on the other team members.

GOALS AND THE COACH/CLIENT RELATIONSHIP

Business coaching places great emphasis on clarifying and achieving goals. Often within the complexity of the organisational environment, the client's overarching goals may be set by a more senior power; where that senior individual may have different worldviews, different paradigms, and differing limiting and empowering assumptions. It is therefore important that, as goals are set, they be related to the intrinsic and extrinsic drivers of the client themselves. The client must have a "living sense" of what their goal may be (Spinelli, 1989). In other words, the goal must be aligned to the values of the individual, as much as to those of the organisation, if it is to be achieved.

A secondary consideration is that goals change for the client over time as the relationship develops. For example, as he grew in competence and confidence over a two-year period, one of my clients working in an international organisation based in Johannesburg, changed his overarching goal from that of developing strong leadership competence, to being considered one of the most competent business leaders – not just within his own country, South Africa, but in the entire sub-Saharan African continent!

To develop the relationship effectively, the principles and concepts of the Rogerian, person-centred approach is useful to us. This is a relationship-oriented experiential approach, requiring the practitioner to listen with acceptance and without judgement if clients are going to be able to change (Rogers, 1961:33-35). If one of the core aims of the coaching intervention is to help clients understand and manage themselves and their own interpersonal communications, and if we as the coaches are going to enable rather than teach our clients, then our coaching interventions and the coaching process constantly need to have goals in mind, and be able to clearly define the types of goals.

O'Neill (2000:104) maintains that sustaining your goals as a coach gives you more focus. We can identify two specific types of goal: content (what is to be accomplished) and process goals (how the coach wants to be in a session). If you as coach are aware of your goal, you will stay in response mode rather than revert to automatic mode when your stress is high. The next step is to ensure your goal is related to your client's goal. This is an interesting way to look at goals. Most executive coaches would first identify the client's goals and coach the client accordingly. O'Neill says be very clear about your goal as coach throughout the session so that you lose neither signature presence nor backbone, nor heart.

The coach is responsible to ensure that goal-setting conversations get the best results. However, it is best if goal setting is slowed down to speed up action later (O'Neill, 2000:104). O'Neill differentiates between two kinds of client goals, business and personal, and links the coaching effort to a business result, highlighting and prioritising the business areas that need attention. Business goals are about achieving external results; personal goals are what the leader has to do differently in how they conduct themselves to get the business results. O'Neill (2000) cites Robert Crosby who, on the other hand, defines three types of goals:

1. Bottom-line goals – aligned to the reason the organisation exists.
2. Work-process goals – how the work is accomplished.
3. Human relations goals – how people collaborate to accomplish goals.

O'Neill (2000:104) reflects Hargrove who discussed the use of "breakthrough thinking to achieve stretch goals". In setting goals, O'Neill's interventions are:

1. Which business results are needed?
2. What are the team behaviours needed to be different to accomplish the results?
3. Which personal leadership challenges is the executive facing in improving these results and team behaviours?
4. What are specific behaviours the leader needs to enhance or change in themselves?

IN CONCLUSION

In this chapter, we have examined the purpose and focus of the coaching conversation and the need for it to be a solutions-focused, results-oriented, and systemic process which skilfully develops the client's learning processes. The coaching conversation is an alliance between coach, client and organisation designed to maximise and transform thinking, behaviour and performance.

The coaching conversation provides a thinking environment where business professionals develop self-awareness and a depth of understanding of themselves and others. If coaching embeds newly acquired skills, competence, attitudes and behaviour, unlocking an individual executive's potential, then it suggests that personal and experiential learning is the key.

COACH'S LIBRARY

Goleman, D. (1996). *Emotional intelligence*. London: Bloomsbury.

Hargrove, R. (2003). *Masterful coaching: Inspire an "impossible future" while producing extraordinary leaders and extraordinary results*. San Francisco, CA: Jossey-Bass/ Pfeiffer.

Kline, N. (1999/2004). *Time to think: Listening with the human mind*. London: Ward Lock.

O'Neill, M.B. (2000). *Coaching with backbone and heart: A systems approach to engaging leaders with their challenges*. San Francisco, CA: Jossey-Bass.

Peltier, B. (2001). *The psychology of executive coaching: Theory and application*. New York, NY: Brunner-Routledge.

Peterson, D. and Little, B. (2008). Growth market. *Coaching at Work*, 3(1):44–47.

Spinelli, E. (1989). *The interpreted world: An introduction to phenomenological psychology*. London: Sage.

Weiss, P. (2004). The three levels of coaching. Paper from *An appropriate response*. Available at: www.appropriateresponse.com.

Whitmore, J. (2002). *Coaching for performance: Growing people, performance and purpose*. Third edition. London: Nicholas Brealey.

Whitworth, L., Kimsey-House, H. and Sandahl, P. (1998). *Co-active coaching: New skills for coaching people toward success in work and life*. Palo Alto, CA: Davies-Black.

Yalom, I.D. (1980). *Existential psychotherapy*. New York, NY: Basic Books.

ENDNOTES TO CHAPTER 3

1. Experiential learning in education is seen as an active exploration of the personal, experiential meaning of abstract concepts through dialogue among equals.

4

Working With Question Frameworks

At its core the coaching relationship is a strong personal connection between two individuals that typically occurs out of public view and whose workings may even appear mysterious to outsiders. Coaching is fundamentally a process for facilitating learning and change which is another way to describe development (Ting and Scisco, 2006:36).

Chapter outline

- Structure – working with question frameworks

- Two-stage frameworks

    - Understanding intrinsic motivators and drivers

    - Functional analysis: the ABC of behaviour management

    - Functional analysis

    - Action learning approach

- Three-stage frameworks

    - Contracting

    - What needs work?

- Four-stage frameworks

    - Whitmore's GROW model

    - O'Neill's "executive coaching with backbone and heart"

- Five-stage frameworks

    - Framework for change

    - Working with the CLEAR model

- Six-stage frameworks

    - Nancy Kline's Thinking Partnership®

    - Six-stage Thinking Environment® coaching process

- Eight-stage frameworks

    - Well-formed outcomes (NLP)

- Ten-stage frameworks

    - Business Best Year Yet®

- Developing your own question frameworks

- Coach's library

This chapter explores the range of coaching question frameworks available in the marketplace, for example those of John Whitmore, Nancy Kline and Jinny Ditzler. A framework is a structure that tends to be linear, progressive and visible. A question framework is a sequence of questions with steps or stages. Stages indicate the possibility of nonlinear "movement" between the parts; steps indicate a number of linear or progressive questions as part of its process. The GROW and CLEAR models have developed detailed, linear question frameworks as part of their process.

I describe how to use two-, three-, four-, five-, six, eight- and ten-stage frameworks, including NLP and the Thinking Environment® processes, with examples for understanding. This chapter is designed to have you look specifically at how you can develop your own questioning process.

One of the most difficult paradigms for a coach to understand, as opposed to being a teacher or a therapist, is to not provide answers or solve the client's problems for them. The greatest gift you can offer is to help the client "consider ideas, approaches, strategies, behaviours, and other approaches and actions" (Ting and Scisco, 2006:51) not previously considered. Although, as I have outlined, coaches typically don't offer advice, clients will sometimes ask for an opinion, information or guidance. It is important, in the circumstances, that the coach gives the required support or observation without telling the client what to do. The client's own insight and learning is crucial for change to happen.

STRUCTURE – WORKING WITH QUESTION FRAMEWORKS

Whether your practice is aligned or not to a specific coaching model, your question framework creates a structure for the coaching conversation. Each individual coaching session synchronises with the overall journey you embark on with your client. I will refer to the "coaching intervention" as the questions, observations and challenges that the coach makes during the coaching conversation with the client.

There needs to be a clear structure to your conversation and, although in this chapter we examine creative uses of existing question frameworks, we also explore coaching models in depth in Chapter 5, and examine how question frameworks are integrated into those models. The purpose of this chapter is to consider various linear question processes to help coaches explore client issues from a neutral perspective, one that is non-directive of the client.

Specific sequences of questions are useful for the business coach, either as a way to get started with a new client, or simply as a tool to be used as part of their own coaching model. Common experiences, which shape the culture of a society, may impact on those frameworks that are more useful to you than others. South Africa is a complex, multi-cultural society, yet within organisations, there will be commonly shared values, beliefs and assumptions about leadership, management, responsibility, experience and language.

There are also subtle influences on organisational culture and individual behaviour due to the mix of history, family background, language, religion and education within an organisation. Another important factor may be whether an organisation works with an individual or collective attitude to leadership and management. Within South Africa, there is often a mixture of the two.

The culture of the coach may also differ from the culture of the client. For example, I originate from a results-driven, action-oriented, continual-learning American culture, which emphasises the "individualistic, egalitarian, performance-driven, comfortable with change, and action-oriented" (Hoppe, 2004:135 cited in Ting and Scisco, 2006:133).

This may reflect a belief about leadership and development that may need to be aligned with the client if their cultural assumptions reflect a collective rather than an individual focus. This collective preference could put more emphasis on relationship-oriented group results. We discuss the impact of diverse cultural experiences and various cultural frameworks on the coaching context in Chapter 6. What is important is for the coach to be open and flexible to the assumptions, beliefs and culture within the client organisation.

The following examples of question frameworks are generic. It is up to the individual coach to determine where and when these frameworks may be useful as a structure for a coaching conversation, or simply a tool to be used within the conversation. I indicate at the end of the chapter where you can find more information on each framework.

For the remainder of this chapter we will look at two-, three-, four-, five-, six-, eight- and ten-stage question frameworks to begin to understand the basics about coaching interventions. My aim is to help you to look at how – and what – you do as a business coach to develop and expand your own competence through new learning.

TWO-STAGE FRAMEWORKS

In the early 1990s, when I first started to coach team leaders and executives who headed the teams I was training, I worked with simple question frameworks (two-, three- and four-question frameworks). The first question framework I worked with was a two-stage framework, which ultimately led to an understanding of the core components of emotional intelligence, i.e. self-awareness, self-management, social/relationship awareness, and social/relationship management (Goleman, 1996).

At that time, I used this two-stage question framework to help clients determine their underlying values, beliefs and feelings as a preparation for setting goals and understanding their own intrinsic drivers and sources of stress and conflict at work. It was an insightful position to begin a coaching conversation as it went to a deeper level than just understanding what was working, what was not working and what (if anything) could be done differently. This two-stage framework looks at intrinsic drivers or motivators and helps us to understand if the client's goals are in alignment with their key drivers.

Understanding intrinsic drivers or motivators

This simple two-stage framework provides an insightful position from which to begin a coaching conversation. Part of the briefing before doing this exercise is to talk with the client about the difference between intrinsic and extrinsic motivation. Motivation is intrinsic to our underlying values, beliefs and feelings. The coach wants to find out what constitutes those internal or intrinsic drivers for their client. I explain to the client that external (or extrinsic) motivators come into action when someone else tries to tap into or engage our internal motivators, to encourage us or make us want to do something.

The questions help the client to discover their own intrinsic drivers or motivators, and help both coach and client to identify whether the client's personal and organisational goals are in alignment with their personal and professional internal drivers. As suggested in Chapter 2, the team and the organisation depend on the individual achieving their goals. In order to do so, goals must be in alignment with internal drivers or motivators, otherwise there will be internal conflict or stress.

When I demonstrated this in front of a group of learner practitioner coaches, they were surprised at the depth of the answers. This is because the coach is uncovering the individual's core feelings, values and beliefs. These can touch on individual existential anxieties. It will be very difficult to achieve the individual's goals without harnessing their intrinsic drivers. This process is important, as the individual's motivators must be aligned not just to their own goals, but also to the goals of the team and the organisation.

Typical responses are intangibles which cannot be measured e.g. achievement, balanced life, peace of mind, recognition and acknowledgement, a higher purpose, affiliation, financial security, honesty, integrity, balance, freedom to choose, doing something of value, and giving something back, support, and teaching.

If you use this question framework, explain to the client that external motivators come into effect when someone tries to "engage" our internal motivators, to encourage us or to make us want to do something. Examples of extrinsic motivators are the working environment, feedback, recognition and titles, salaries and bonuses, personal health plans, holiday leave, education and training, an overall salary package, and benefits such as a company car or share options.

To understand what makes the client tick and what drives them, and before setting goals, it is important, firstly, to understand values, beliefs and feelings that underpin their individual behaviour. As coach, you are looking for the intangibles, the unmeasurables. If the client replies with a measurable goal (such as a specific salary or titled position in the organisation), ask "What is important about that?" (you are helping them to search for an intangible such as financial security or recognition/acknowledgement). As I indicated in Chapter 2, for each motivator, the coach can ask "What's important about that?" Another important question for the coach to ask is "Anything else?" At the end of this activity, ask the client which motivator, if achieved, would allow the rest to follow:

1. **What is important to you professionally?** What is important about that? Anything else?

2. **What is important to you personally?** What is important about that? Anything else?

Other applications of this framework are to ask questions relevant to a particular project or issue, such as:

1. What is important to you about your job/this project?
2. What is important about that?
3. Anything else?

Functional analysis: the ABC of behaviour management

Cognitive psychology

Cognitive psychology is the study of the mind and its patterns, and has to do with memory, perception, formation of language and the roles of various brain functions. Cognitive psychology focuses on conscious rather than unconscious thinking processes. It is used to help people learn to notice and change their own thoughts with powerful emotional and behavioural benefits. The philosophy behind cognitive psychology is that what you choose to think determines what you feel and what you do. Specific thoughts create and control feelings, and thinking is largely within the realm of individual control.

Behavioural psychology

If learning in the coaching environment can be defined as the process that leads to potential behaviour change, then behavioural psychology is useful to us as it looks at how internal states and external stimuli influence our behaviour. Ultimately, the behavioural approach is useful because "frequently a powerful and successful person possesses one or two sets of dysfunctional behaviours that cause repetitive difficulties" (Peltier, 2001: xxiii). The underlying belief is that "if something happens to you repeatedly, you are probably reinforcing it in some way". In other words, behaviour is a "function of its consequences" (Peltier, 2001:44).

The strength of the cognitive behavioural approach is that it encourages measurement (always welcome in any organisation), and identifies when small behavioural changes can make an impact on executives in high positions. The flip side is that it can be problematic to identify and quantify specific behaviours to be changed, and it can be difficult to break down new behaviours into something that is measurable and easy to learn.

Functional analysis

A two-stage question framework derived from cognitive behavioural psychology is functional analysis. The results from functional analysis help clients to learn about their own behaviours, the effect the environment has on how they think and behave, and which new behaviours may motivate change in themselves and others.

In functional analysis, the coach helps the client to clarify a specific behaviour that needs to change, and identifies what precedes the behaviour, and what are the consequences of such behaviour. This helps the client to decide which changes (if any) can be made to the **antecedent** in order to change the **behaviour** and the **consequences**. The antecedent is what precedes behaviour; behaviour is what behaviour the client wants to change; consequences refer to things that happen right after the behaviour to change. In this questioning process, the coach helps the client to think not just about their behaviour – but also about the thought process which impacts that behaviour.

Stage 1: Identifying the old behaviour

Antecedent: What precedes the behaviour the client wants to change?

Behaviour: What is the behaviour the client wants to change?

Consequence: Which things happen right after the behaviour the client wants changed?

Stage 2: Identifying the new behaviour

Antecedent: What can the client do or say differently (i.e. changing their behaviour) that will make a positive change to their behaviour?

Behaviour: What will the new behaviour look like?

Consequence: Which things may happen right after the new behaviour?

Action learning approach

Action learning is used by hundreds of companies around the world. These companies employ action learning for strategic planning, developing managers, creating high-performance teams and becoming learning organisations. Action learning is a dynamic process to solve problems while focusing on what needs to be learned and how learning can benefit the individual, the team and the organisation overall.

Action learning helps you respond more effectively to change. Developed by Professor Reg Revans in England, action learning took off when adopted by Jack Welch at General Electric in the USA. Action learning is an experience-based approach to developing people that uses work on meaningful problems as a way to learn. Action learning typically comprises the following activities: experiential learning, creative complex problem solving, acquiring relevant knowledge, and co-learning group support.

Stage 1: The problem

When the client has a problem to identify, understand and resolve, ask them to work through the following questions:

1. Why does the problem exist?
2. When does it happen? When is it worse?

3. Which other problems does it cause?
4. Why is it difficult to solve?
5. Who is responsible?

Stage 2: The solution

Working with the client, take the same problem and talk only about the solution:

1. How would you like the situation to be?
2. If the problem were solved, which things would be happening?
3. What parts of the solution are happening now?
4. Which resources do you have?
5. What are some ways you can use the resources to help bring about more of the solution?

This is a very useful question framework to use with group coaching. The teams work in small groups, first with the problem questions, followed by the solution questions. The two stages are important. For clear thinking to happen, the problem and the solution stages need to operate separately. It is a useful two-stage process, as individuals often need to articulate what is wrong before being able to think through possible alternative options or solutions. For example, in one of my media client organisations, the leadership team found this a very useful framework to help resolve situations that went awry with customers. Rather than having an "inquiry" into what had happened, how much money was lost, whose fault it was – the team began to use this as a thinking process. It moved them away from a "blame" culture to a solution-seeking, collaborative culture.

THREE-STAGE FRAMEWORKS

Contracting

There are a variety of question frameworks available to the business coach, and I refer to some of the better known ones to help you use them creatively, referring to those I don't explore in depth but which may be useful to you. These are useful for coach practitioners, and for managers who prefer to use a coaching style with their direct reports. A useful three-stage framework to use during the contracting session follows.

Stage 1: What does the client need to change and do?

The coach and client meet to decide the potential for a coaching relationship. Coach and client also meet with the sponsor (i.e. the line manager, HR or OD department) to agree on the basic parameters of the coaching relationship (timing, fees, objectives and confidentiality agreements).

Stage 2: How will the client go about changing?

The coach, client and sponsor contract together on the methods they'll use to improve the client's capabilities, and the performance measures that they'll use to assess progress.

Stage 3: How do we make the learning stick?

The coach and client agree how they will embed new behaviours, highlighting the impact of such behaviours on the individual, team and organisation. Also agreed is the structure of the development plan to be created that will visibly show up results achieved as part of the coaching journey.

What needs work?

A simple three-stage question framework will assist you as coach/manager to understand the power of asking questions as opposed to telling. This emphasises the importance of developing active listening skills and opens up the coaching conversation to the client's key concerns in their job and life as a whole.

These questions open up the individual's thinking on a subject where they are stuck, or where they cannot see a situation clearly, as well as helping the client to identify the core issues the coaching journey will tackle:

1. What is working?
2. What is not working?
3. What (if anything) can you do differently?

Case study: What needs work?

A recent experience has led us to re-evaluate the balance between the simple "use of questions" by the coach, and the importance of the "relationship" between coach and client, and the way that relationship develops. One of my students and I demonstrated this elegantly simple coaching process in front of a larger group of 20 students. I asked the student the three simple questions:

- What's working?
- What's not working?
- What, if anything, can you do differently?

The purpose of the demonstration was for observation and feedback on what had worked and what had not worked between coach and client, and to learn how important specific questions are in the process.

As it turned out, how the questions were asked, and how attentive and focused the coach was on the client, and the coach's ability to "sit" with the client in her thinking space, proved to be the most powerful parts of the process. I interrupted the process several times to turn back to the group to discuss where coach and client were in the process. As long as the client knows explicitly during teaching demos what is to happen (i.e. that the coach will stop and turn to the audience periodically), the client will go right on thinking until the coach turns back to the conversation.

In this three-question process, the client's core values started to be uncovered. The question process allowed a key value, "health", to pop up. As it turned out, it was the crucial value. What allowed the client to explore this value (which had been held internally but which was never made explicit or articulated in action, commitment or taking responsibility) courageously was the non-judgemental focus and complete attention of the coach on the client through the most difficult moments in the coaching conversation.

So, the integration of the question framework with the key components that help to build the relationship seems fundamental to the success of the coaching intervention. The coach helps to create the space for the client to feel safe, even when surrounded by 20 fellow students.

FOUR-STAGE FRAMEWORKS

Whitmore's GROW model

GROW and CLEAR are models as they metaphorically represent a coaching process. GROW indicates growth through goal setting, and CLEAR signifies clearing the client's presenting issue. However, because both models allow you to design a framework of questions in preparation prior to the coaching conversation, they are both useful to describe in this chapter.

John Whitmore's GROW model is a basic four-stage coaching process which easily structures a goal-setting session with the client, and adds greater depth to the coaching conversation. It is useful for learner coaches who need to understand the importance of structure, deep listening and how to ask questions. Although it is primarily a goal-setting tool, it can be used in many different formats. The essence of Whitmore's four-stage question framework is "to unlock a person's potential to maximise their own performance" (Whitmore, 2002). It is helping them to learn rather than teaching them:

Stage one: What is your **G**oal?

Stage two: What is the **R**eality?

Stage three: What are your **O**ptions?

Stage four: What **W**ill you do?

Although many master executive coaches think the GROW model is very simplistic, its importance derives from the fact that Whitmore identified three essential concerns of coaching: developing self-awareness, taking responsibility for learning, plus the use of questions as the coach's primary tool. The questions that can be used in each of the four stages are useful, not just for setting goals, but also for developing an understanding of the very basics of a coaching question framework. Whitmore's rationale behind the GROW model is fundamental: to build awareness and responsibility in the client.

Stage one: What is your goal?

Outline the client's key goals for the year, their overarching goals, and then the goal for this particular coaching conversation. GROW is about working with the elimination of external and internal obstacles to goal achievement. Furthermore, help the client to identify the type of goal; i.e. performance goal, end goal, dream goal (Whitmore, 2002:59):

- What would you like to get out of the session?
- Where do you want to be by the end of our time together?
- What would be the most helpful thing for you to take away from the session?

Stage two: What is the reality?

Here the coach invites the client to tell their story as it relates to this goal. The coach should invite self-assessment, and the question could be, "What is happening for you right now as it relates to this goal?" At this point, the coach may take the client back to redefine the goal if it is not specific enough, then to clarify the current situation. Whitmore suggests the reality questions provide the most straightforward means of self-assessment. He suggests rarely using "how" and "why" because they invite analysis and opinion. Asking "why" invites defensiveness and keeps the client in the conscious thinking process. Whitmore suggests reality questions that emphasise the value of action and the difference between action and thinking:

- What action have you taken on so far?
- What were the effects of that action?
- What are the internal obstacles?
- What are the internal blocks?
- What assumptions could be limiting your thinking?

Stage three: What are your options?

This focuses on what the client could do. This will encompass possible action plans and strategies, a development of some alternative perspectives, and brainstorming options. What could the client do, from realistic to fantastic thinking? The options stage of GROW is not about finding the right answer; it is about creating as many courses of action as possible. Whitmore focuses on the implicit assumptions that people carry around with them – again the arena in which I prefer to work with clients. Examples of implicit assumptions are:

- I can't do it.
- We've never done it like that before.
- I will never get permission to do it like that.
- They won't give me the budget to spend.
- No one in the team has the time to fix it.
- I expect the competition have already thought of it.

The options phase is to stop the client from finding reasons why not to do something. It is to encourage the brainstorming of options without judgement and to eliminate assumptions that stop the client from achieving what they want to achieve. Some alternative questions for the options phase are:

- What if you had a large enough budget?
- What if you had more staff?
- What if you knew the answer? What would it be?
- What if that obstacle did not exist? What would you do then?
- What do you really want?
- What are all the different things you could do to achieve it?
- What else?
- What are you willing to commit yourself to?
- What are the advantages and disadvantages?

Stage four: What will you do?

Step four refers to what clients will do. What did they learn? What are they going to do differently? What can change? This is the practical, summing up and writing down of the action steps to be taken to achieve the goal set originally under "G". This stage moves the client into decision mode with precision and detailed timelines (Whitmore, 2002:89–90). It is about "will" – what **will** the client do? Hence the questions:

- What are you going to do?
- When are you going to do it?
- Will this action meet your goal?
- Which obstacles might you meet along the way?
- Who needs to know?

- What support do you need?
- How and when are you going to get that support?
- What other considerations do you have?
- Rate the percentage of certainty you have that you will carry out the actions as agreed.

O'Neill's "executive coaching with backbone and heart"

Mary Beth O'Neill (2000) focuses on patterns of behaviour and coaching conversations with leaders to develop their business goals. Her style is action-focused and systems-oriented. She makes many suggestions about the framework within which the executive coach works and suggests a sequence of questions to help the coach intervene successfully with the client.

O'Neill describes the essence of coaching as "helping leaders get unstuck from their dilemmas and assisting them in transferring their learning into results for the organisation". She has coined the term "signature presence" (O'Neill, 2000:xiii–xiv). Signature presence means "using one's presence in the moment at the time of intervention".

A four-question sequence

According to O'Neill (2000:5–7), the coach's question framework needs to embrace four essential ingredients with complementary questions:

1. **Which business challenges are you facing? How much time have you got?**

   How can you be results-oriented in relation to a leader's problem?

2. **What keeps you from getting the results you want?**

   What do you need to work or do to be a partner to the leader?

3. **What is challenging for you about this situation given the disappointing results?**

   How can you develop an ability to engage the executive in specific leadership challenges?

4. **What specifically do you expect from your team that would directly lead to higher results; and what will be required of you to produce those results through your team?**

Here, link team behaviours to bottom-line goals, pointing out the need to set specific expectations for their teams.

The journey of the individual executive and the coach are parallel journeys. You are helping that individual to find more of their own signature presence; at the same time you are being clear, objective and staying aligned with their issue.

FIVE-STAGE FRAMEWORKS

Framework for change

Peltier (2001) states that one of the reasons people feel they cannot change is that they would have to acknowledge they were previously wrong. He mentions the components of emotional intelligence (self-awareness, self-regulation, motivation, empathy, social skills) and uses Goleman's definition of emotional intelligence: "the capacity for recognising our own feelings and those of others, for motivating ourselves and for managing emotions well in ourselves and in our relationships" (Goleman, 1996:317). An intervention suggested by Peltier (2001:139), based on Silberman's (1986) model for change, I have rephrased as a coaching question framework:

Stage 1:   What is the situation now?

Stage 2:   What is the situation as you want it to be?

Stage 3:   What will keep the situation from changing?

Stage 4:   What action steps can you take?

Stage 5:   What resources are needed to help you make the change?

Working for change

Stage 1: What is the situation now?

One of my female executive clients, Sibongile, was working in a male-dominated engineering environment. She realised that it would be difficult for her to accelerate her learning and development without the mentoring or sponsorship of a senior executive. Although she had been put forward for several leadership development programmes, she was not making progress within her own division of this large corporate.

Stage 2: What is the situation as you want it to be?

The situation that Sibongile aimed for was not necessarily a promotion. She had attended several of the leadership and management development programmes offered within and outside the organisation; however, she did not have any direct reports other than those with a dotted-line responsibility. She wanted to practice the skills that she had learned on the various programmes, but had no way to build her competence or capacity. Those who had a dotted-line responsibility to her were about 10 to 15 years her senior. She had worked two years in the organisation, and her direct reports had each completed up to 10 years.

Stage 3: What will keep the situation from changing?

We spent an entire coaching session on this question. As Sibongile developed in self-awareness, she realised that she was the only one who could effect change. She was waiting for something to be offered to her, based on merit and her good work during the previous two years. However, unless she built alliances, and communicated her management development aspirations, nothing would happen.

There was another difficulty: her line manager was ineffectual and not particularly interested in her achievements or developmental aims. As far as he was concerned, she was in a coaching relationship, and he needn't do anything further for her except increase her salary year after year.

Stage 4: What action steps can you take?

She decided to put together her own leadership development plan, making sure that it aligned with divisional and organisational values. Part of the plan was to build her network within the organisation, which was sizeable and international. As we devised the plan, working step by step, she identified the skills and competences that were areas for improvement; and she identified her skills and competences not being utilised. As a business analyst, she realised that she needed to find a mentor outside of the organisation to help with her development. She wanted to move into an international position eventually, so began to build her network in the international office. She continued to work on her management and interpersonal skills to manage her tendency to "introversion", and began taking classes in a foreign language to improve the possibility of eventually moving into that market.

Stage 5: What resources are needed to help you make the change?

The resources she required were:
- finances for the various programmes which she personally funded;
- a sponsor for the organisation's upcoming management development programme;
- time and energy to apply herself to learning a foreign language on a weekly basis; and
- a health and fitness programme to begin to achieve a greater work/life balance.

Finally, she realised that her networking and alliance building skills were most useful to her, catapulting her into greater "visibility" within the environment. This paid off, and she was offered responsibility as project manager on a sizeable project. This would give her the chance to build her contacts across diverse organisational functions and to "project manage" a team of people. This framework moved the client from frustration, to a sense that she was in control of her own career path.

Working with the CLEAR model

CLEAR metaphorically represents a process to help the client "clear" a presenting issue. CLEAR is an acronym for **contracting, listening, exploring, action** and **review.** CLEAR provides a slightly different perspective on what to focus on in a coaching session, providing a sequence of questions to help the coach move progressively from contracting to reviewing learning, actions and decisions made. This is a very useful and straightforward framework for managers to use with direct reports.

STAGE 1: Contracting: Opening the discussion, setting the scope, establishing the desired outcomes, and agreeing the ground rules

CLEAR looks not only at the goal of the session but allows for wider contracting issues such as time available for both parties as well as specific ground rules to be observed, such as confidentiality. Questions to ask are:

- How would you like me to coach you today?
- What helps you learn?
- What blocks your learning?

STAGE 2: Listening: active listening as a catalytic coaching intervention helps the client develop their understanding of the situation and generate personal insight

- What am I hearing in the content of the words?
- What am I hearing that isn't being said?
- What isn't being heard or said?
- What could I ask that would help the client to reflect?

As a guideline, **listen** 75 per cent of the time and **speak** only 25 per cent of the time in your coaching session. Rather than focusing on your next response, concentrate on what the individual is trying to communicate through the content of their message: their non-verbal signals, metaphors, stories and limiting assumptions. In this context, you can paraphrase or reframe the client's words to clarify understanding and to avoid your own assumptions.

STAGE 3:   *Exploring 1: Helping the client to understand the personal impact the situation is having on them and Exploring 2: Challenging the client to think through possibilities for future action in resolving the situation*

All behaviour is driven by what we think or feel, and it usually has a wider implication than the specific incident or event. Exploring can be used to help the client understand their own assumptions about other people's behaviour as well as their own:

*   Has this happened before? When has anything similar happened before?
*   What was the outcome/result?
*   How did your behaviour/reaction affect the situation?
*   What did you feel when so-and-so said ... or did ... ?
*   What outcome would you prefer?

STAGE 4:   *Action – supporting the client in choosing a way ahead and deciding the next step*

In Stage four, the client should ideally figure out the next steps for themselves. Be careful not to advise an action or behaviour that worked for you in similar situations. Your experience might be invaluable and useful, but it does not necessarily mean that your way is the best way for the client to learn or change behaviour. In experiential learning the client's insight is the best indicator of change:

*   What do you think you can do?
*   What, if anything else, could you possibly do?
*   How will this (action step) help you achieve your goal?

STAGE 5:   *Review – closing the intervention, reinforcing ground covered, decisions made and value added. The coach also encourages feedback from the client on what was helpful about the coaching process, what was difficult and what they would like to be different in future coaching sessions*

This stage adds reflection, which is a missing ingredient in the wrap-up stage of GROW. Summarise what was discussed and agreed and ask the client to reflect and review the process:

- What worked for you in this session?
- What did not work?
- What else would you have preferred either of us to do or say?

SIX-STAGE FRAMEWORKS

Nancy Kline's Thinking Partnership®

Nancy Kline's question framework comprises a six-stage process underpinned by ten components or behaviours, positive philosophical choice, and incisive questions. One of the key theories which determines how we work with clients in the "coaching conversation" is that of "positive philosophical choice". Kline's Thinking Partnership® is based on the "chosen philosophical view that human beings are by nature good: intelligent, loving, powerful, multi-talented, emotional, assertive, able to think through anything, imaginative and logical". Kline says that "behaviour to the contrary is seen as the result of assumptions generated over a lifetime by events, conditions and attitudes in a person's environment" (Kline, 2005:4). The Thinking Partnership® model is based on positive philosophical choice and 10 thinking components:

1. **attention** (listening with interest and without interruption);
2. **equality** (treating the other as a thinking peer; keeping agreements and boundaries);
3. **ease** (offering freedom from internal rush or urgency);
4. **appreciation** (a 5:1 ratio of appreciation to criticism);
5. **encouragement** (moving beyond internal competition);
6. **feelings** (allowing sufficient emotional release to restore thinking);
7. **information** (supplying facts; managing organisational denial);
8. **diversity** (welcoming divergent thinking and diverse group identities);
9. **incisive questions** (removing assumptions that limit ideas); and
10. **place** (creating a physical environment that says to the other, "You matter").

Six-stage Thinking Environment® coaching process

In Kline's Thinking Environment® sequence, the crucial work is to identify and replace limiting assumptions with a more powerful worldview by choosing one core limiting assumption at a time that is relevant to the presenting issue. Kline's framework is based on six stages of questioning (Kline, 2005:4–21):

1. **Exploration** (What do you want to think about?)
2. **Further goal** (What would you like to accomplish in the rest of this session?)
3. **Assumptions** (What are you assuming that is stopping you from [insert goal])?
    *   What is the key assumption?
    *   Is that assumption true?
    *   What are your reasons for thinking that? (Look for alignment with positive philosophical choice, logic and information).

    Transition question:
    -   (If it is true or possibly true): That is possible, but what are you assuming that makes that assumption hold you back from [insert goal]?
    -   (If it is not true): As [insert untrue assumption] is not true, what are your words for what is true?

    Invitation question:
    -   Given that that assumption is stopping you from achieving your goal, what could you more credibly assume that would help you achieve your goal?
    -   Would you be interested in choosing that view for a few minutes?
    -   So, it is not true that [restate the untrue limiting assumption]. What would be your words for what is true (for a liberating alternative to that assumption)?

4. **Incisive question** (if you knew [insert true liberating assumption] how would you [insert goal]?)
5. **Recording** (client records incisive question and action to be taken).
6. **Appreciation** (key component: what quality do you respect/admire in each other?)

According to Nancy Kline (1999/2004:100–1), team effectiveness depends on the calibre of thinking the team can do. Yet most teams do not operate within a thinking environment with the 10 components necessary to enhance quality thinking and decision-making.

Teams are the most strategic place to begin organisational change, but the limiting assumptions of each team member and the limiting assumptions of the group as a whole need to be identified and replaced with empowering assumptions.

Although this is one of the purest coaching question frameworks I have encountered, its ultimate success in the coaching context is in the client's implementing the goals that are set as a result. This question framework helps us to understand the process of identifying limiting assumptions and replacing them with more empowering assumptions. This is a transformative process for the individual client.

In the Thinking Environment® question framework, awareness and insight is the context within which the coach works with the client to identify, understand and change those limiting assumptions that are most getting in the way of the client's taking responsibility, setting goals, taking action, growing and learning.

EIGHT-STAGE FRAMEWORKS

Well-formed outcomes (NLP)

NLP is a cognitive behavioural representation system. **Neuro** refers to the nervous system (the mind), through which our experience is processed via five senses: visual, auditory, kinaesthetic, olfactory and gustatory. **Linguistic** refers to language and other non-verbal communication systems through which our neural representations are coded, ordered and given meaning. This includes pictures, sounds, feelings, tastes, smells and words (self-talk). **Programming** refers to the ability to discover and utilise the mental programmes that we run (our communication to ourselves and others) in our neurological systems to achieve our specific and desired outcomes.

NLP interventions are based on the NLP communication model and can include third-position thinking, circle of excellence, rapport exercises and setting well-formed outcomes. NLP is based on the clinical practices and research of Alfred Korzybski (General Semantics 1930–40); Paul Watzlawick (Linguistics 1950s); levels of language and theory of logical types (logical levels); Richard Bandler (Computer Linguistics); John Grinder (Gestalt Linguistics); Milton Erickson (hypnosis); Gregory Bateson (syllogism);

Fritz Perls (Gestalt Therapy); and Virginia Satir (family therapy) (McLoughlin and Stout-Rostron, 2002).

Well-formed outcomes: practical exercise

NLP can be defined as how to use the language of the mind to consistently achieve our specific and desired outcomes. The various ways to achieve a well-formed outcome are well documented in the NLP literature. The following question framework will assist the coach in setting well-formed outcomes with the client.

1. **Stated in the positive:**
    - What specifically do you want?

2. **Specify present situation:**
    - Where are you now?

3. **Demonstrable in sensory experience:**
    - Evidence procedure.
    - How will you know when you've got your outcome? Imagine you have it now:
        - What are you seeing having got it?
        - What are you hearing having got it?
        - What are you feeling having got it?
        - What are you doing having got it?
        - What will others be seeing, hearing and feeling that lets them know that you've got it?

4. **Is it congruently desirable?**
    - What will this outcome get for you or allow you to do?

5. **Is it self-initiated and self-maintained?**
    - Is it only for you? (You cannot set goals for others. You can only set goals for yourself.)

6. **Appropriately contextualised:**
    - When, where and with whom do you want it?
    - When, where and with whom do you not want it?
    - For how long do you want it?

7.   **What resources are needed?**

  *   What do you have now, and what do you need to get your outcome?

  *   Have you ever had or done this before?

  *   Do you know anyone who has?

  *   Act as if you have it.

8.   **Ecology check:**

  *   For what purpose do you want this?

  *   What will you gain or lose if you have it?

  *   Is it worth the cost to you?

  *   Is it worth the time it is going to take?

  *   Is this outcome in keeping with your sense of self?

An alternative well-formed outcomes exercise

Here is a version for setting well-formed outcomes advocated by Peter McNab (2005):

1.   **What do you want?**

  *   Is it stated in the positive? Is it initiated and controlled by you? Is it sensory-based?

2.   **Where, when and with whom do you want it?**

  *   Have you considered different contexts? Is it ecological? Is it sensory-based?

3.   **How will you know that you have it?**

  *   Is it sensory-based, appropriate, and timely?

4.   **What do you get out of your current behaviour?**

  *   What will you lose? How will you maintain this in your desired state?

5.   **Ecology #1**

  *   How will your outcome affect other aspects of your life? Who and what else will it affect?

6.   **Ecology #2**

  *   Under which conditions would you not want to implement your goal?

7.   **What (if anything) stops you having your desired state already?**

  *   If so, what additional resources do you need?

8.   **What are you going to do? When are you going to do it?**

  *   Give appropriate detail with the first step precisely defined.

TEN-STAGE FRAMEWORKS

Business Best Year Yet®

Best Year Yet® is both an individual and a team coaching process. Business Best Year Yet® works with a ten-stage coaching intervention to create aligned individual and team plans by identifying and replacing limiting paradigms, creating a new vision, aligning organisational strategy with the team's top 10 goals.

The coach helps the individual or team to set goals and develop new guidelines, new values and a new empowering paradigm or vision. Not dissimilar to the Nancy Kline Thinking Environment® process, the central focus is on the moment of change (transformation of a disempowering paradigm to an empowering one). The 10 questions help the coach to focus the client first on the past 12 months, and second on creating a new vision for the next 12 months. This is a useful one-on-one coaching tool, as well as a tool for a team coaching process. As coach, you can use the 10 questions developed by Jinny Ditzler (1994), which follow, as a question framework to help the client to set goals that will reflect their new paradigm or mindset.

Having worked with the Best Year Yet® process for nearly 10 years, I have described each of the 10 steps for you to use in an individual coaching process. For those who want to use the team coaching process, you will need to contact Best Year Yet®. For more information on this process developed by Jinny Ditzler, refer to her book, *Your Best Year Yet: The 10 Questions That Will Change Your Life Forever* (1994).

Best Year Yet® coaching exercise

1. **What were your accomplishments over the last 12 months?**
   - What was the secret of your success?
   - What worked?
   - Why were you able to achieve what you did?
2. **What were your biggest disappointments and frustrations in the last 12 months?**
   - What didn't work and why not?

- What would have worked better?

3. **What did you learn?**
   - What can you learn from your own excellence?
   - What can you learn from those things that didn't work?
   - Pick three and turn them into guidelines for your next 12 months.

4. **In what way do you stop yourself from achieving your best, and how can you change?**
   - What is it that you do and say that stops you from achieving?
   - What do you say to yourself (write it down!) to justify these reasons or excuses?
   - Pick the most powerful one or two that would create the greatest change if they worked for you rather than against you. Now brainstorm the words that would turn it into a future-oriented, powerful, positive way forward.

5. **What is it that gets you up in the morning, motivated and ready to go?**
   - What is important to you about work? About home? About life?
   - Choose those unmeasurable values: such as achievement, recognition, health, being loved, giving something back – these are the intangibles that are really driving you.
   - Which ones most represent who you are?

6. **Which key hats do you wear, professionally and personally?**
   - i.e. owner, manager, boss, employee, partner, peer, husband, wife, mother, father, son, daughter, sister, brother, friend.
   - Choose the top seven, and add a reflective eighth (e.g. "my coach, my mentor, my tutor").

7. **Which hat (or role) needs to be your major focus to make the next year your best one yet?**

8. **Write down three goals for each role.**

9. **From your list, choose your top 10 goals which will make the difference for you.**

10. **Now, what will most help you to achieve them?**

DEVELOPING YOUR OWN QUESTION FRAMEWORKS

In this chapter, I have introduced you to a range of question frameworks that help structure the business coaching conversation. It is useful for you to begin to develop your own range of questions as they relate to your coaching model. At the end of each session with a client, write up your reflections on the conversation, making a note of the overall structure of the conversation and the sequence of questions that you used. In the next chapter, we explore various coaching models available in the business environment today, and coaching question frameworks that are specific to those models.

Question frameworks are simply tools for you to structure the coaching conversation. As you develop your work with your clients, choose question frameworks that are suitable to your personal style of working and the needs of your client. Gradually, as you begin to refine your own coaching model, it will become clear which questions are most useful to you.

One of the core skills of the business coach is the ability not just to ask questions but to ask incisive questions that will help the client to explore their own attitudes and assumptions about themselves and others in the workplace. Having done so, they are better able to develop an awareness of self and others, which in turn allows them to manage relationships more successfully.

What is shown to be transformative and to create the greatest change in the coaching conversation is the identification and transformation of limiting assumptions into empowering assumptions through the use of a question process.

Change happens when the client transforms limiting assumptions into empowering ones – and then commits themselves to action as a result. The coach's job is to understand this process and to help the client create empowering assumptions – and thus a new attitude or mindset – which could be the beginning of a new paradigm or worldview. This can take place at any stage of the coaching process.

However, there needs to be a high degree of trust between the coach and the client. The relationship needs to be strong. It is in the safety and confidential nature of the coach/

client relationship that the client will feel free to be challenged by their limiting thoughts, feelings or behaviour (Stout-Rostron, 2006c:225).

During the coaching conversation, the process of asking questions has to be done from a point of no prejudgement or assumption, really clarifying and understanding the thinking of the client. This is difficult, as each individual operates within their own worldview and limiting paradigms, and each coach approaches the coaching conversation with their own assumptions and biases, and must therefore learn to bracket such assumptions and biases and put them aside. This is a core skill for a coach: to learn to bracket their own assumptions and biases (Stout-Rostron, 2006c:147). For example, if as a practitioner you are going to reframe or say something about the client's process, just describe it, do not impose your assumptions on what they are saying. This is a difficult but crucial point for a coach.

The coaching conversation, ultimately, seems to be less about the mechanics of the coaching intervention than about the art of integrating pure, sheer presence and non-judgmental attention on the client, combined with the skill of asking the right question at the right time. It is the development of awareness that leads to knowledge and action. The coaching intervention is simply the bridge between reflection, awareness, learning, knowledge and action.

COACH'S LIBRARY

Bandler, R and Grinder, J. (1992). *Reframing and the transformation of meaning.* Moab, UT: Real People Press.

Dilts, R. (2003). *From coach to awakener.* Capitola, CA: Meta.

Ditzler, J. (1994). *Your Best Year Yet: The 10 questions that will change your life forever.* New York, NY: Warner.

Goleman, D. (1996). *Emotional intelligence.* London: Bloomsbury.

Goleman, D. (2002). *The new leaders: Transforming the art of leadership into the science of results.* London: Little, Brown.

Kline, N. (1999/2004). *Time to think: Listening with the human mind*, London: Ward Lock.

Kline, N. (2004). Keynote address, in *Coaching in a Thinking Environment*. Wallingford: Time to Think.

McDermott, I. and Jago, W. (2001). *The NLP coach: A comprehensive guide to personal well-being and professional success*. London: Piatkus.

McNab, P. (2005). *Towards an integral vision: Using NLP and Ken Wilber's AQAL model to enhance communication*. Crewe: Trafford.

O'Connor, J. and Seymour, J. (1990). *Introducing NLP*. London: Aquarian/Thorsons.

O'Neill, M.B. (2000). *Coaching with backbone and heart: A systems approach to engaging leaders with their challenges*. San Francisco, CA: Jossey-Bass.

Peltier, B. (2001). *The psychology of executive coaching: Theory and application*, New York, NY: Brunner-Routledge.

Revans, R.W. (1983). *The ABC of action learning*. Bromley: Chartwell Bratt.

Ting, S. and Scisco, P. (2006). *The CCL handbook of coaching: A guide for the leader coach*. San Francisco, CA: Jossey-Bass.

Watzlawick, P. (1978). *The language of change*. New York, NY: Basic Books.

Whitmore, J. (2002). *Coaching for performance: Growing people, performance and purpose*. Third edition. London: Nicholas Brealey.

5

Exploring and Understanding Coaching Models

Listening and observation are key skills for the business coach. Developing the skill of observation is partly to develop the ability to be "inside" the coaching conversation, and to be "observing" the conversation. It is to take up a meta-position, while never leaving the micro level of being present for the client (Stout-Rostron, 2006c:152).

Chapter outline

- Models
- Coaching tools and techniques
- How many models to use?
  - Purpose, Perspectives, Process model
- The coaching conversation and the coaching journey
  - Nested-levels model
  - The expert approach
  - "You have all the answers" approach
  - Learning level
  - Ontological levels – being and becoming
  - Learning
- Learning conversations
  - Three levels of intervention – behaviour, underlying drivers, root causes
- Four-quadrant models (Hippocrates)
  - Insights four-colour model
  - Domains of Competence model (Habermas)
  - Ken Wilber's four-quadrant Integral Model
  - Questions in the four quadrants
  - GROW and CLEAR models
  - EQ model
  - Kolb's Experiential Learning model
  - Using Kolb's four modes of learning

<table>
<tr><td></td><td>-</td><td>Hudson's Renewal Cycle model</td></tr>
<tr><td></td><td>-</td><td>I-T-O (Input, Throughput, Output)</td></tr>
<tr><td>•</td><td colspan="2">The U-process</td></tr>
<tr><td></td><td>-</td><td>Scharmer's U-process</td></tr>
<tr><td>•</td><td colspan="2">In conclusion</td></tr>
<tr><td>•</td><td colspan="2">Coach's library</td></tr>
<tr><td>•</td><td colspan="2">Endnotes to Chapter 5</td></tr>
</table>

MODELS

Today, coaches are trained in an eclectic range of coaching models. This chapter explores a cross-section of models that influence the work of business and executive coaches worldwide. I highlight the work of Daniel Goleman, John Whitmore, David Lane, New Ventures West, David Kolb, Frederick Hudson, Cummings and Worley and Ken Wilber.

Coaching models help us to understand the coaching intervention from a systems perspective, and to understand the need for "structure" in the interaction between coach and client. Models help us to develop flexibility as coach practitioners. They offer structure and an outline for both the coaching conversation and the overall coaching journey – whether it is for 20 hours, six months, a year or more. However, although models create a system within which coach and client work, it is imperative that models are not experienced as either prescriptive or rigid.

The coaching conversation is about the client, not the coach. If the model is too prescriptive, it means the coach has their own agenda to fulfil, rather than attempting to understand the client's issues. In this chapter, I discuss four-quadrant models, circular and U-process models. I explore the flexibility you have to combine models and to construct your own if you so wish.

A model represents a system with an implied process. It is a metaphor or analogy used to help visualise and describe the journey. Models systemically visualise or represent a process that cannot be directly observed. In other words, a model represents more than what you are looking at. If you can develop a model that encompasses the coaching conversation and the entire coaching intervention, you will begin to work with considerably greater ease within your practice. This is how we will look at models in this chapter.

A coaching model is representative of what happens, or will happen, in the coaching conversation (micro) and in the overall coaching intervention or journey (macro). I recommend here simple models that can represent both the micro and macro coaching interventions.

COACHING TOOLS AND TECHNIQUES

What is a coaching tool and what is a coaching technique? A **tool** is an instrument used to produce certain results; the tool is what you engage with as a coach inside the coaching conversation. For example, a hammer and nails are tools used to build a house; the tools you work with in the coaching conversation are profiles, assessments, questions, reframing statements, listening, question frameworks and models. A **technique**, on the other hand, is the technical skill, ability or competence you have developed to use that tool. For example listening is a tool, and active listening is a technique. This is where your experience, expertise and hours spent coaching come into effect. Often your tools and techniques fall into a specific part of your model's process.

The model is the process you use to work with your client. It embodies all of your tools and techniques, including the question frameworks I discussed in the previous chapter. Although you might be dying to explain your model to your client, they might not be particularly interested! They might be more interested in the tools and techniques that they will directly observe and experience with you. Often, if you are coaching other coaches, they will want to be debriefed on which tools, techniques and models you have used when working with them.

So, a model is a simple representation of the journey which can encompass the skills, experience and expertise coach and client bring to the coaching conversation. Part of the model may include the actions the client takes as a result of your coaching conversations when they go back into the workplace, and their own inner work throughout the entire coaching journey as they develop greater self-awareness and adaptability.

HOW MANY MODELS TO USE?

There are varying degrees of thought when training coaches. Some schools train their coach practitioners to use only one coaching model. Other coach training schools teach a variety of models and advocate choosing one of them, or learning how to flexibly integrate a few models to develop your own.

The key purpose of this chapter is to introduce you to a variety of models (not all) for your own learning and development. If you prefer one particular model that is taught in the marketplace, it is essential to go through the training to ensure you have a depth of understanding in its use. Eventually, you may want to choose whether to work with one model, an integration of several models or to develop your own. That is not for us to prescribe. There are many valuable and useful models available to you.

Whatever you decide, I believe that knowledge is power, and the more understanding of available models you have, the more intelligent your choice will be. When I teach coach practitioners in models and question frameworks, I look at how to integrate different models to construct your own. However, my purpose in this chapter is simply to explore a variety of coaching models and to give examples of how to facilitate a coaching conversation with each one.

Purpose, Perspectives, Process model

The key principle I want to convey is that it is essential to adopt a structured approach to your coaching conversation. This does not mean that you cannot let the conversation grow and be explorative – I mean structure in a big-picture way. That is the beauty of any model: having the freedom to explore within each part of the model. The Purpose, Perspectives, Process model (see Figure 1) was developed by David Lane of the Professional Development Foundation (PDF) and the Work-Based Learning Unit at London's Middlesex University (Lane and Corrie, 2006).

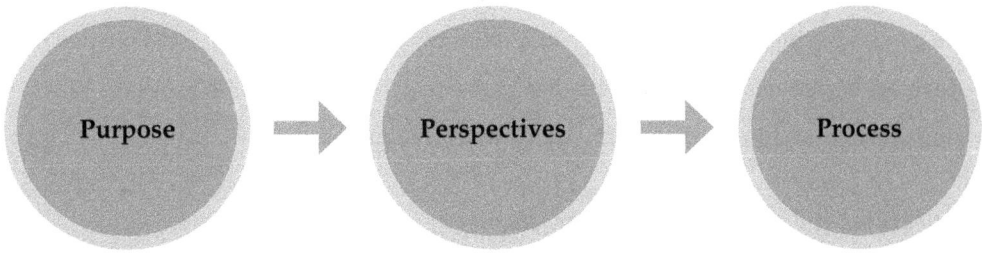

Figure 1: Purpose, Perspectives, Process

Source: Lane and Corrie (2006)

Purpose (where are we going and why?)

What is the purpose in working with the client? Where are you going with this client? What does the client want to achieve? Where do they want to go in their overall journey with you as their coach?

For example, one client working in the telecoms industry said in our first session together, "I need your help because everybody in the organisation distrusts me and I'm in a pretty senior position. What can I do about it? I'm highly respected by those subordinate to me in position and disliked and mistrusted by those superior or equal to me in position." As coach, your questions will relate to client purpose, i.e. "Where are we going, and what's the reason for going there?" It is usually better to ask a "what" question rather than a "why" question. For example, "Why are we going there?" sounds intrusive and can create a defensive posture on the part of the client. "What" questions help to create a bigger picture of the journey; "what" creates perspective. This client's purpose was to "build alliances and trust with peers, colleagues and superiors throughout the organisation".

Part of the client's purpose will be aligned with the questions they bring to the coaching process. Their questions are often related to "why" they want to go where they want to go, and they are testing you to see if you can help them to arrive at their final destination. Your job is to understand what is motivating them, what is driving them. For example, I worked with a group of people whose underlying purpose was to build a business partnership together in the field of leadership development. They peppered me with questions as to how they could achieve what they had set out to achieve as their overarching strategic purpose. My job was to understand their vision and the driving interests underlying their vision. With the telecoms client, for example, his purpose was to develop better relationships with his peers and colleagues, and building alliances became his overarching theme in the work we did together.

Perspectives (what will inform our journey?)

What perspectives inform the journey for both coach and client? What informs our journey, i.e. what informs the client and what informs the coach? Both coach and client come in with their individual backgrounds, experience, expertise, culture, values, motivations and assumptions that drive behaviour.

I recently had a call from a potential client within the energy industry. He was a general manager and asked if we could just chat. We chatted about his perspective on his background, experience, career and his current job. We discussed his perspective in terms of his position within the organisation, his style of leading and managing his team of people, the impact and influence of his age on his career prospects, and finally he said, "I have got as far as I can get with what I know now – and I need to know more, somehow".

We then discussed my perspective, i.e. what informs the way I work with clients, what informs my experience and expertise and, based on our mutual perspectives, he asked, "Would we have some kind of synchronicity or a match in order to work together?" He wanted to understand what models, tools and techniques I used as he wanted to create his own leadership development toolbox for his senior managers. He also wanted to understand how to handle mistakes: did I make them and what would my education, training and work experience bring to our conversation?

One of the things I am very careful of with clients is never to "over-talk" my perspective. The coaching intervention is about **them**, not you. Perspectives are informed by both the client and the coach's cultural and structural interpretation of the world – defined by their family, education, learning, qualifications, faith, spirituality, experiences, expertise, personality traits, values, feelings, motivations, assumptions and behaviour. In this first contracting conversation, we worked through the model beginning with perspectives:

Purpose – what he ultimately wanted from the coaching experience;

Perspectives – how we might bring our two worlds together; and

Process – how we would work together to achieve his outcomes.

The process (how will we get there?)

Using this model helped me to begin to understand the above client's needs, to develop rapport, and to identify not just his overall outcomes but a way to begin working together. At this stage of the model we contracted, set boundaries, agreed confidentiality matters, outlining the fee paying process and the development of a leadership development plan. We also agreed on timing (how often we would see each other and the individual client's line manager). What assessments would be useful for the individual client to complete? How would we debrief those profiles? We also discussed potential coaching assignments and timing for the overall contract (including termination and exit possibilities if either party was unhappy) and explored how to obtain line manager approval. Finally, we set up a separate meeting to agree the process with the line manager and the Group HR Director.

A model is a metaphor for the journey and embodies a structured process. This model can help you in three ways: to contract with the client, to structure the entire coaching journey, and to guide your coaching conversation. Out of the specific conversation about process emerged the client's purpose, the way our perspectives fit together to help him to achieve his purpose, and the process within which we would work to achieve the outcomes desired.

This model can be used for the regular coaching conversations you have with your client. The client arrives and brings into the conversation a possible "menu" of topics to be discussed, or even just one particular topic. One of my clients in the media came to me one day saying, "My purpose today is to understand why I am sabotaging my best efforts to delegate to my senior managers" (purpose). As the coach, I wanted to understand all of the perspectives underlying the client's aim for this conversation (perspectives), as well as identifying the various tools or techniques that could be used in the process.

In this instance, I suggested that we use the Nancy Kline six-stage Thinking Environment® question framework to explore his goal (process). After an hour of exploratory thinking, my client identified a "further" goal for the session. The questions in this process led him to articulate assumptions never actually voiced before. We moved eventually from a disempowering assumption to a liberating assumption that allowed him to identify action steps to delegate skilfully and artfully in a format that he would adhere to.

THE COACHING CONVERSATION AND THE COACHING JOURNEY

This model can represent the process for just one coaching conversation, but it can also represent the overall journey. For example, the client comes in with their **purpose**, "I would like to work with you; no one else will work with me as they find me too difficult". This client's purpose became to find a coach who would work with him, to help him to identify how he could not just develop the interpersonal skills to work successfully with others – but to demonstrate his new learning through visible behaviour change at work. The coach's and the client's **perspectives** will be unique and different. In working with the client, you bring not just perspective, but your observations as to how this client seems to be working within the organisational system.

In terms of process, the coach may ask the client to do a range of assessment profiles, or you may shadow the client at work to experience how they facilitate meetings, and interact with customers, subordinates, superiors and colleagues. This way you can make observations (your perspective), being careful not to interpret as a therapist would, and ask questions that would enable the client to develop self-awareness and self-management skills and competences that will ultimately lead them to interact more successfully with others in the workplace.

Nested-levels model

The next model was developed by New Ventures West (Weiss, 2004). This model introduces the concept of horizontal and vertical levels in coaching models. It is a "nested-levels" model. Although somewhat different from the U-shape model, which I discuss later in this chapter, it is based on a similar idea of depth. The nested model works first at the horizontal level of "doing", eventually moving into deeper "learning" one level down; reflecting about self, others and experience at a third "ontological" level where new knowledge emerges about oneself and the world (Figure 2).

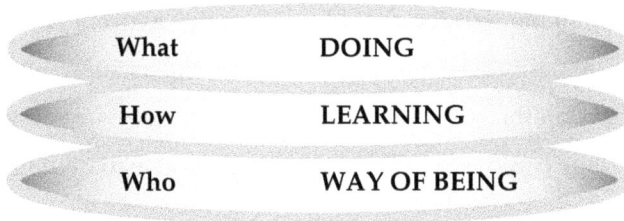

What	DOING
How	LEARNING
Who	WAY OF BEING

Figure 2: Nested-levels model

Source: Adapted from Weiss (2004)

In her web article, Pam Weiss talks about the two different camps of coaches. In jest, I call them the Jo'burg versus the Cape Town camp. The Jo'burg camp says, "I'm the expert, let me fix you". The Cape Town camp says, "You are perfect and whole and have all of your own answers". However, each of these camps falls short, even though coaches often fall into one camp or the other. The role of coaching is actually about developing human beings. It is not really about "expertise" versus "you already have all your own answers".

The expert approach

Clients are not broken and do not need fixing as the experts might think. Clients may be anxious, stressed, nervous, overworked and even narcissistic – but they don't need fixing. They are mostly healthy human beings going about their jobs and lives, experiencing their own human difficulties. Your job as coach is to help the clients to "learn" for themselves so that when you are no longer walking alongside them, they have become "self-directed" learners (Harri-Augstein and Thomas, 1991) and do not need you anymore. The second view about "expertise" also has limitations. The role of expertise is that, as coach, you are an expert; but coaching is not about the coach giving all the answers; that tends to be the role of the consultant, i.e. to find solutions for the client.

"You have all the answers" approach

The "you have all the answers" assumption is partially true; but there are several limitations according to Weiss. The first one is that we all have blind spots, and it is your job as coach to help the client to identify their blind spots. Secondly, it's perhaps a bit of "mythical" thinking that the client has all of the answers already; the flip side of that argument is that, if it does not work out, the client assumes blame and fault. In other words, "If I have all the answers, I should be able to do it myself without help". If that is not the case, they could feel, "Oh dear, if I am not able to do it myself, then I'm a failure".

Both of these approaches are "horizontal"; in other words they skim the surface of the work you can do with the client. Both help people to maintain the lives they currently have. The expert "Jo'burg" approach helps the client to do it better, faster, more efficiently, and the "Cape Town" approach may withhold the coach's insights and observations, which could help to build the client's awareness of their blind spots. What is important, rather than "fixing" the client, is the skill of "observation" on the part or the coach. There is no problem in helping the client to **do** it better, faster or more efficiently – that is often what the organisation hopes for in terms of performance improvement. However, it is important for the client to gain the learning they need to address blind spots and to build their own capacity and competence.

Learning level

If you continue to help people to accomplish tasks, achieve goals and to keep on "doing", they risk falling into the trap of being "busy" and possibly overwhelmed. They may, however, not necessarily get the "learning" they need to develop self-awareness and self-management. I know all too well about this trap of being excessively busy. If we keep "doing" without reflection we eventually burn out. To keep individual executives performing better and better, they need to work at one level lower – at the level of learning. They need to **learn how** to "do the doing" better. As soon as an executive begins to work with a coach, they begin the possibility of working at one or two levels deeper.

As coach you will be asking questions to help clients reflect, review and gain useable knowledge from their experience. In this model, the higher levels don't include the lower ones, but the lower levels include the higher ones. So, we need to help clients address their purpose one level down, at the level of learning. At this level you may ask questions such as, "how are you doing; what are you doing; what are you feeling; how are your peers/colleagues experiencing you/this; what is working and what isn't working; what is useful learning for you here; what needs to change and how?"

Ontological levels – being and becoming

The third and fourth levels of coaching intervention are that of who the client **is** and who the client **wishes to become** in terms of thinking, feeling and behaviour (I have added the level of "becoming"). Your questions move from "what do they need to do", and "how do they need to do it" (**doing**), to "how does their style of learning impact on how they do what they do; what do they need to learn in order to improve thinking / behaviour / feeling / performance / leadership" (**learning**); to questions about "what do they need to understand and acknowledge about themselves, who are they, how do they be who they are, and what needs to change (**being and becoming**)?"

Case study: levels of learning

My client, working in the field of IT technology security, wanted to lead and manage his team more effectively, and to build trust not just with team members but also with colleagues, superiors and clients (**doing**). In order to do so, he needed to identify what the interpersonal skills and competences were where he already had "unconscious competence", and which new skills and competences he needed to learn in order to build alliances and develop better relationships (**learning**). Even more so, he needed to understand who he is, what his essence is, what do people sense about him, how do others perceive him, and how does he behave when perceiving others (**being**), as well as who he wanted to become (**becoming**) in terms of his thinking, feeling and behaviour.

We agreed to do a range of assessment profiles, including a 360° feedback, for him to gain a sense of how others experienced him in the workplace. He was surprised to learn that he was experienced negatively as someone who barked orders, was impatient to the point of intolerance, and seemingly had no empathy for real feelings and people's individual lives. This helped him begin to identify who he was perceived to be and who he needed to become in terms of his behaviour if he was to achieve his goals (**doing**).

One of the ways we began to identify how to go about changing (**learning**) was from my observations of him in the workplace, at social business occasions, and inside the coaching conversation. Gradually, this executive client began to take a greater interest in others, beginning to articulate his assumptions about his team's capabilities and learning to understand how his assumptions were sabotaging the process of learning for his direct reports. Although the process took over a year, this executive became clear about his own style of learning and those of his team. He slowly began to engage differently with others at all levels in the workplace. Although trust cannot be easily built, his behaviour enforced the perception that he was proactively trying to change. This encouraged his direct reports, peers and superiors to be confident that his "being different" was something he was working on even if it was not perfectly embodied.

Case study: Doing

Another client, a senior leader in the financial sector, was an authoritative but gentle giant, whose size was somewhat alarming to his subordinates and direct reports. He embodied a sense of self-assurance and exactitude, which kept people at a distance. On top of that, he lost his patience with fair regularity. The original purpose of our work together was to begin to manage his "short fuse", in fact, our goal in working together was to help him develop "a longer fuse" that would impact on how he behaved (**doing**). We first identified how his short fuse impacted on his performance and on that of his team, and we looked at quite a few specific examples to identify what triggered his short fuse and loss of temper. Once we had identified the triggers, we could begin to look at how to change them.

So, what assists people to get things done? Above all, it is about clarifying goals, creating action steps, taking responsibility and being accountable. In order to perform more effectively, we need to help clients shift down a gear to learn how to work with competence (a set of skills) rather than just learning a specific new skill.

Learning

Your job as the coach is to help the client be open to possibilities of learning something new, and to help them relate to themselves and others at a deeper level. With my financial client, at the level of "learning", we identified his need for a greater sense of self-confidence. It was important for him to feel that he could deal with ineffective behaviour and performance at work. His effective handling of difficult situations would be visible to the more senior authorities upon whose recognition he depended if he was to move upwards in the organisation. He needed to know that he had the skills and competence to get people to perform at their best. Executives in the corporate world usually know how to play the game of politics, but they often don't know how to win over the people who drive results for them.

This client began to develop a greater set of interpersonal skills and competences. These helped him to build a bond with his direct reports and their subordinates. They began to trust that he was bringing change to the division and gradually, due to his hands-on style, they began to trust their new perceptions of him. He grew in leadership competence, managing team forums and regional road shows for the staff. As he developed leadership competence in his direct reports, he also gradually built bridges with staff. He was willing to understand the challenges faced by employees in the field.

> ### Case study: Addressing the person versus the issue
>
> Another client, employed on the technological side within the energy industry, was working about 60 hours a week, driving two hours a day, and doing an MBA part-time. On weekends, he had to find time to study and to be with his family. He and his wife had a new baby. On Sundays, he refereed a football team for disadvantaged kids. How high were his stress levels? We identified his need to learn how to create balance in his life, and to find a way to bring exercise, diet and nutrition into the equation – just thinking about it made him more stressed! He also needed to learn to let go of control. Eventually he found an entrepreneurial young man who was willing to drive him back and forth to work during the week. This freed up two hours a day when travelling that he could devote to study, sleep or emails.
>
> On the football field, he took to running with the boys. He and his wife also bought an exercise bike, which everyone in the family began to use. They worked out an economic way to add fresh vegetables and fruit into their diet. For the client, it was about learning how to "do the doing" better; at a deeper level becoming the more balanced person he wanted to be. This shifted the gears in the coaching relationship. It was a move from simply addressing the issue to addressing the person.

To use this model, you could ask questions such as:

1. What is it that the client wants to **do**? What is their aim or purpose in working with you?

2. What do they need to **learn** in order to make the change? What in their thinking, feeling and behaviour needs to change in order to do the doing better? How can they use their own experience to learn what is needed?

3. How do, and how will, their thoughts, feelings and behaviour impact on how they "**be** who they are" and "who is it that they want to become"? In this way, we work at horizontal and vertical levels. At the end of the day, the client's new attitudes, behaviour, motivations and assumptions begin to impact positively on their own performance and their relationships with others.

What is our aim with this model? Is it to shift any limiting sense of who they are so that they can interact and engage with the world in new ways? As the client begins to shift, it has an impact on others with whom they interact in the workplace. It also means addressing issues systemically, from a holistic perspective, whether it revolves around health, stress, anxiety, performance or relationships with others. Our task as coaches is to widen the circle, enlarge the perspective of the client, and help them to learn from their own experience to reach their potential.

LEARNING CONVERSATIONS

One of the core areas where coaches work with clients is that of learning. If you are guiding, directing and giving your clients all the information they need, it will be difficult for them to ever be free of you. From your first conversation as a coach, you should be trying to work yourself out of a job – in other words, to help your clients learn to be without you. Harri-Augstein and Thomas (1991:27–29) define learning as follows: "From birth each person strives to understand; grows and develops; reaches for greater awareness; constructs personal worlds; achieves at least some needs and purposes; invests new patterns of thoughts and feelings; acts to validate these; builds new personal worlds, habitations into stable routines; survives; declines; lives through personal and social crises ..."

Eventually, as a result of three to four coaching sessions with my clients, we complete a learning contract (adapted from Learning Conversations)[1] to fully integrate the learning with goals set and commitment to action. We continue to refine this throughout our contract:

1. **Vision** – Refine their vision: where is the client going?
2. **Strategy** – Outline the strategy: how is the client going to achieve the vision?
3. **Outcomes** – What are the specific outcomes that need to be accomplished in the next few weeks in order to work towards achieving the vision and putting the strategy into action?
4. **Learning** – Help the client summarise what was gained from the session in order to help underline self-reflection, continuing to help the client understand that they are responsible for their own thinking, their own doing, and their own being.

If **learning** "is the conversational construction, reconstruction and exchange of personally significant, relevant and viable meanings with awareness" (Harri-Augstein and Thomas, 1991:23), then **meaning** and **experience** inform our learning. Individuals learn something, take two steps forward, three back, and a few more forward. Although learning is an uncomfortable space until competence is developed, it is critical that learning is significant and relevant to the journey. It is helpful if the client embodies new learning personally and physiologically. It is about helping them to reconstruct their own thinking and feeling to gain perspective and become self-directed learners.

The conversation with your client centres on what is meaningful to them. If significance and relevance are to emerge from your coaching conversation with them, your conversation is going to be around what they need. It has nothing to do with what you need or think they need. What do they need to learn; what is significant and relevant to **them**? It doesn't matter what is relevant to you; it matters what is relevant to them. So, it is important to be aware of your own assumptions in the coaching conversation.

Three levels of intervention – behaviour, underlying drivers, root causes

This concept is introduced in the *CCL Handbook of Coaching* by Ting and Scisco (2006:19–21). The coaching framework of nested levels with which we worked above identified **doing, learning** and **being**. This framework can be adapted in another way for the coaching conversation. Instead of looking at **doing, learning** and **being/becoming**, we can look at **behaviour, underlying drivers** and **root causes**. It is important to be careful here due to the mistaken impression that coaching is therapy. Coaching is not therapy, although it can be therapeutic. Often when things go wrong it is due to poor practice on the part of the coach, perhaps from not setting proper boundaries (Ting and Scisco, 2006:19). The coaching waters deepen gradually, moving from the behavioural to the underlying drivers and root causes (Figure 3).

BEHAVIOUR

UNDERLYING DRIVERS

ROOT CAUSES

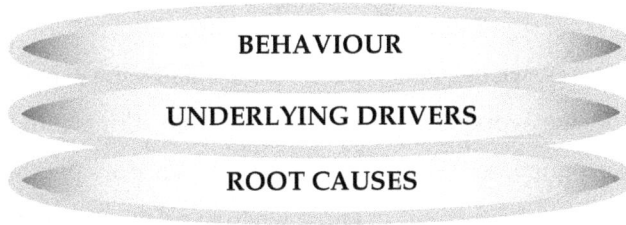

Figure 3: Levels of coaching intervention

Source: Adapted from Ting and Scisco (2006)

Behaviour

If we work at the level of behaviour, we look at observable actions: what the client says and does, what they don't say and do and their verbal and non-verbal language. Typically, the questions to ask are "what's working, what's not working, and what could you do or say differently?"

Sometimes behaviour is connected to difficult life experiences. Or, perhaps there is a family history of psychological disorders, such as addiction or chemical abuse. We need to differentiate between these behaviours and those associated with intrinsic drivers. This will be apparent through the ease and degree of consciousness with which these behaviours can be discussed.

Underlying drivers

If we work at the level of underlying drivers, we are looking at the client's personal style, orientation (introvert or extravert), culture, worldview, assumptions, values, beliefs, core needs and life experiences. Remember the two-stage exercise we did in Chapter 2? The question was "What is important to you about your professional and personal life?" You may spend the entire coaching journey helping clients to be aware of their underlying drivers and assumptions which impact on behaviour. It is at this level where it is useful to look at any assessment profiles your client has completed, which may identify conscious and unconscious thinking, feeling and behaviour.

Root causes

If we look at root causes, we begin to work with the client's life experiences, most often their experiences in the workplace. However, they may bring into the conversation traumas they have experienced. There may even be a presence of a psychological disorder, and it is therefore critical for a coach to know when to refer a client to a therapist. Ting and Scisco (2006:23) suggest a few guidelines: (a) when the client needs to delve into past life experiences, and (b) when the client needs to relive and heal past wounds. It is at the level of root causes that coach and client may start to identify repetitive patterns of behaviour that need to change for the client to be successful. For example, a history of losing one's temper, taking things personally, or creating conflict in the workplace.

A great way to start any coaching intervention is to ask the client to tell their life story. The coach begins to understand some of the client's current issues and presenting challenges, and begins to observe the client's patterns of thinking, feeling and behaviour. Because we work with Kolb's theory of "understanding experience in order to transform it into useable knowledge", this model helps us to determine the context in which the person is operating, where the individual and systemic problems may be occurring, and how the organisational values and culture impact on individuals and teams. It is at this level that the coach's ability to observe, challenge and ask appropriate questions can be most transformational.

FOUR-QUADRANT MODELS (HIPPOCRATES)

It is thought that the first quadrant model was Hippocrates' Model of the Four Humours. Although today medical science has moved on from the diagnostic aspect of Hippocrates' theory, his behavioural observations remain so relevant that many modern personality studies are based on Hippocrates' theory of the four humours: sanguines, cholerics, melancholics and phlegmatics (Stout-Rostron, 2006c:A40–A41). The model equates the liquids in the body with the four seasons and four elements: black bile, earth and autumn represent melancholics; phlegm, water and winter represent phlegmatics; blood, air and spring represent sanguines; yellow bile, fire and summer represent cholerics. Before exploring other four-quadrant models, it is useful to understand the model of the four humours (Figure 4).

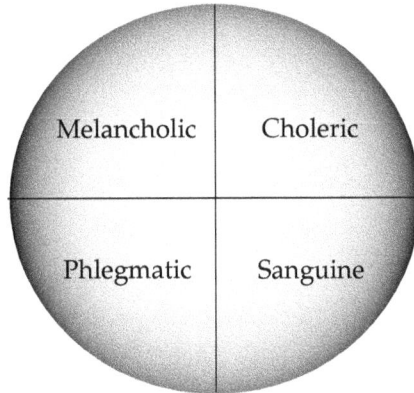

Figure 4: Hippocrates' four humours

Source: Stout-Rostron (2006c: A40-A41)

In terms of temperament:

Cholerics: appear to be tough-minded natural leaders (choleric refers to the bile, which Hippocrates thought controlled anger). Cholerics are known to have a short fuse and are referred to as A-types.

Sanguines: are outgoing, optimistic, high energy and fun-loving (sanguine means blood and is related to optimism and high energy).

Phlegmatics: observe from the sidelines and tend to comply with other's demands (the term originates from bodily phlegm, which was thought to make a person steady, peaceful and passive). This profile is seen as the cool dude, very laid back.

Melancholics: like orderly lives and are prone to mood changes (melancholy represents black bile and melancholics therefore have a tendency to depression). Melancholics are considered to have depth of intelligence; this profile is sometimes noted as that of a typical artist.

Insights four-colour model

The Insights model is based on the four colour quadrants of the Insights profile (blue, red, yellow and green). The four colours are used to represent "energies" that interact with the personality, and the subsequent archetypes (observer, reformer, director, motivator, inspirer, helper, supporter, coordinator) are an aid to understanding oneself (see Figure 5). The Insights profile is the result of extensive psychological research, particularly Jung's work on the personality. In 1921, Carl G. Jung published *Psychological Types*, and the Insights Discovery profile (with some similarities to MBTI®) is based on this aspect of Jung's work (Insights, 2008).

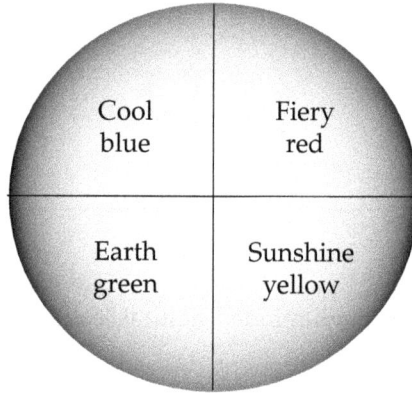

Figure 5: Insights Jungian model (circularity and quadernity)

Source: Stout-Rostron (2006c: A40-A41)

The colour energies on a good and a "not so good" day are:

UR Fiery red: Positive, affirmative, bold, assertive (Upper Right quadrant):
(bossy, aggressive on a bad day).

LR Sunshine yellow: Cheerful, uplifting, spirited, buoyant (Lower Right quadrant):
(idealistic, feet not on the ground, over-enthusiastic on a bad day).

LL Earth green: Still, tranquil, calming, soothing (Lower Left quadrant):
(sickly sweet, needy on a bad day, over-sentimental, over-sensitive).

UL Cool blue: Showing no bias, objective, detached (Upper Left quadrant):
(Lacking empathy and compassion on a bad day).

We can also represent Hippocrates' model using the colours of the Insights framework (Figure 6):

Cool blue	Fiery red
Earth green	Sunshine yellow

AUTUMN Black bile	SUMMER Yellow bile
WINTER Phlegm	SPRING Blood

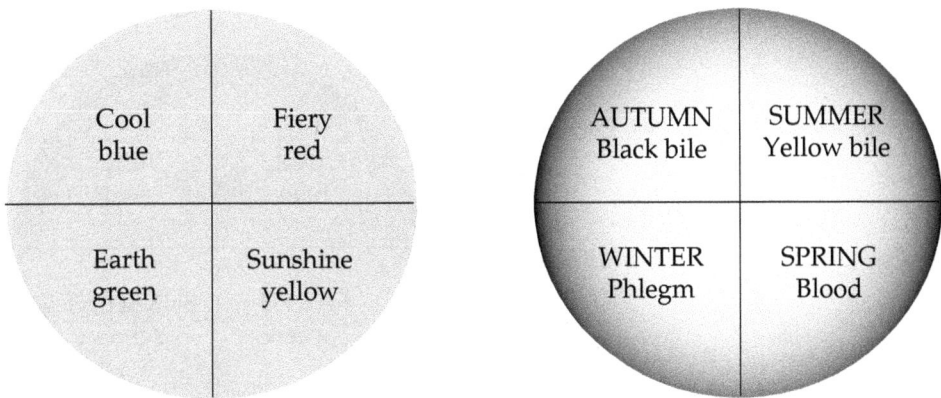

Figure 6: Hippocrates' quadrants with Insights colours

Source: Adapted from Insights (2008) and Stout-Rostron (2006c)

Our system of knowledge and beliefs can be seen as a set of **paradigms**. In the coaching conversation, we are often looking to identify and shift disempowering paradigms. This profile looks at conscious and less conscious personas; **introversion** and **extraversion**: Jung's attitudes/orientations; **thinking** and **feeling**: Jung's rational functions; **sensing** and **intuition**: Jung's irrational functions. This profile identifies eight archetypes within the circle, and four energy colours in the over-laying quadrants (Figure 7). These archetypes and the profile itself is only one of many useful assessment tools, which can be used as an assessment tool at the beginning of a coaching intervention.

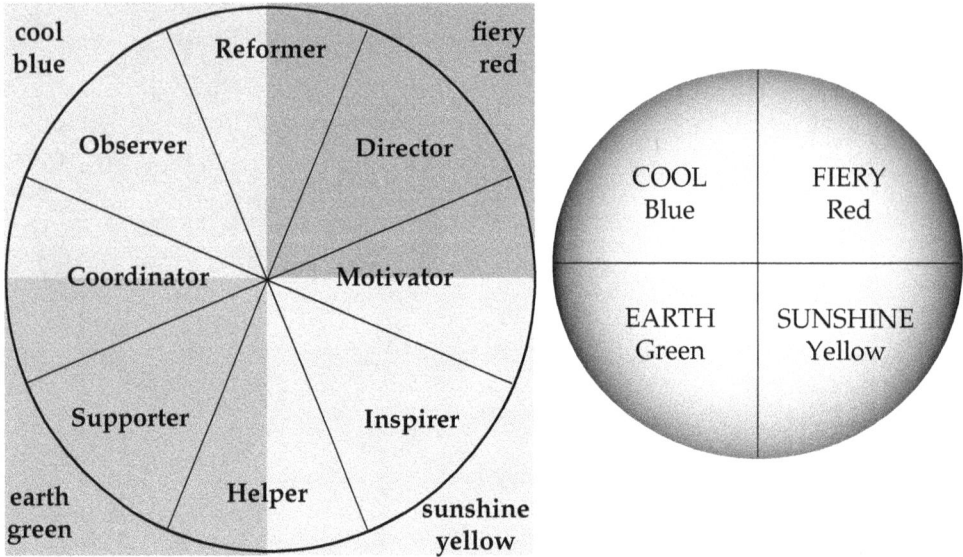

Figure 7: Insights Jungian model (circularity and quadernity) showing the eight primary Insights types

Source: Adapted from Insights (2008) and Stout-Rostron (2006c)

In this chapter, we explore coaching with models structured in a specific way. The four quadrant models are based on the Jungian Insights model, with "interior" on the left, i.e. what is not visible individually and collectively; and on the right, what is made visible through behaviour, i.e. what is external individually and collectively. In the Insights model above, thinking is in the top two quadrants (blue and red), feeling in the bottom two quadrants (green and yellow); the left-hand quadrants represent the interior, and the right-hand side the exterior of the individual and the collective.

Domains of Competence model (Habermas)

Part of a coach's discipline is to be able to use and understand models to structure the coaching intervention, helping the client to develop self-awareness and to change behaviour. Habermas's Domains of Competence model (Figure 8) is a precursor to understanding Wilber's Four-Quadrant Model. Habermas' model defines the "general structures of communication" that enable clients to engage in successful interaction (Wilber, 2000b:82–83). Habermas defined three domains of reality in the world that exist concurrently: I, We, It.[2] The right-hand drawing below is the original example in James Flaherty's *Coaching: Evoking Excellence in Others* (Flaherty, 1999:83). I have adapted it to a holistic model for our use on the left.

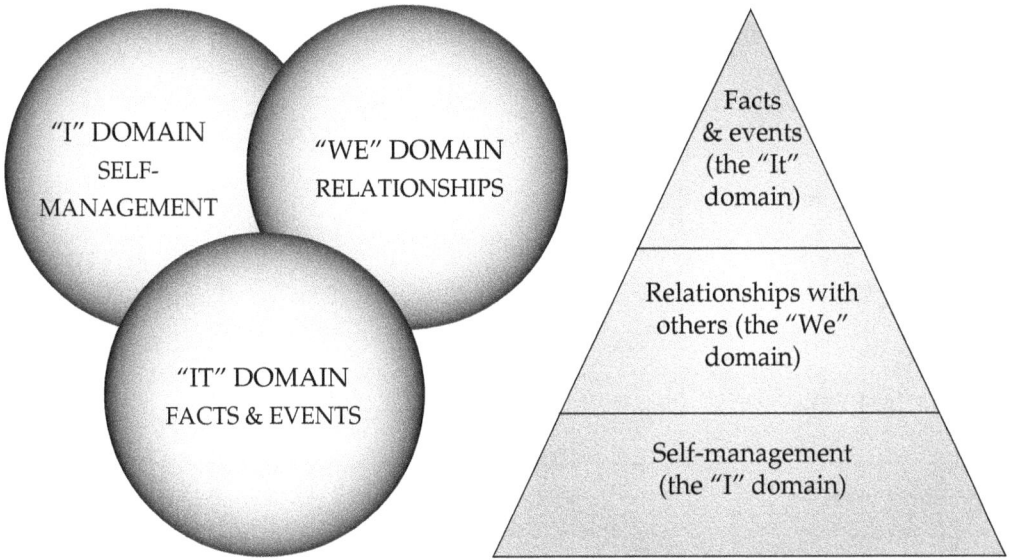

Figure 8: Habermas' Domains of Competence

Source: Adapted from Weiss (2004) and Flaherty (1999)

I: The domain of the individual

This domain relates to the subjective world of the individual who sees the world through their own eyes. Access to this domain is through self-observation and the development of self-knowledge. The skills required are those of self-observation, self-knowledge, self-management, self-remembering, self-consistency and daring. The competences are purpose, self-knowledge, self-correction and persistence. The basis of this domain is subjective and the qualities are those of vision, passion, integrity, trust and curiosity.

We: The domain of the collective or the community

This is the collective view of how we see the world. This view is embodied in social practices, roles, rituals, meaning, narratives and values that determine what is possible. Access to this domain is through dialogue, conversation and relationships. The skills required to access this domain are listening, speaking, setting standards, learning and innovating (Braaten, 1991). The competences are relationship, communication, leadership and inspiration. The basis of this domain's reality is "subjective". The qualities of this reality are empathy, reliability, openness, and faith.

It: The domain of the external or objective world (Wilber, 1996)

This domain is that of science and technology, objective nature, empirical forms and processes. It deals with objects, and access to this domain is by becoming observant, analysing, predicting and building models. The competences of this objective domain are processes, technology, measurement and statistics, and the qualities of this domain are rigour, objectivity, persistence, creativity and focus.

Practical exercise

Our clients operate in all three of these domains, and we can devise questions in each to further client development. As an exercise, devise questions that you could ask, relevant to each domain. These questions are to help your clients understand the lens through which they see the world, and to help them begin to think about, experience and see the world through others' eyes. James Flaherty says this model represents the essential domains of life in which a "leader must be competent" (Weiss, 2004). Examples of possible questions:

I Domain: How can you continue your own self-development? What are your short-term and long-term goals? How can you balance both work and personal life? What are your blind spots and how can you work with them?

We Domain: How can you use your skills of communication and persuasion to inspire people to action? What is your value to the team? How can you build competence in the team having lost a valued member? What are the values and goals of your team?

It Domain: What are the processes that are working in the organisation? What technical processes need to be written up for your training manuals? What processes are not being strictly adhered to and how can you best apply them?

Ken Wilber's four-quadrant Integral Model

Ken Wilber has written prodigiously about the evolution of his model, and various adaptations of his Integral Model are taught in South African coach training institutions. Wilber's Integral Model is an elegant way to map the essentials of human growth and development – socially, psychologically and spiritually. Wilber integrates five factors essential to facilitating human growth which he calls **quadrants**, **levels**, **lines**, **states** and **types**. However, in this book, we are going to work only with his four quadrants, which refer to the subjective and objective realities within each of us (Figure 9).

Wilber's (2006:17) philosophy is that "every level of interior consciousness is accompanied by a level of exterior physical complexity". In other words, the more consciousness we have in the interior, the greater our corresponding understanding of the complexities of the exterior world. If as coaches we are helping clients to learn from experience, then it is important that we understand the **I** (inside the individual), the **we** (inside the collective), the **it** (outside the individual), and the **its** (outside the collective) (Wilber, 2006:20–21).

"I" Inside Individual Interior Intentional Subjective Self & Consciousness **I**	**"It" Outside** Individual Exterior Behavioural Objective Brain & Organism **It**
"We" Inside Collective Interior Cultural Inter-subjective Culture & World view **We**	**"Its" Outside** Collective Exterior Social Inter-objective Social System & Environment **Its**

Figure 9: Ken Wilber's model

Source: Wilber (2006:36–39)

My purpose is to help you design coaching questions that emerge within each of the quadrants, to develop your client's growing consciousness in their interaction with "self" and the "world". All four quadrants can show growth and development. Wilber explains that the unfolding four quadrants can "include expanding spheres of consciousness ... Self and culture and nature can all develop and evolve" (Wilber, 2006:25). All four quadrants need to be taken into account if we want to work as integrally as possible with our clients, helping them to integrate perspectives and awareness.

Initially, to use this as a coaching process, we can look at the types of questions you might ask clients within each quadrant to build perspective on themselves and their own issues. This is a very complex model and we are working with it in its formative stages. We can devise questions from a macro and a micro perspective, whether for contracting, for the overall coaching journey, or the individual coaching conversation. Try to devise your own questions before looking at the examples listed after the following descriptions of each quadrant (Figure 10).

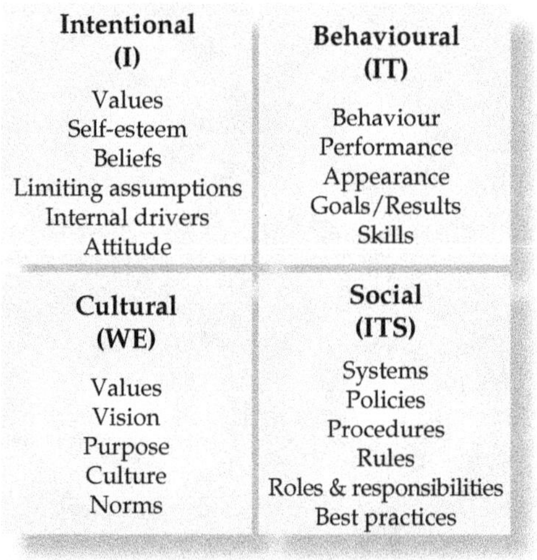

Intentional (I)	Behavioural (IT)
Values Self-esteem Beliefs Limiting assumptions Internal drivers Attitude	Behaviour Performance Appearance Goals/Results Skills
Cultural (WE)	Social (ITS)
Values Vision Purpose Culture Norms	Systems Policies Procedures Rules Roles & responsibilities Best practices

Figure 10: Ken Wilber's Integral Model

Source: Adapted from Pampallis Paisley (2006)

Upper Left (UL)

I (UL) is inside the individual, i.e. self and consciousness; the individual's values, vision, their purpose, their culture, their norm. In this model, the upper left (UL) is **interior, individual** and **intentional**. The internal you is represented by your values, your beliefs, your morals, your feelings, your emotions, your self-confidence and self-assurance. The UL represents what goes on inside of you and is not visible to the external world.

Upper Right (UR)

It, the UR quadrant is described as **exterior, individual** and **behavioural**. The UR shows how your values, beliefs, feelings and emotions show up through your behaviour and interaction with others in the external world. It is outside the individual, i.e. to do with the body, brain and behaviour. This is how the individual shows up in their behaviour with another individual out in the world; it is their interpersonal skills, competences, what they say and do; what they don't say and do. Once this behaviour is visible, i.e. what you say and do, and what you don't say and do, this behaviour is represented in the upper right quadrant (UR).

Lower Left (LL)

We, the lower left, is **interior, collective** and **cultural**. **We** is inside the collective, i.e. culture and worldview of the organisation or the society; the values, culture and beliefs of the team, organisation, society, nation of which the individual is a part. This is represented by an awareness of your relationships with others, with the values and beliefs of the collectives in which you operate.

For example, your organisation (superiors, subordinates, peers) or family, or within the communities of your spiritual life – these collectives all share similar values. Your organisation may, for instance, be underpinned by family values or health or may be capitalising on consumer needs with which you are in alignment.

Lower Right (LR)

Its (LR) is outside the collective, i.e. the social system and its environment. This is represented by the systems, rules, regulations and procedures within the corporate environment and society within which the client works. The lower right quadrant (LR) is represented by the **exterior collective** and the **systems** within which you live and work, i.e. the rules, regulations, processes and procedures that operate within your family, society, workplace, region, nation and the world. The shared values and the shared relationships meet each other in harmony or conflict in this quadrant.

Teams or companies within the system are, for example, able to work collaboratively. Or on the other hand, due to gender inequalities, an organisation may only pay lip service to the development of women in leadership, pulling candidates from training and development programmes without understanding the negative impact it might have on women wishing to move into management roles within that organisation.

According to Wilber (1997), these four quadrants enable us to map every phenomenon, every interest, every area and every process in life according to internal and external processes. As coaches, we can use this model to help clients to understand themselves, developing self-awareness and a conscious awareness of their interior life. Coaches can also use this model to help clients understand the impact of their interactions with others in the external world, and the way they manage themselves and their relationships within the cultures and systems (family, community, organisation, society and nation) within which they live and work.

We can relate this model to the four quadrants of the EQ model. In the upper left is a developing **self-awareness**, which people do not see. That self-awareness shows up in your behaviour. In the upper right are your interactions with other individuals (**self-management**). In the lower left is your developing awareness of values, beliefs, feelings and culture (**relationship awareness**), and in the lower right, managing relationships at a systemic level (**relationship management**), i.e. how teams or companies interact within an organisation, and how families work together in a family system.

Case study: How the quadrants are represented – in society

In South Africa during May 2008 we experienced a flood of violent, xenophobic behaviour. It had been brewing on the individual interior level (UL) for many years among individuals who felt discriminated against in society. As Jonathan Faull wrote in the Cape Times: "Many poor, urban citizens of South Africa's cities feel under- or unrepresented, buffeted by the tides of poverty, subsistence, criminality and the desperate competition for resources and opportunity ..." (Faull, 2008). In poorer areas, foreign nationals have grouped together by nationality to protect themselves and to continue to live within a semblance of a culture that they understand (LL). Locals, nationals and foreign nationals have managed to co-exist with each other with the odd external flare-up or demonstration of conflict at an individual level (UR) and between cultures (LR). The recent xenophobic attacks have been at a systemic level (LR): mobs and criminal gangs have instituted an array of violent attacks against poorer, isolated foreign nationals. The attackers' sense of frustration and discrimination shows up in the attacks on individuals (UR) and on groups of foreign nationals (LR). The sense of despair is due to a lack of jobs, housing and the continuing poverty within which many continue to live.

> **Case study: How the quadrants are represented – In the workplace**
>
> Recently, I have been working with an executive, Ben, in a retail manufacturing industry that has a history of success. Ben's divisional performance (LR) and his individual performance (UR) have always been rated as excellent. However, in the last two years, Ben has suffered an extreme loss of self-confidence and worrying health problems. This was due to working with a destructive line manager whose behaviour was extremely negative over a two-year period. This line manager undermined Ben constantly, shouting and humiliating Ben in meetings (LR), as well as displaying constant aggressive behaviour one-on-one (UR).
>
> Eventually, the constant undermining of Ben began to impact negatively on his performance (UR). The work between coach and client (UR) has been to rebuild the confidence and self-esteem of this individual by increasing his levels of self-awareness (UL). The coach instituted a 360° feedback (LL) and discovered that Ben was highly thought of throughout the organisation (LL). However, the organisation was very concerned about Ben's mental and physical health (UL). Gradually, through a combination of one-on-one coaching conversations between coach and client with Ben and various senior executives to whom he reports (UR), and coaching conversations in the collective team (LR), Ben has begun the process of working on his confidence and his health by learning new interpersonal skills and competences (UR), developing greater self-awareness of his own and others' assumptions (UL).

Questions in the four quadrants

What are the questions we can ask in each of the four quadrants to use Wilber's four-quadrant model in the coaching process? Devise your own questions before looking at the examples below (Figure 11).

Upper Left (UL):   What is going on for you; how are you thinking and feeling?

Upper Right (UR): Where are you in relation to the other?

Lower Left (LL):   How would you describe the culture, values and relationships in your organisation?

Lower Right (LR): Where are you in relation to the system/world in which you live and work?

INDIVIDUAL

What's going on for you?

What's important to you personally/
professionally?
What is motivating you?
What is working for you?
What's not working for you?
How does this make you feel?
What are your goals?
What would that goal feel like?
What do you think about that goal?
What is your feeling about that?
What is your understanding?

*Where are you in relation to the
other?*
(actions and behaviours)

What are you doing and saying?
What are you not doing or saying?
What could you say or do
differently?
What would it look like?
What would it feel like?
How are you perceived?
How would you see the other behave
if you changed your behaviour?
How can you consistently work with
your new behaviour?
What will get in your way?

Interior   **Exterior**

*How would you describe the culture
and values in your organisation?*

What are the team's values?
What are your team goals?
How do your values and goals fit in
with those of the team?
What is the impact of these values on
the team, organisation and society?
How do others interact with you?
How are you feeling in relation to
others?
What makes you comfortable/
uncomfortable in the work
environment?
What impact have the company
changes had on people's morale?
What's not being spoken about in
your organisation?

*Where are you in relation to the
system/world within which you live
and work?*

What needs to change?
How would your team function if
your goals and those of the team
were congruent?
What systems block communication?
How does the performance
evaluation system work?
How can your team impact on the
organisational system?
If your team did x … what would the
impact be on …?
What else goes on in the system?
What has changed in your
environment?
How is the economic downturn
affecting your customers and
company overall?
What is impacting your company's
overall performance expectations?

COLLECTIVE

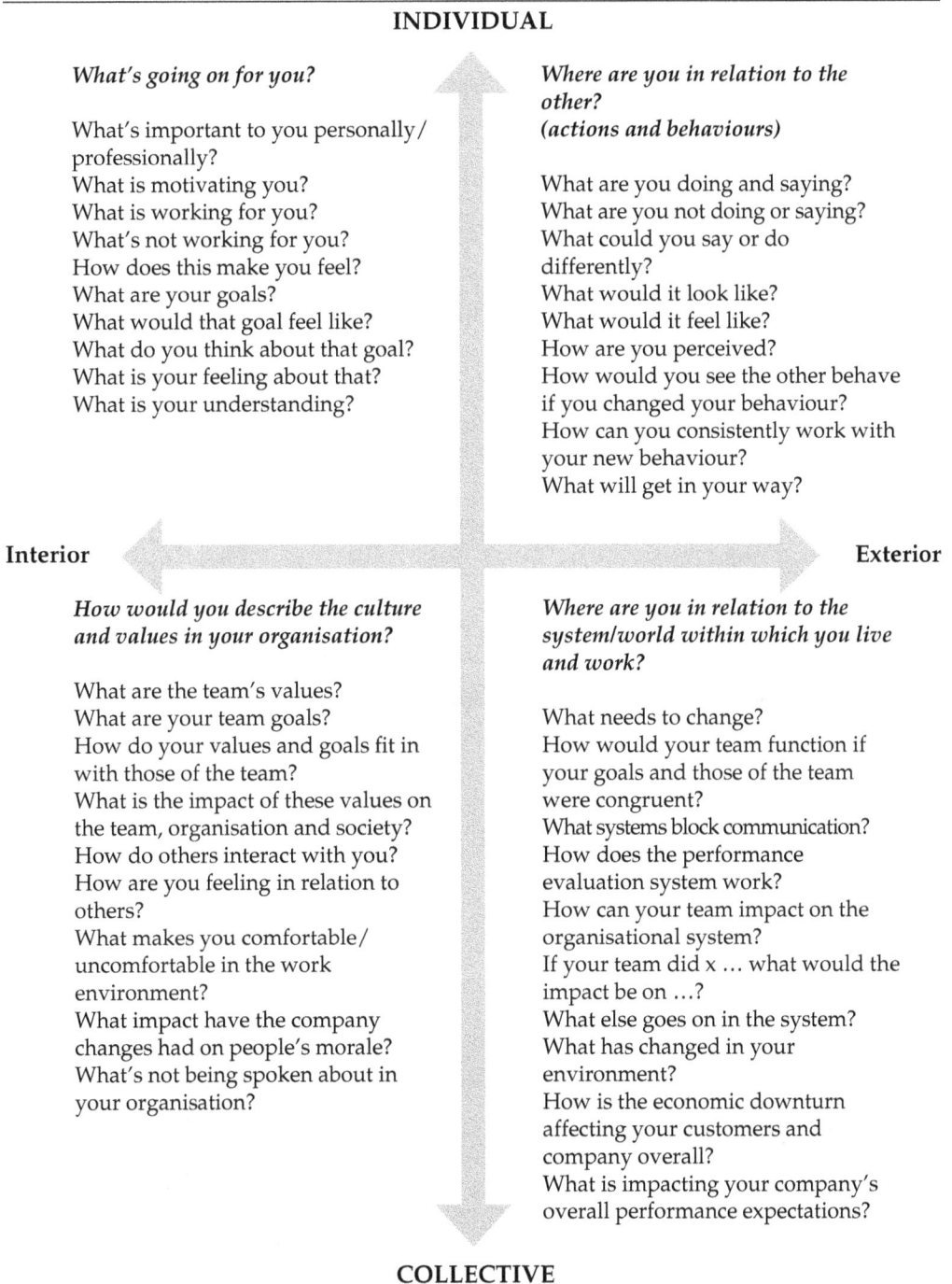

Figure 11: Questions in Wilber's quadrants

Source: Questions devised by author to fit Wilber's four quadrants

GROW and CLEAR models

John Whitmore developed the GROW model, which we explored in the previous chapter, as an excellent goal-setting process. GROW is confusing as it has been described as both a model and a question framework. It actually is a model representative of the coaching conversation, i.e. it is a metaphor for the growth which you hope your clients will experience in the overall coaching journey. It is a model representative of the process of that growth using a goal-setting framework of questions that hopefully leads to awareness, responsibility and change. GROW can be used as a goal setting process: identifying a goal, discussing the client's current reality, exploring the client's options, and summarising outcomes and what the client will actually do differently.

CLEAR as a model implies a contracting process, identifying the rigour of listening, exploring the client's issue at depth, asking questions throughout the coaching process, and finally reviewing where the client is at the end of the coaching conversation. In the previous chapter we explored the sequence of questions that can be thought about prior to the coaching conversation using CLEAR. However, the general rule with models, is that questions emerge during the conversation itself as they relate to the context, complexity and situation of the client.

EQ model

The EQ (Emotional Intelligence) model developed by Daniel Goleman (1996) provides fuel for investigation inside the coaching conversation, usually starting with questions about self-awareness and self-management, moving at a later stage to develop relationship awareness and relationship skills (such as interpersonal communication, managing people, and handling conflict). I have overlaid the EQ model with the Insights and Ken Wilber's (2006) four quadrants (left side for intrinsic, right side for extrinsic; individual in the north, collective in the south) (Figure 12). This EQ model can represent the journey you and the client engage in together. The coach uses the EQ model to help the client learn how to manage themselves and relationships. The coaching journey begins with developing the self.

As clients develop **self-awareness**, they become more aware of what they say and do, and how they engage with others (**self-management**). As they begin to engage differently with others they gain an understanding and awareness of the culture, values and beliefs that exist within that organisation, and the diverse relationships operating concurrently in teams (**relationship awareness**). As their awareness grows, they also become more aware of how the system operates, how teams cooperate with each other or not, and how units, divisions, staff, customers and stakeholders interact with each other (**relationship management**) (Figure 13).

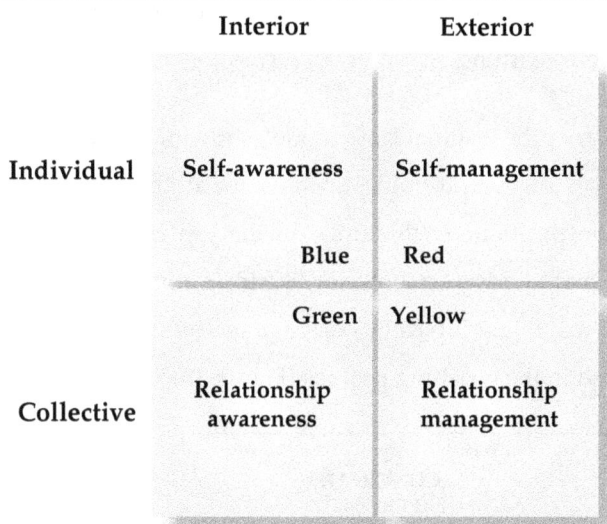

	Interior	Exterior
Individual	Self-awareness	Self-management
	Blue	Red
	Green	Yellow
Collective	Relationship awareness	Relationship management

Figure 12: EQ model, a four-quadrant adaptation

Source: Adapted from Goleman (1996), Wilber (2006) and Insights (2008)

Self-awareness ➜	*Self-management* ➜	*Relationship awareness* ➜ *(Team awareness)*	*Relationship management* ➜ *(Team management)*
Knowing self	Inter-personal behaviour	Organisational culture (values, beliefs, feelings)	Team behaviour; Client management
Resistances	Communication skills	Environment	Conflict management
Purpose	Management skills	Politics	Systems integration

Figure 13: Emotional intelligence: competences and associated skills

Source: Stout-Rostron (2006c)

Kolb's Experiential Learning Model

The coaching conversation is essentially reflecting on experience. Coach and client reflect the client's experience and behaviours, devising new thinking, feeling, behaviours and actions. Kolb says that learning is not just an active, self-directed process, but also a process where knowledge is created through the transformation of experience (Kolb, 1984:42). Sometimes you just cannot get the learning on your own, which is where the role of a coach or mentor comes in. The coaching conversation helps to transform their experience into workable knowledge; learning then becomes an "emergent experience" within a cycle of continuous learning.

Below is my adaptation from the original Kolb model, showing the learning modes and integrated learning styles. However, for our purposes, for all the four-quadrant models used in this book, I have positioned "thinking" in the top right and left quadrants; "feeling" in the bottom two quadrants; "interior/intrinsic" on the left, and "exterior/extrinsic" on the right. Thus, following Kolb's original model (Figure 14), is the version of Kolb's model to be used in the coaching process (Figure 15).

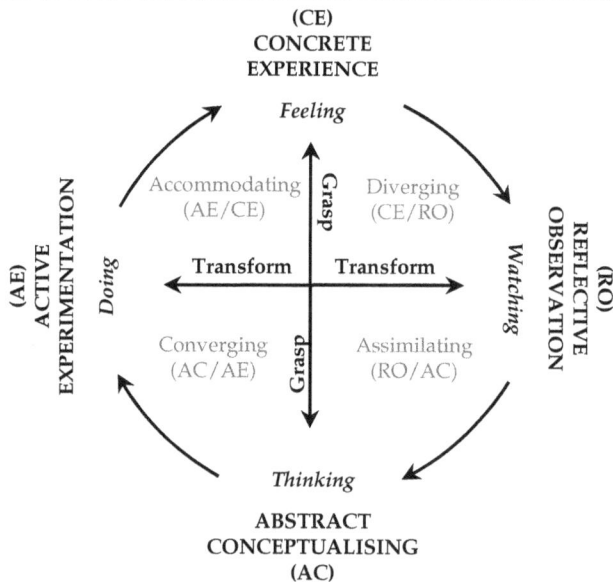

Figure 14: Kolb's original Experiential Learning Model

Source: Adapted from Figure 3.1 in Kolb (1984:42)

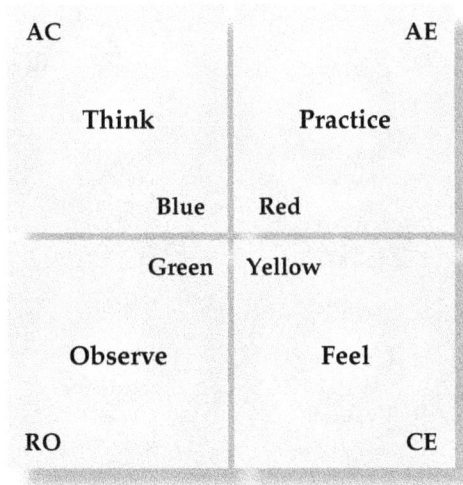

Figure 15: Kolb's Experiential Learning Model

Source: Stout-Rostron (2006c)

Using Kolb's four modes of learning

This is a very useful coaching model, as all clients come into the coaching conversation with their concrete experiences. Coach and client reflect and observe, think and theorise based on the client's observations, and agree what new thinking, feeling and behaviour need to take place back in the working environment (Figure 16). If the client stays in doing, action and concrete experiencing (e.g. if we coach continuously without reflection, observation and evaluation) it would not be possible to gain new learning (for both coach and client). Many businesses get stuck because they create business plans, put them into action and complete them, but do not take enough time out to review and evaluate. The integration of the quadrants into learning styles is explored in depth in Chapter 6 on diversity, personality and culture.

KOLB

AC		AE
Think Conceptualise Meaning		Practice Experiment Try Out
Blue	Red	
Green	Yellow	
Observe Watch Evaluate		DO Experience Feel
RO		CE

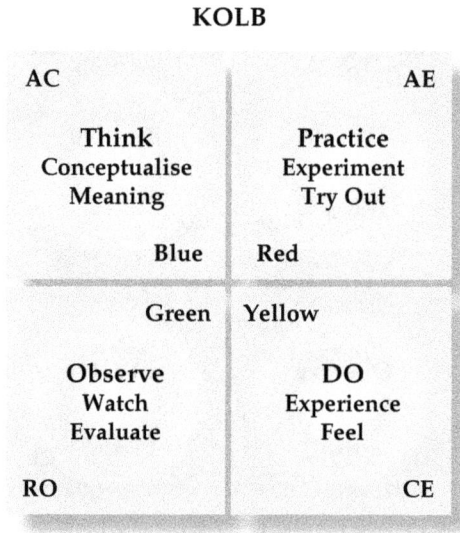

Figure 16: Coaching with Kolb's Experiential Learning Model

Source: Stout-Rostron (2006c)

The basis of this learning process in coaching is to integrate the four adaptive modes of Kolb's learning model (concrete, abstract, reflective and conceptual). Kolb (1984:41) insists that knowledge is the result of "grasping of experience and transforming it into divergent, assimilative, convergent and accommodative knowledge". A further definition of the coaching conversation could be "an integration of reflection and thinking on action and experience". Kolb's definition of each of his experiential learning quadrants is particularly helpful:

CE (concrete experience) is about feeling and experiencing;

RO (reflective observation) is about observing and watching;

AC (abstract conceptualisation) is about thinking and conceptualising; and

AE (active experimentation) is about doing and being in action.

Kolb's model can be used to structure the coaching conversation and the coaching journey overall. We gain knowledge through our own experience; each individual filters their worldview through their own experience. In reflecting on our concrete experiences, we can transform experience into some kind of useable knowledge. Some people prefer to step into the experience itself; others prefer to watch, reflect and review; some like to conceptualise, hypothesise and theorise; others like to experiment with doing something new. All four work in conjunction with each other. Essentially, each one of us integrates all four learning modes, but we tend to have a preference for one or two.

What Kolb's four learning modes indicate

Concrete experiencers: adopt a receptive, experience-based approach to learning that relies heavily on feeling-based judgments. CE individuals tend to be empathetic and "people-oriented". They generally find theoretical approaches to be unhelpful and prefer to treat each situation as a unique case. They learn best from specific examples in which they can become involved. Individuals who emphasise concrete experience tend to be oriented more toward peers and less toward authority in their approach to learning. They benefit most from feedback and discussion with their coach and peers.

Reflective observers: adopt a tentative, impartial and reflective approach to learning. RO individuals rely heavily on careful observation in making judgments and prefer learning situations such as lectures that allow them to take the role of impartial objective observers. These individuals tend to be introverts and require a typically greater reflective approach to the coaching session. Coaching needs to be very reflective for them to access the learning needed to move forward.

Abstract conceptualisers: adopt an analytical, conceptual approach to learning that relies heavily on logical thinking and rational evaluation. AC individuals tend to be oriented more toward things and symbols and less toward other people. They learn in impersonal, authority-directed learning situations that emphasise theory and systematic analysis. They are often frustrated by, and benefit little from, unstructured "discovery" learning approaches, such as activities and role plays. The coach needs to be able to provide a structured thinking approach to the session, and could use the Kolb model to help the client to access the other learning modes.

Active experimenters: adopt an active, "doing" orientation to learning that relies heavily on experimentation. AE individuals learn best when they can engage in such things as projects, homework, developing new techniques inside the coaching conversation that they can take back out to the workplace, and in group discussions. They dislike passive learning situations such as lectures, and tend to be extraverts. AE clients can be active and noisy and may require focused energy in the coaching environment.

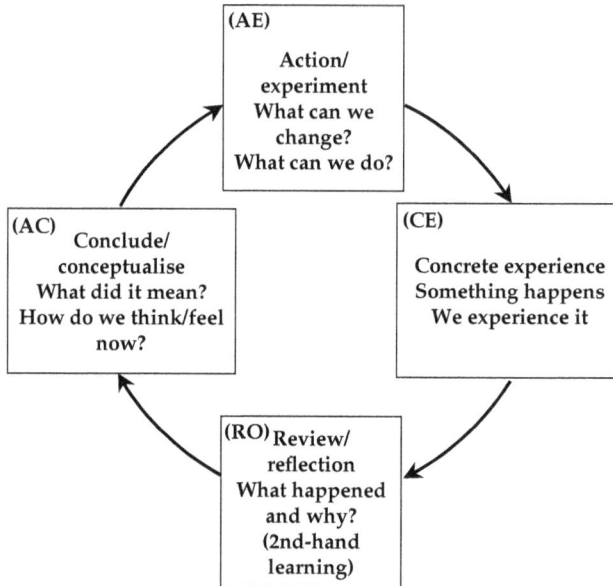

Figure 17: Kolb's adult learning cycle

Source: Adapted from Kolb (1984:42)

Case study – Using Kolb's learning modes as a coaching process

In the case study below, the coach's comments are in italics; the clients are in standard type. The coach determined during a previous coaching session that it would be useful with this client (who was a coach) to work with a specific concrete "coaching" experience, as the client had had trouble using the Kolb process as a coaching model.

The aim of the coaching conversation below was to help the client to understand the four modes of the Kolb experiential learning process to use with his own coaching clients. Having read the definitions of each learning mode and the following case study, think about how you can use this model in certain coaching situations.

What is your goal? To build my confidence in the coaching process and to pay attention to structure; and to do so I want to try to understand how to use the Kolb model as a coaching process.

OK, so would you like me to use the Kolb model for this conversation, and then we can reflect back at the end to understand how we moved through the four modes, from concrete experience, to reflective observation, abstract conceptualisation and active experimentation? Yes, and would we always start with concrete experience?

Not always; it depends on what the client needs. You said that you have a specific experience that you wish to start with, so I am suggesting we begin with your specific concrete experience. Okay, let's go.

Concrete experience (CE)

Can you tell me a little more about this goal, sharing your experience so that I can understand the issue? I want to explore the triggers that prompt me to be too hasty when I am coaching. Usually, as I end the coaching conversation, I find that I have been very judgemental of the client, and I always rush to close. In other words, I make way too many assumptions. I want to understand what I can do to guard against rushing.

So tell me a little more about what happens that makes you rush in this coaching session. If you like, tell me a little about both your thoughts and feelings, as well as what you feel physically in your body as you coach. I feel helpless, frustrated, with a huge sense of urgency and anxiety, feeling that I need to get it done at a high level.

Anything else? It's useful to look at what you are thinking and feeling, whether it's anxiety or a sense of urgency. Looking at this one specific instance may be a really useful way for us to look at what happens, not just in this instance, but also when this has happened to you in previous coaching sessions. Yes, it's a similar experience in all of my coaching sessions.

One of the words that you used earlier was "assumptions". Yes.

Can you remember any of the things you assume as you begin to feel that anxiety? Can you visualise or feel yourself back in that situation and describe how you are experiencing it? Yes, some of the assumptions are that I might not be able to help; that I should already know the answers; that this is too difficult already.

And your goal during the coaching session for yourself is? I want to complete the Kolb coaching process and give value to the client.

Reflective observation (RO)

Let's now look back at this experience as something you've experienced in the past. When you were in the coaching session, what triggered your assumptions? I cannot recall; only that **time** seemed to be one of the triggers.

So when time became a trigger, what kinds of things were you assuming? That I should jump in with answers for the client; that I should make suggestions about what they should do; and that perhaps I'm not the right person to do this; and also I sort of feel like they "need fixing". *When you got to the end of the session what did you assume?* That I hadn't completed stuff and that I hadn't really acknowledged them, or something about them.

So, as we reflect on this, it seems that you actually had some clarity on your own thinking and feeling which can be useful for us to learn from. Is there anything else about your assumptions that got in your way? Just that I spend so much time thinking about my own thoughts that I am not listening effectively to the client.

And what would you prefer to do? I want to focus on the client. I want to let go of my thoughts.

Okay, so what can we learn from this that will help you learn next time? I think that I need to find a way to centre and focus before I start the coaching conversation, so that I am entirely focused on them throughout.

*You spoke earlier about having your attention in several areas at once as identified as the three streams of attention in Nancy Kline's Thinking Environment® (Kline, 1999/2004). I would like to do that; be focused on them, know what my responses are and still create an environment conducive to coaching.

If you are able to do that, will you experience the coaching conversation differently from your current experience? Yes, I will feel that I can add value to the client, which is what I want. And I feel that this process may be perfect for me to use.

What do you mean by perfect? I think it is structured yet has flexibility, and I think I can trust the process.

And so if you were to have faith in this process, how would that help you? ... Anything else, now that we are reflecting? What else do you think you need to learn from this specific experience? I think it's about self-balance.

Can I just check that I understand what you mean by "self-balance"? For me, self-balance forges self-respect and respect for others.

So self-balance in the coaching relationship is self-balance for the coach as well as self- balance for the client? What I'm going to suggest is that we move from reflection on this specific conversation to think about and conceptualise what the conversation may look and feel like if there is self-balance for both coach and client? Great, I'm happy with that. I think that if I have dealt with some of the assumptions that we have discovered then that will help, but also I need to feel centred and balanced before entering into the conversation.

Okay, shall we overturn some of these disempowering assumptions before moving on? Yes, please ...

(Coach and client identify the key limiting assumptions, and the coach helps the client to identify if they are true or false, identifying several more empowering assumptions and ways to think. They then move into the next phase using the Kolb experiential learning process.)

Abstract conceptualisation (AC)

Do you mean, noticing and observing what you think and feel, and letting go of assumptions that might disempower both you and the client? Yes, I need to focus on the client, knowing that if I just listen that that in itself is empowering and gives some space for thinking together.

So, you want to refocus and give attention back to the client. What else? I need to find some way to ... create a sense of groundedness, like being rooted but still flexible.

Some of the language you use is sometimes reflective of NLP.[3] So I wonder if it is "anchoring" you are thinking of? Yes, I need some sort of physical anchor to move me out of my head to be able to create a focus on listening and being present for the client at all times. That will help me shift some of these assumptions. Can you help me with that?

Sure, tell me what would work best as an anchor for you? A question, a thought, something you do physically with your hands? That would be the simplest and not distract the client.

In other words, you need to use something physical and tangible to take the focus off your own disempowering thinking? Yes, that would be perfect. I don't want to get up and pace up and down as that would be distracting. I want to do something that calms both my mind and my body.

Okay, so that would help you to refocus; sounds useful. (Coach and client agree on the anchor, and the coach helps the client to create an anchor that will work in every coaching conversation to create focus). *Anything else that would help you to refocus on the client?* No, that is perfect.[4]

Do you think that this one gesture will be enough to help you anchor and refocus on the client? Yes.

OK, so in the coaching conversation, this will help to manage self-balance; what else would be useful to think about in terms of self-balance for the client? Well, actually it was an assumption to think the client needs self-balance. It's actually me who needs it, so I think this is a start!

What else might be useful – to think about how you use your self-balance and refocus back on the client? I don't know.

It's a tough one. My observation is that if this has happened once it may happen again. So in what way could you work going forward? It's something about being present for the client in the way I frame questions and reflect back what they are saying. If I am "anchored" I will be easily able to do it because I know that I have done it before.

Great, so essentially to refocus and give attention you would need to fire your anchor. In the same way, if self-balance continues to come up, will the other reflective practices that you have prepared help you? Definitely, and this is how I will use them ...

Anything else that when you conceptualise the coaching conversation would be helpful to you? Yes, I will ...

Anything else that would be helpful for you to focus on the client?

Active experimentation (AE)

So we've been working on conceptualising and moving away from your disempowering thinking. Shall we think about how you actually could do it differently, and think differently, when coaching? Yes, let's try it.

So now we will actively think about how you would do it. Let's start by thinking about how you would have done the old conversation differently ... I would be so focused on the client that I am hearing what she has to say, and I am actually thinking about where we are in the process, in terms of structure, in the coaching conversation.

Can you think of something coming up to think about how you would do it differently? Yes, in fact I am going to practice this at home first, focusing on the kids as they tell me about their school day. I'm going to fire my anchor and listen to my wife. Usually I just interrupt and don't let any of them finish what they have to say. I guess I'm fixing them too! I think it's a practice that I have to begin first at home in order to make it something that begins to come naturally.

That sounds great – it's always hardest to do any kind of new thinking and behaviour at home. Also, I think I need to use my anchor to put on the "pause button". In other words, I need to pause before I say anything. This is something I need to experiment with.

Pushing the pause button sounds like a great anchor. How will you reflect how effectively you are in pressing the pause button? Perhaps I should make a few notes ...

Would you like to write down some of these new active practices, and in our next session, we can reflect on what has worked for you? These are useful new practices. (Client makes notes). *Is there anything else you would like to do to actively experiment with doing something differently?* No, I think this will do and I am already developing some awareness of myself that will help with self-balance. I think actually that I may keep a small journal at the end of the day that will help me to adopt these practices. I have several coaching sessions with new clients before I see you again, and I will reflect on what's worked and what hasn't when I see you next.

Fine, anything else that comes to mind that would be useful going out into the world and doing it differently? No, I like this process and just want to reflect a few minutes on how we went through the four modes of the Kolb process, and how I might use it and my anchors in my next coaching session. If we could do that, then I think I'm all set. Thanks.

Great, let's finish with that. Okay, let me think it through with you. We seem to have stepped into the "concrete experience" itself when you asked me to think about how I felt, what I was thinking, and what I was assuming in that one specific coaching conversation with my client. We then moved into a reflective space, as I reflected on those thoughts, feelings and assumptions and we thought about what I had learned from that session in reflection. We then talked about the coaching conversation in a kind of thinking manner, i.e. we conceptualised a different way forward, and in fact we moved into active experimentation as we developed anchors. So, in fact, we already have begun to experiment. Then we worked with anchors and talked about how pause buttons can best be put to use at home and in my next coaching session. I have an action plan and will report back on how I do in our next session. I think it's about more self-awareness, focusing on the client, thinking about new behaviour as I am beginning to think and feel differently.

Is there anything else you need from this conversation? No thanks.

Can I ask what you gained from working with this process? I think that I understand the Kolb model better, particularly the conceptualisation stage, and I feel quite comfortable to try it in a coaching session for myself.

Reflecting on the case study

In the above coaching conversation, the coach first helped the client determine his goals for the session, and structured the conversation using the Kolb model. The coach made sure that she constantly clarified the way forward with the client, not moving before he was ready. Furthermore, she tried to mostly use the client's words. Once or twice she reframed what the client had said to check whether she had understanding. The coach referred to thinking, feeling and assumptions right through the conversation, having picked that up from the client. And, to end the conversation, the client reviewed the cycle, reiterating the **experience**, what was **reflected**, what the new **concept** was to work differently in the coaching conversation, and how they **experimented** with a way forward. Using this model, the coach was able to help the client articulate how he experiences the world, and where his levels of discomfort were in the coaching process. The coach also confirmed that NLP was part of his experience before they worked to develop new anchors; previously, disempowering assumptions were his anchors. In all of these ways, the coach was able to safely create an environment to use the Kolb model, which the client wished to learn as a coaching structure. Finally, the coach moved from the specific situation to create anchors and an understanding of how to use the Kolb model in a coaching situation i.e., she moved from the specific to the general.

Hudson's Renewal Cycle model

Frederick Hudson's (1998:79) model is useful in order to understand an adult's experience of life and change. Hudson's renewal cycle can be used to structure the coaching conversation and the overall journey. I have placed Hudson's four quadrants where they are most aligned to the Insights four colours (Figure 18). The quadrants integrate relatively well with the Insights four colours: yellow for "getting ready" to go back into the world, red for actively "going for it", blue for the "doldrums" and green for "cocooning". Often when you overlay one model over another, it is not always a perfect match.

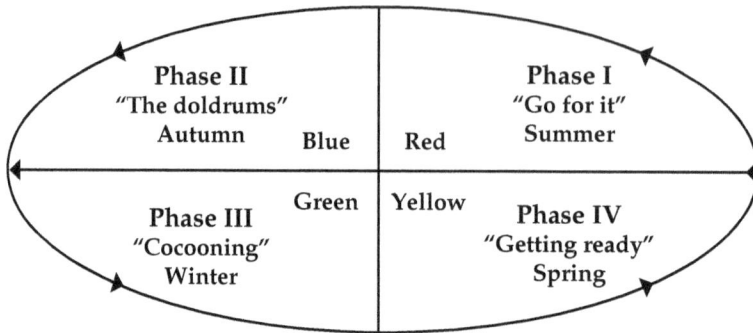

Figure 18: Hudson's four stages

Source: Adapted from Hudson (1999:106) and Insights (2008)

As a coaching model, the coach can start wherever is most useful for the client, and in whatever sequence is needed (Stout-Rostron, 2006c):

1. **Go for it (summer)** – In phase one, the individual is purposeful, active, busy, committed, optimistic, and energised as a team player.

2. **Doldrums (autumn)** – In phase two, the individual is bored, restless or feeling stuck, reactive, in denial, angry, sad, pessimistic, low in energy, a loner, and resistant to change.

3. **Cocooning (winter)** – In phase three, the individual is turned inward, meditative, experimenting, exploring, disoriented, healing, quiet, deconstructing and reconstructing the self, tapping into core values, tapping resilient emotions, spiritual, and doing inner work.

4. **Getting ready (spring)** – In phase four, the individual senses a new purpose, searching, networking; this phase is creative, free and uncommitted, naively optimistic, recovering perhaps forgotten childlike and spontaneous abilities.

We can create an analogy for each of these phases with the seasons of the year. As in autumn, the client is in the **doldrums,** in the dark and resistant to change. **Cocooning** is like winter, where the client is deconstructing, reconstructing, doing some inner work, meditative. **Getting ready** is like spring, and the client is seeking new purpose, searching, maybe looking for that new job, the inner child is at work. **The going for it** phase is like summer, where the client is busy with a new sense of purpose, committed and optimistic and energised.

Case study: Using Hudson's model for coaching

The doldrums

A young woman who wanted to change careers, Shannon, came to me for coaching. Shannon wanted to work with someone who could understand the passion she had for her AIDS NGO work, and could help her think about what the next step in her career should be. Although qualified as a lawyer, Shannon was working in marketing and promotions rather than on the legal side. She was in the doldrums, working about 12 hours a day, exhausted, not feeling that she was working at a senior enough position to make a difference. She was highly committed to the work she was doing. In some ways, I was also a mentor for her. One aspect of a mentor's job is to introduce the client to their own network to help the client to build alliances and relationships. This moves them the next step in their career. In our first session, we talked about the doldrums, which is how she described her current thinking and feeling, and what was different to when she first began her work in this NGO.

Cocooning

In our next few sessions, we talked about her need to do a bit of **cocooning**, to sit back and reflect, using the coaching sessions as a space to do so. We agreed she would **cocoon** as long as it took. We thought about the following questions:

- What do I really want to do?
- Shall I stay or leave my job?
- Do I want to leave South Africa to pursue my studies?
- Would that be the right thing to do?
- Can I grow my skills and education by staying in South Africa?

Eventually Shannon realised she thought she was ready to begin to think about making a move from her current job, but she was not yet willing to leave the projects in which she was immersed.

Getting Ready

We met a few times, and gradually she began to articulate a possible way forward. As we moved into the **getting ready** phase, she looked at her options and decided that she would first begin to build her network, and create relationships that could open doors for her. She attended a few courses, including a master class in the Thinking Environment® with Nancy Kline, and participated in several business breakfasts on Leadership Skills for Women. She made contact with the two NGOs with whom I had contact, searching for opportunities to continue her education by studying and working abroad. She was clear that her ultimate aim was to return to South Africa with new skills that could be applied to the AIDS organisations. I knew two people in the NGO world who were potential employers. Shannon met with these two international NGOs who had offices in South Africa although their head offices were in the States.

After a period of about six months, Shannon thought she was ready to move into action. This would normally be the **go for it** phase. However, was she ready to go for it? She applied for a scholarship to study further at Georgetown University in Washington DC. When she was accepted, her words were, "I don't understand why I am not jumping for joy. It is an incredible opportunity, I am going to get a visa for four years. I am going to study in the States. I am going to have a research job. What is wrong with me? It's right there." The question always worth asking is, "What does the client need now?" Here she was ready for a change but, although a fabulous opportunity was within her grasp she could not understand why she didn't just "go for it".

Going for it

We talked about what she needed in order to get back into action. She decided to stick with her current NGO job. There were projects still to complete before she could move out of the country and take up the scholarship. She felt she could not let her colleagues down by not implementing her current programmes. In this way, she revitalised her passion for her current job. We discussed ways to create boundaries to manage her working hours. In speaking to her several months later, I learned that she was on track to take up the scholarship the following year. Her intention was to return to South Africa when she was qualified, accepting a new and more empowering role.

I-T-O (Input, Throughput, Output)

Models in coaching are very useful to us as a way to structure the entire coaching intervention, and the individual coaching conversation. However, all models must provide flexibility, not rigidity. The following model is an open systems model developed for change management by Cummings and Worley (2004). It is used by i-Coach Academy, and is taught in their Masters in Coaching degree in the UK, USA and South Africa. This model can easily be used to structure the coaching conversation, or to structure the overall coaching intervention (Figure 19).

Figure 19: Input, Throughput, Output

Source: Cummings and Worley (2004)

Input (Why)

As a coach (and for the client), where do you come from and what are you **informed** by? This is the **input** part of the coach's framework, the **why**. It assumes the "input" or beginning stage of the coaching conversation between coach and client. Input is what informs you as a coach, the underlying theories you are working with, your experience and expertise, your philosophy and values, and the constructs that underpin your worldview. Questions you might ask the client in the input stage are:

- What is on the menu for our conversation today?
- What do you want to think about?
- What are your key issues or challenges?
- What are your priorities?

Throughput (How / What)

The **process** the coach uses in the coaching conversation is the **throughput** of the coaching framework. It is the **how**, in other words, what the coach actually does in the coaching conversation. This second stage, throughput, is represented by the tools, techniques, models, processes, mechanics and systems the coach brings into the coaching conversation. Typical questions you could ask may be:

- What are your observations about your thinking?
- What are your questions about your thinking?
- What can you learn from your thinking?
- What are you assuming that is stopping you / limiting you / holding you back?
- What makes that stop you?

Output (What for / purpose)

The third stage is the purpose (**what for**) in the coaching process and relates to the client's **outcomes**. **Output** represents the actions, goals, results and measurements expected from the coaching conversation, including an outline of what the client has learned, will do differently and goals set.

Output is represented by the results, objectives and outputs which the client gains from the coaching conversation. It is represented by the client arriving at their desired outcome. Output relates to where the client is going, how results can be measured and what has changed as a result of the coaching. Typical questions might be:

- What action are you now going to take?
- What has changed in your overall vision, strategy and goals?
- What is the overall learning this session?
- What will you do differently as a result of today?

Contracting with I-T-O

To contract the overall journey, coach and client discuss what each brings to the relationship, and the overall aim of coaching for the client (**input**). Coach and client then discuss how the coaching will take place: timing, boundaries, fees and the tools and techniques to be used by the coach, and the way the client would prefer to work (**throughput**). They also discuss the overall results and outcomes the client hopes to achieve from the coaching intervention, results that need to be visible to the organisation, and thinking, feeling and behaviour that the client would like to change (**output**).

As a rule, when using this model, I start the coaching conversation with **input**: "Where are you now?" "Where do you want to get to by the end of this conversation?" "What do you want to talk about?" "What's on the menu for today?" Once we have identified what needs to be worked on, I move into throughput: using whichever question frameworks, tools or techniques are relevant to the process. For **output**, we summarise actions, learning and outcomes from the conversation.

Case Study – I-T-O

Input

With one of my current executive clients, Rosalyn, coach and client chatted for an hour about where Rosalyn was in her personal and professional life. She felt that she was somewhat chaotic in her approach to her new position as Director of Transformation for her organisation. After an hour's thinking, she identified her goal for the coaching session: "I'd like to create a transformation workshop that can be facilitated throughout the entire organisation. So, I need to do some thinking around how I can do it and who can do it for me, and whether I should ask you to do it for me. Or, should I hire an external consultant? I'm thinking about creating a series of national transformation workshops. What do you think?" Coach and client agreed to work on an outline for the workshop as a start.

Throughput

The coach asked the questions that would help Rosalyn to think through a framework for the one-day programme. Coach and client identified the assumptions that were stopping Rosalyn from thinking she was the person to facilitate the transformational workshops. We discussed who might be the facilitator, and it emerged that she was the right person: she had the relevant skills, organisational knowledge, experience and an understanding of diversity and empowerment

---

in South Africa. She also had a better understanding of organisational culture than an external consultant might have. We agreed that, as her coach, it was more useful to her if I simply helped her to design the programme.

Output

To conclude, we reflected on what she had gained from the session. She concluded that she felt empowered to be both designer and facilitator for the first pilot session with the board. She decided to think during our next session about how to develop other facilitators for the process. She wanted to be the trainer of the facilitators. She also decided to put forward a proposal for a deputy who would help her with administration and policy-making. She came to the conclusion that transformation needed to start at the top, otherwise the complexity of transformation would not be fully embraced. We summarised her action steps, finished the outline for the programme, and explored how she could present her ideas to the board.

THE U-PROCESS

The U-process is sometimes known as the process of transition, while many have also experienced it as similar to Kubler-Ross's cycle of grieving, or as a mid-range change theory. Kubler-Ross's stages of death and dying are denial and isolation, anger, bargaining, depression and acceptance. This stage theory has been controversial, primarily because the theory denies the individuality of human beings and other needs of the dying, such as having some control in their own treatment and destiny, the role of culture, religion, personality, family dynamics and so on (Gorle, 2002). Although the staging theory has experienced limitations in its interpretation, in the coaching field this U-process is more typically represented in Scharmer's U-process.

Scharmer's U-process

In the process of transition, the client can move from anxiety, through happiness, fear, threat, guilt, denial, disillusionment, depression, gradual acceptance and hostility to moving forward.

The change process

The U-process is considered a mid-range change theory with a sense of an emerging future. Scharmer's process moves the client through different levels of perception and change, with differing levels of action which follow. The three main elements are sensing, presencing and realising. These represent the three basic aspects of the U (Figure 20).

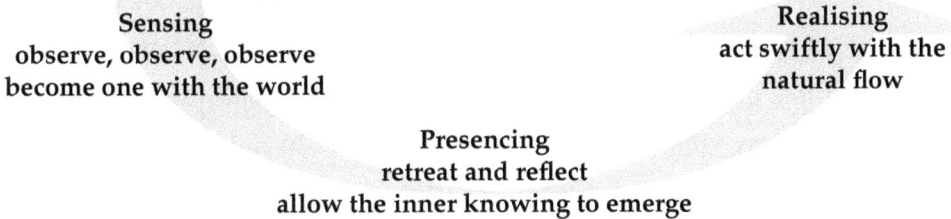

Sensing
observe, observe, observe
become one with the world

Realising
act swiftly with the
natural flow

Presencing
retreat and reflect
allow the inner knowing to emerge

Figure 20: Scharmer's U-Process Model

Source: Adapted from Senge, Scharmer, Jaworski and Flowers (2005:88)

This process helps the client to work at different levels of perception and change, and allows different levels of actions to follow. All three are extensions of the learning process. As the coach and client move into the U, **sensing** is about observing and becoming one with the world; **presencing,** moving to the bottom of the U, is about retreating and reflecting and allowing an inner knowing to emerge; and **realising** as you move out of the "U", is about acting swiftly and with a natural flow from the knowledge and understanding that has emerged.

The U-theory suggests co-creation between the individual and the collective – i.e. the larger world. It is about the inter-connection or integration of the self with the world. At the bottom of the U, as described by Scharmer, is the "inner gate" where we drop the baggage of our journey, going through a threshold. The metaphor used here is that of "death of the old self", and "rebirth of the new self", the client emerges with a different sense of self. A lovely dialogue between Wilber and Scharmer is on the web where they discuss the seven states and the three movements in this one process (Dialog on Leadership, 2007).

Superficial learning and change processes are shorter versions of the U-movement. In using this as a coaching process, the client moves downwards into the base of the U, moving from acting, to thinking, to feeling, to will. This is to help the client to download with the coach, to let go and discover who they really are, to see from the deepest part of themselves, developing an awareness that is expanded with a shift in intention.

Otto Scharmer, in his article, "Addressing the blind spot of our time", an executive summary of his book, *Theory U: Leading From the Future as it Emerges,* describes the U-process as five movements: co-initiating, co-sensing, presencing, co-creating and co-evolving. Scharmer describes this as moving "first into intimate connection with the world and to a place of inner knowing that can emerge from within, followed by bringing forth the new, which entails discovering the future by doing" (Scharmer, 2007). The following case study demonstrates the five-step process.

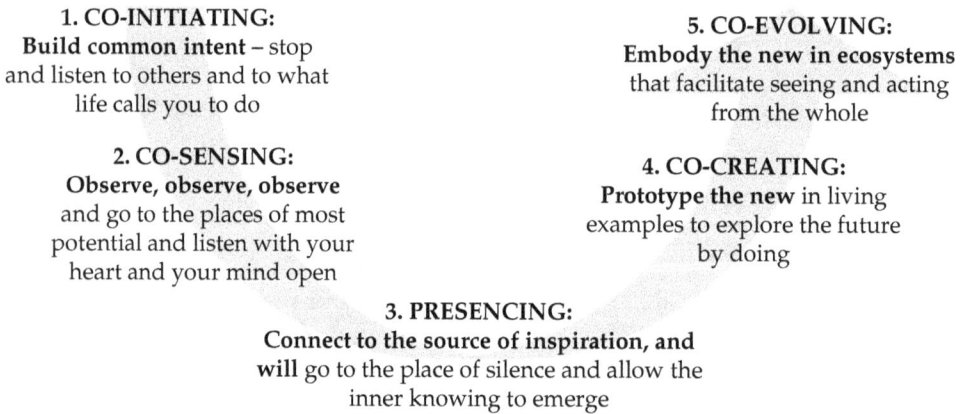

---

1. CO-INITIATING:
Build common intent – stop
and listen to others and to what
life calls you to do

5. CO-EVOLVING:
Embody the new in ecosystems
that facilitate seeing and acting
from the whole

2. CO-SENSING:
Observe, observe, observe
and go to the places of most
potential and listen with your
heart and your mind open

4. CO-CREATING:
Prototype the new in living
examples to explore the future
by doing

3. PRESENCING:
Connect to the source of inspiration, and
will go to the place of silence and allow the
inner knowing to emerge

Figure 21: U-process case study

Source: Scharmer (2007:6)

Case study – The Global Convention on Coaching (GCC)

From July 2007 until July 2008, Marti and I took part in the Global Convention on Coaching. I was chairperson of the GCC's Working Group on a Research Agenda for Development of the Field, and Marti participated in the Working Group dialogue process. The GCC has been established to create a worldwide collaborative dialogue for all stakeholders in coaching. The ultimate aim is to professionalise the industry. Nine initial working groups were formed by the GCC's Steering Committee to discuss critical issues related to the professionalisation of coaching, producing "white papers" on the current realities and possible future scenarios of these issues.[5]

1. Co-initiation

Co-initiating is about building common intent, stopping and listening to others and to what life calls you to do. In the Working Group on a Research Agenda, the group built common intent by first setting up the group, defining their purpose and beginning to discuss the process that they wanted to use for their dialogue.

It was agreed that the chairperson and facilitator would invite specific individuals to join the Working Group, and those members would suggest other individuals who might have a key interest in the research agenda for the field (i.e. the emerging coaching profession). The group began their online dialogue, once all had accepted the invitation and the use of their user names and passwords for the online web forum on the GCC website. It was agreed that there would be three communities working together, the Working Group and the Consultative Body (to be developed) on a Research Agenda, and the Steering Committee who were responsible for all nine portfolio committees.

2. Co-sensing

Observe, Observe, Observe. Go to the places of most potential and listen with your mind and heart wide open. The chairperson and the facilitator of the Working Group had to learn to co-facilitate, observing each other's skill and competence. They had to be willing to listen to each other, observing each other's style in facilitating an online dialogue. They needed to create the group, and to facilitate the way forward with the group, learning to take constructive criticism and appreciation from each other, guiding the group forward without being prescriptive. Both chairperson and facilitator agreed to co-chair the process, remaining mentally and emotionally open to each other's divergent opinions, ways of being and styles of interpersonal communication, whether working with the group online or by phone.

3. *Presencing*

Connect to the source of inspiration, and will. Go to the place of silence and allow the inner knowing to emerge. Each individual in the process read, reflected and regularly added their thoughts and feelings to the online forum. Debate, conflict and agreement emerged – with chair and facilitator taking responsibility to keep the group on track without being prescriptive. The chair and facilitator had to connect, each one to their own individual source of inspiration and to bring that together as one voice to guide the group.

4. *Co-creating*

Prototype the new. In living examples to explore the future by doing. This entailed harnessing the energy of the Working Group to draft a current reality document of their online and tele-conference dialogue which took four drafts. They brought in a facilitator for the Consultative Body who entered the Consultative Body dialogue at Stage 1 (co-initiating), but entered the Working Group dialogue at Stage 3 (presencing). Trying to move forward with their own Working Group process, yet move the Consultative Body from Stage 1 to Stage 2 (co-initiation to co-sensing) was a complex and parallel process. The chairperson and facilitator enlisted the help of a copywriter and editor to manage the writing process of the white paper during Stage 4 (co-creating).

5. *Co-evolving*

Embody the new in ecosystems that facilitate seeing and acting from the whole. The final stage of the process was the physical gathering at a convention in Dublin. This took place in three stages: pre-convention, during the convention and post-convention (post-convention work has just begun). Several months prior to the convention, all nine working groups began to work together online and by telephone to share their own varied stages in the U-process; in this way they learned from each other as they gathered momentum moving towards Dublin, the culmination of their year-long project. Some groups had lost participants during the 12 months through disagreement; others managed to harness the energy to move through each of the stages together. The culmination of the process took place at the convention. The three processes were:

- **Pre-convention**: Preparation for the presentation of a white paper by nine committees; this was for their committee's current global reality and future possible scenarios for their topic.

- **Convention**: Physical presence, dialogue and debate in Dublin with each of the working groups. This was paralleled with the virtual online feedback on a daily basis from those online yet not able to attend the convention.

- **Post-convention**: Continuation of the process with a new format. The work to take place in diverse groups regionally and nation-wide, to proceed to the next step building the emerging profession of coaching.

This worldwide process is ongoing. This U-process is applicable to large innovation projects where the unfolding takes place over a long time; a year in this instance. The team composition in such projects as this will change and adapt to some degree after each movement: the working group had lost and added new members, whereas the consultative body was a looser entity with only certain members playing a strong role. This was a process of discovery, exploring the future by doing, thinking and reflecting. As Scharmer explains, it facilitates an opening. Facilitating an opening process involves "the tuning of three instruments: the open mind, the open heart, and the open will" (Scharmer, 2007:8–9).

At any one time there were three U-process journeys taking place: within the working group, the working group interacting with the consultative body, and the working group interacting with the steering committee.

IN CONCLUSION

Coach practitioners have a great deal of flexibility when working with coaching models. In this book, we work from an experiential learning premise because the client always brings their experience into the coaching conversation. The client's experience is underpinned by a range of factors, including culture, education, life experience and personality.

In this chapter we explored a few models that hang on a framework of circularity, quadernity and the U-shape. As it is not possible to work with every coaching model available in the marketplace, we have not delved into Maslow's triangular model, Beck and Cowen's spiral dynamics model, Ned Herrmann's four-quadrant, whole-brain business model, or Will McWhinney's Paths of Change model. I leave those for you to explore, and hope that you have gained a sense of the flexibility models can offer the coach practitioner, as well as the elasticity in overlaying one over another. Simplicity is the prerequisite.

I hope that this chapter has introduced some new learning and the curiosity to experiment with new structures within your coaching conversations. It may be that you add one or two of these models into your coach's toolkit; or that you register for a coach education and development programme to learn to work with a new model for your continuing professional development.

COACH'S LIBRARY

Cummings, T.G. and Worley, C.G. (2004). *Organization development and change.* Eighth edition. Mason, OH: South-Western College Publishing.

Flaherty, J. (2008). Detail of Habermas' domains of competency. Available at: coaching. gc.ca/documents/ coaching_essential_competences_for_leaders_e.asp.

Goleman, D. (1996). *Emotional intelligence.* London: Bloomsbury.

Harri-Augstein, S. and Thomas, L.F. (1991). *Learning conversations, self-organised learning: The way to personal and organisational growth.* London: Routledge.

Hudson, F.M. (1999). *The handbook of coaching: A comprehensive resource guide for managers, executives, consultants, and human resource professionals.* San Francisco, CA: Jossey-Bass.

Insights Model. (2008). Available at: www.insights.co.uk.

Kline, N. (1999/2004). *Time to think: Listening with the human mind.* London: Ward Lock.

Kolb, D. (1984). *Experiential learning: Experience as the source of learning and development.* Upper Saddle River, NJ: Prentice Hall.

Lane, D.A. and Corrie, S. (2006). *The modern scientist-practitioner: A guide to practice in psychology.* Hove: Routledge.

McLoughlin, M. (ed.). (2006). *Sharing the passion: Conversations with coaches.* Cape Town: Advanced Human Technologies.

Scharmer, C.O. (2007). Addressing the blind spot of our time: An executive summary of the book by Otto Scharmer, *Theory U: Leading from the future as it emerges: The social technology of presencing.* Excerpt from www.theoryu.com.

Senge, P., Scharmer, C.O., Jaworski, J. and Flowers, B.S. (2005). *Presence: Exploring profound change in people, organizations and society.* London: Nicholas Brealey.

Ting, S. and Scisco, P. (2006). *The CCL handbook of coaching: A guide for the leader coach.* San Francisco, CA: Jossey-Bass.

Weiss, P. (2004). The three levels of coaching. Paper from *An appropriate response.* Available at: www.appropriateresponse.com.

Wilber, K. (2000a). *A theory of everything: An integral vision for business, politics, science and spirituality.* Dublin: Gateway.

ENDNOTES TO CHAPTER 5

1. "Learning conversations" refers to research into learning conversations and self-organised learning, developed by S. Harri-Augstein and L.F. Thomas (1991:24).
2. See James Flaherty's excellent detailing of Habermas' domains of competency at: coaching.gc.ca/documents/coaching_essential_competences_for_leaders_e.asp.

3.	"NLP (neuro-linguistic programming) provides psychological skills for understanding the mental processes and patterns we use to achieve results. NLP addresses how we use our senses to think, how language relates to thought, and how our thinking strategies control our experience and achievements. NLP provides a practical understanding of how the brain works: how people think, learn and motivate themselves to change. It is essentially about how we process information, and how this manifests itself in behaviour. It is how we use the language of the mind to achieve specific desired goals. Like many learning tools, NLP refers to how you organise your mental life: the basis of all learning" (Stout-Rostron, 2002:117).

4.	"The process of anchoring involves linking a specific sight, sound or touch with an experience that is present. For example, a situation in which you are associated. This process enables you to use the anchor to re-access the same experience" (McLoughlin and Stout-Rostron, 2002:48).

5.	Each group's white papers were presented at the Dublin GCC in July 2008. This case study summarises the working group process of the research agenda. This was a 12-month online dialogue process, with the addition of monthly telephone conversations from the beginning of 2008.

6

Diversity, Personality and Culture

with Marti Janse van Rensburg

This is a general introduction to a vital subject that all business coaches need to get to grips with. It is not an academic assessment or designed for those who are already experts in the field and may be running specialist diversity workshops. This is for the general practitioner who needs to reflect on their own levels of awareness and approach to diversity, personality and cultural differences.

In this chapter we explore the various themes of diversity, personality, cultural and gender issues, learning and thinking styles. It is up to you to cultivate self-awareness, continuing your own professional development and applied practice when working with diversity and cultural issues in an organisational context. An integrated understanding of this chapter's core themes can only enhance your success as a business coach.

This chapter is aimed at deepening your understanding and providing helpful pointers on which to reflect. It is strongly recommended that you enhance your understanding through your own personal development and diversity work. Every practitioner needs to expand their own ability to work with business clients who may well see the world through a very different perspective. For those who wish to study further there are recommended resources at the end of the chapter.

The importance of acknowledging diversity is increasingly recognised in our globalised world. Yet in South Africa many coach practitioners continue to find they still work in a very "white" world. Here Sunny Stout-Rostron introduces the subject of diversity and power relations, looking at how assumptions limit individuals and groups – while Marti Janse van Rensburg comprehensively explores race, cultural and gender issues, personality traits, learning and thinking styles.

Chapter outline

- Diversity
- Diversity and social transformation
    - Workplace transformation
- Background and similarities
- Themes of diversity
    - Race
    - Gender
    - Communication styles
    - Language and linguistic patterns
    - Religion
- Cultural differences in the workplace
    - Individualism versus collectivism
    - Context
- Personality differences
    - Personality profiles
- Learning and thinking styles
    - Thinking styles
    - Learning styles
    - Honey and Mumford
    - Decision-making styles
- Bringing it all together
- Coach's library
- Endnotes to Chapter 6

DIVERSITY

Diversity is about difference: in equality, power, and worldview.

Equality and power are in many ways related. Power creates its own self-justifying worldview. This often becomes an unexamined rationalisation for the dominant group's power. The mirror image of this is that it negates the view of those without power. Thus it can be very difficult to get those with power to see the prejudiced limits of their bias – particularly their limiting assumptions about the powerless – because it is precisely that which justifies their monopoly of power. On the other hand, to achieve full equality – politically, professionally and personally – those without power also need to come to grips with their own limiting assumptions (often dictated by those who have had power over them). In both cases, for the powerful and the powerless, being able to discard such limiting worldviews is liberating.

On an individual level, many problems are also fuelled by our own self-limiting assumptions. We see through the filters of our own worldview, as we are all products of our personal histories, language, culture, experience, education, gender and social conditioning.

Having worked for many years with Nancy Kline in the Thinking Environment®, as business coaches we have tried to help ourselves and our clients to explore the roots of their own discriminatory attitudes and behaviours. We do this by starting to examine "untrue" limiting assumptions that society and organisations make about people on the basis of their "group" identities and their place in the hierarchy of work and society (Kline, 1999:88–89).

Although people live and work in a diverse world, we have become suspicious and mistrusting of our differences. In doing so we discriminate against, and disempower, others on the basis of their difference, rather than welcoming these differences and encompassing other worldviews to enhance our own.

When working with a client in the coaching conversation, it is useful to help them to learn how to remove the limiting assumptions they hold about themselves, others and the systems in which they live and work – such as their organisation and society as a whole. We actually need diversity in order to approach difficult situations with fresh thinking. Only true liberating assumptions can free individuals and groups and help them to reclaim their self-esteem and influence. This of course means developing an awareness of our own prejudices, biases, limiting thinking and life conditioning.

Nancy Kline defines diversity as "difference and equality" (Kline, 1999:87). To truly honour diversity requires genuinely diverse thinking with an appreciation for difference, an elimination of reprisal for difference, and crucially highlights authority issues (who has the power?) and the fundamental issue of individuals being encouraged and permitted to think for themselves.

In working with teams in the thinking environment we often ask, "do we think better if there is an amount of diversity, safety and openness; and if so, why?" (Kline, 1999). One answer is that diversity simply gives us a more complete picture of reality. Another question is, "if the norm is power in organisational teams and in societal groups, how can we create 'safety' to help people to think clearly?" (Kline, 1999). An answer to this question is that, "we think best in the midst of diversity" (Kline, 1999). To appreciate the power of diversity, however, we need to operate from a foundation of really believing that people are created equal. We all need to work on developing an internal ease in the world of difference that we face everyday.

There is diversity in experience, race, ethnicity, background, education, culture, history, language, faith, belief, capability and disability. It is crucial in the working environment to help individuals become aware of all the groups they identify with – particularly the less visible. The circuits of discrimination are complex. Everyday we witness (or experience) instances of prejudice or bias, driven by untrue limiting assumptions that everyone in some way carries with them, sometimes knowingly, often unconsciously.

Our purpose here is to help business coaches begin to develop awareness of this complexity, and through your own inner journey to be able to identify and name all the diversity issues that face you and your clients on a daily basis.

Transforming limiting assumptions

This is a simple but powerful exercise that we learned working with Nancy Kline. The late, wonderful Margaret Legum and her business colleague, Dorrian Aiken, have been instrumental in taking this work to greater depths within organisations in South Africa. First identify your own untrue limiting assumptions; only then can you begin to help your clients to do so.

The following exercise is one used when working with diversity in a Thinking Environment (Kline, 2005). Make a list of the groups with whom you identify, and about whom society makes assumptions that limit the power, confidence and dignity of each of those groups. Of those groups choose the three that you most identify with, and list the assumptions made about those groups that are most limiting to their power, dignity, happiness and influence. Choose the one assumption you believe is the most limiting; do you think it is inherently true for this group? What instead would be your words for what is a liberating, true alternative assumption?

Finally, ask yourself, "if you and the world knew that truth, what would change for you and the world?" The assumptions that we hold about ourselves can be the most limiting. In working through this, and similar exercises, you can start to develop an acute awareness of the preconceptions, limiting assumptions and prejudices that you work with everyday.

What happens when it goes wrong?

How can we deal with the situation when diversity goes wrong practically? Diversity mistakes can be emotional – and when any situation becomes emotional, individuals often lose perspective. If business coaches can help clients to develop greater emotional intelligence, particularly self-awareness and self-management skills, any diversity situation can be improved.

Working with the EQ model that we explored in Chapter 5 can be helpful. Questions to ask your client are: What are they thinking and feeling; what are they assuming and is it inherently true; what is working; what is not working? How can they use their own self-awareness to bring perspective to the situation? How might they manage what they say and do differently to create a better result and to manage any conflict that has arisen? How will their new behaviours impact on the values and culture of the team and the organisation, and ultimately on the business, and business processes?

Working with diversity in business can also go beyond cultural differences, bringing in a range of other perspectives. For example, in business it is rare for the marketing and finance functions to see eye to eye, or to have the same intention of outcome. Marketers and accountants not only occupy different functions in the organisation, they will have developed differences in personal and professional worldviews.

DIVERSITY AND SOCIAL TRANSFORMATION

In *Using Experience for Learning*, Costas Criticos (1996) reflected on the social and political conditions in South Africa, exploring how apartheid affected the experience and learning of all members of its society. Criticos writes about the challenges facing South Africa as a result of the apartheid years. He points out that two of the most important South African institutions that challenged the apartheid government and created space for dialogue were the churches and the universities.

His description of apartheid describes a pathology of racist oppression. This pathology was created by the tension "between contradictory experiences and contradictory explanations of society" (Criticos, 1996:157). He explains that even so "learning" can live inside the conversations and dialogues that are produced by these tensions. Criticos' chapter explores the liberating nature of experiential learning in South Africa. However, it is clear that very different learnings emerge from such dramatically divergent experiences as those of the powerful or those of the powerless.

Whether you are a privileged or previously disadvantaged person, the nature of recent historical experience in South Africa is so momentous and all pervasive that it must inform – whether consciously or unconsciously – many of our attitudes as well as the everyday realities that we face.

Workplace transformation

Affirmative action in business is a controversial topic. But the statistics tell their own story. According to the September 2008 Employment Equity Commission report, there is still "gross under-representation of Africans, 'Coloured', and people with disabilities in key areas of the labour market" (Johwa, 2008:4).

There are fluctuating, sometimes even regressive figures for black representation. The number of blacks "decreased 8.7 per cent to 41.3 per cent of the total in professional and middle management level; Africans declined 14.9 per cent to reach 24.1 per cent" (Johwa, 2008:4). Apparently, the largest gains are by white women in the corporate marketplace, which has led the Commission's Chair to recommend that white women be removed from the definition of affirmative action's "graduation principle" as the "prejudice against white women cannot be compared to that suffered by black women" (Johwa, 2008:4).

Althea Banda-Hansmann, Human Resource Development Project Leader at the South African Petroleum Industry Association (SAPIA), says that the "race and gender representation as revealed in the 8th CEE Annual Report shows that institutionalised racism is still in place in corporate South Africa". Banda-Hansmann suggests that the slow progress that is reflected in top and senior management levels is apparent in the under-representation of designated groups at management, professionally qualified and technically skilled levels. If business stays committed to transformation and diversity in the workplace, this commitment will require a great deal of support from the business coaches working at all levels in the corporate marketplace. In particular, she emphasised "it will require constant insight, deep understanding and compassion about individual and group histories that define South Africans" (Banda-Hansmann, 2009, pers.com.).

Workforce diversity will continue to be an important topic for continued transformation in South Africa. As it provides a huge opportunity for change, this remains an important arena for executive coaching – and thus requires those coaches to be skilled in managing all aspects of diversity.

In the rest of this chapter, Marti discusses other diverse influences such as race, language, gender, personality and thinking styles that can help us to work with greater knowledge, understanding and wisdom with our clients in a coaching environment.

BACKGROUND AND SIMILARITIES

Leading in a multicultural and diverse environment is like playing several instruments. It partly calls for different attitudes and skills: restraint in passing judgement and the ability to recognise that familiar tunes might have to be played differently. Our natural tendency is to watch the world from behind the windows of a cultural home and to act as if people from other countries, ethnicities, or categories have something special about them (a culture) but home is normal. Awareness means the discovery that there is no normal position in cultural matters (Hofstede, 2005:ix).

We can all trace our ancestry back to Africa about 150 000 to 200 000 years ago when we shared a common ancestor or mother (Kaessmann and Pääbo, 2002).

During an ice age approximately 80 000 years ago, a group of early humans left Africa for Yemen. These people, an estimated 250 of them, created all the other races in the world today. About 70 000 years ago some of this group moved to the Indian sub-continent, and continued into Indonesia and Australasia. With the thawing of the ice age, humans moved into the interior of Asia and Europe and only arrived in Europe approximately 42 000 to 43 000 years ago from India and the Middle East (Olson, 2007).

The final migration was roughly 15 000 to 35 000 years ago during another ice age, when some of the hominids inhabiting the Arctic went into North and later South America (Olson, 2007). This means that the entire populations of Europe, Asia, Australasia and the Americas are descendants from the estimated 250 people who left Africa all that time ago. This is why among rugby players, Lote Turquiri (a Melanesian from Fiji) is more closely related to Stephen Larkham (a white Australian) than George Gregan (who was born in Zambia).

The complexity for South Africa was shown on a TV programme.[1] Satirist Pieter-Dirk Uys's paternal ancestor originated from the Iberian Peninsula 13 000 years ago after the last ice age. His maternal ancestors belonged to one of the commonest lines in Africa, associated with Bantu-speaking people. In contrast, comedian Marc Lottering's maternal line originated from a hunting family in the Dordogne region of France 20 000 years ago, while his paternal ancestor is Eurasian. Under apartheid in South Africa, Marc Lottering would have been classified as "coloured", yet he has European ancestry. Pieter-Dirk Uys, who would have been classified as "white", has European and Bantu ancestry.

Given our common ancestral lineage, how did we develop our obsession with difference? How we appear to each other has become more important than how we feel, taste and smell. We have become acutely sensitive to small differences which we use to evaluate and judge others. We attach importance to gender, race and other attributes such as height, size and dress sense, basing our decisions and judgements on our assumptions.

We create groupings around these differences in order to belong – whether to race, gender, a religious group, and the sports clubs or community associations that we join.

Unfortunately, in the process, we also create assumptions about other groups and their relative hierarchy to our group. We tend to associate power with other groups, as an aspiration ("I want to belong to that group"), or because we fear that our choice might be incorrect. This often leads to judgement, for example, that the other group is "wrong" or "inferior". This habit has sparked many religious and ethnic conflicts and wars.

THEMES OF DIVERSITY

Diversity themes

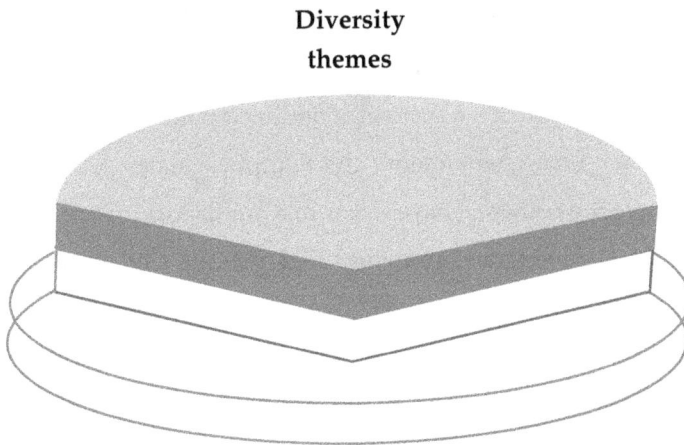

Figure 1: Themes of diversity

To understand and manage diversity we need to look at the various elements that constitute difference, first looking in greater detail at race, gender, language and religion.

Race

Although skin colour is a surface adaptation to climate conditions, it still makes a huge difference to how we see people ... and how we see ourselves.

Race differentiation is particularly pertinent in South Africa because of our history. I once gave a client in South Africa an article, "Dear White Boss" (Caver and Livers, 2002), which he said he could have written himself. A compilation of the experiences of African Americans in the USA, the article expressed feelings of alienation, and how some felt they could not trust their white colleagues or bosses to support them when they made mistakes. As a result, these individuals did not feel they could contribute fully at work. One African American manager said: "The executive team saw me, not as a seasoned strategist, but as an authority on race relations" (Caver and Livers, 2002). Another story, told by an inebriated white colleague over dinner, was that blacks get too many breaks and are not smart enough to be in executive positions. Not dissimilar to what I hear from my black clients in South Africa are comments such as: "If I am quiet, I am told I am not assertive enough – and when I speak up, I am told I am too aggressive".

Ramphele (2008:73) defines racism: "Racism is essentially the use of the concept of 'races' to establish a hierarchy of power relationships by assigning value to categories of people defined as inferior or superior. It is a socio-economic and political mechanism that justifies treating fellow human beings as 'others'." As Ramphele states, we assign value either inferior or superior to the "other". I have found that South African companies often value the skill and expertise of foreigners more than that of locals. Companies typically ask for a foreign coach for their very senior executives, ignoring the fact that South Africans have possibly more experience in diversity than most foreign coaches. The decision is not based on skill, expertise and experience, but rather on a value assigned to a different race or culture.

In *Our Separate Ways*, Bell and Nkomo (2001) talk about the experiences of white and black females in the USA. They talk about the journey of women with ambition and armed with degrees: working hard, contributing to the bottom line, proving themselves, putting in excessive time, often at the expense of their personal lives, only to be told to wait for opportunities, while the ones who decide not to leave often find that the rewards are not in line with the costs. They talk about what is different for black and white women, and how black women more readily find their authority questioned. These are not only relevant to this country; they are worldwide issues.

In South Africa, race does not just refer to white and black but also to ethnicity, culture and background. Factor in upbringing, and the similarities and differences might be surprising. Several years ago, I worked with one of the partners of the MIL Institute[2] at CIDA[3]. One of the activities concerned diversity. The group consisted of black students only. The feedback in terms of diversity was not simply white/black race issues but also difference in eating habits and preconceived notions of other ethnic groups. The students recounted stories about porridge, eaten with either salt or sugar, and how they had been brought up with specific views about Zulus versus Xhosas.

Other race-related differences concern eye contact, greetings and apologising. Westerners view lack of eye contact as offensive or shifty, whereas African cultures regard it as a sign of respect. Loud conversation between Africans is a sign that no secrets are withheld, while Westerners regard it as bad manners. Generally speaking, greetings with Europeans are a simple habit and carry little meaning. The person who asks you "How are you?" expects a superficial answer. In African culture, it is a ritual that has to be done with respect and attention. One student told how he walked through his village as a child. He stopped in front each person, asking about all the family members and their well-being. This was done every time he walked through the village, even if several times a day.

Africans generally say "sorry" to indicate that they witness your discomfort or pain; "sorry" does not indicate an apology for it. A few years ago, I worked with an American colleague who tripped over a wire on a conference room floor. The technician setting up the computer equipment said "Sorry". My colleague turned around in surprise and said, "It wasn't your fault" and the technician, who was black, just shook his head.

So far, we are looking at differences in terms of race, but there are intriguing similarities. Those of Jewish, Afrikaner and Indian descent use food as a form of cultural and social boding – if you have a crisis, they feed you, and if you celebrate something, they feed you. For Africans, a funeral or a wedding has to provide plentiful food for everyone.

It is no secret that the ethnic debate in South Africa is complex. On a daily basis, there are media stories about people from other African countries who complain that they are badly treated by ordinary citizens and the police in South Africa. As I write this, the dominant story in the news is the ethnic violence in townships in Johannesburg and Cape Town. Dr Mamphela Ramphele in *Laying Ghosts to Rest* references ethnic chauvinism, and the way different ethnic groups in South Africa "experience their sense of belonging in different regions in South Africa" (Ramphele, 2008:98). She cites the example of President Julius Nyerere of Tanzania, who abolished the formal role of traditional leaders in the interest of national unity. This allowed Tanzanians to see themselves as Tanzanians first, in contrast to South Africa where tribal leaders and ethnicity are recognised by the Constitution. "Indigenous laws and practices can only enrich our democracy if they are properly reviewed and aligned to the values we aspire to in our national Constitution. Otherwise tradition will continue to be a source of disadvantage and division" (Ramphele, 2008:98).

How to use this

Self-awareness and practice

Developing self-awareness and personal wisdom only translates into changed behaviour when we decide what to do differently and practice changes first in ourselves and second within the coaching conversation.

- List your assumptions about your own race versus other races; which if any are inherently true?
- What assumptions do you make about the different types of power of your race versus other races?
- What assumptions do you make about your clients, their abilities, habits and potential?
- Which assumptions are stopping you from seeing the potential of your clients?
- Ask your clients how their racial experience affects their view and behaviour towards others, both at work and in their personal lives?
- How is your racial experience impacting the way you coach, and what might be a more liberating alternative view for you to enhance your success as a business coach?

Gender

We know that many women and men diverge in interests, abilities and desires. But is this a problem that should be fixed? (Pinker, 2008:255).

In this section, we explore gender, choices women and men make, and the different ways in which men and women communicate. We also look at how both parties are affected in a business context, and what this would mean for the coach.

South Africa is regarded as one of the most progressive countries in terms of gender representation. The Gender Parity Index (GPI) for 2004 in primary and secondary schools combined was 1.0 (Children's Institute, 2008). This indicates that an equal proportion of boys and girls attend school. However, this does not give any indication of the discrimination against female learners. Of South African cabinet ministers, 43 per cent are female; four of the nine provinces have female premiers; and 40 per cent of local government representatives are women. South Africa ranks 10th out of 130 parliaments worldwide in gender representation, with 32 per cent of parliamentarians female. Yet, gender remains an issue, with the private sector lagging behind. The 2007 *Annual Report* of the Business Women's Association (Ramphele, 2008) showed that only 16.8 per cent of executive management and 11.5 per cent of directors of companies listed on the Johannesburg Stock Exchange were women. Corresponding numbers elsewhere are similar: in 2005, only 16.4 per cent of all corporate officers in Fortune 500 companies were female (Pinker, 2008).

Gender equality is written into the South African Constitution. Nevertheless, "Women are still treated as lesser beings in the name of culture. They are considered minors, possessions of their patriarchal families in many settings, and are denied the right to inherit. Pride in the distinctiveness of African customs is cited as a reason for continuing practices that are in conflict with our constitution" (Ramphele, 2008:75). In addition, South Africa is reputed to have one of the highest incidences of violence against women, including rape, in the world.

Ramphele (2008) quotes a radio programme broadcast during Women's Month (August) in 2007. A young black man in his twenties said, "Women are emotional and illogical. They do not have the intellectual wherewithal to run organisations or companies. They can't make sound decisions unless there is a man they can use as a crutch." This indicates that stereotypes linger. One of my clients, a black woman with three degrees who is highly competent, attests to the prevailing sexism. She asked her boss, a black man, to confirm in writing some discussions they had had. He responded aggressively, warning her that he knew her husband and would tell him how she behaved at work. She left the organisation, and today she is successful in an environment that is respectful of her abilities. The boss in question continues to be successful despite his chauvinism.

In general, most women with whom I work do not want to be treated differently. What they want is choice and equal opportunity, equal responsibility and equal pay.

Aiming for balanced representation might not be the ideal solution, even if it seems to be the obvious one. Pinker (2008) wrote about research on this issue in the USA, Canada and Europe. The research findings might be useful in a South African business context. Pinker says that her book is about what women want and why they want it, and asks whether it makes sense to use men as the base model when we talk about women at work. She shows distinct differences in the psychological profiles of men and women: learning problems, attention deficit disorder, and autism spectrum disorders are four to ten times more likely to occur in boys, whereas anxiety and depression are twice as likely in girls. Despite learning disabilities, boys tend to be successful in adult life, while the girls, despite forging ahead of the boys in social skills and learning, usually choose different paths from those that would give them lucrative careers and status.

Pinker (2008:10) points out that "Equal opportunity doesn't necessarily lead to equal results". Currently women outnumber men at universities throughout the developed world. Women far outnumber men in veterinary science, pharmacy, law and medicine. In the awarding of business degrees, the numbers are equal, while more degrees are awarded to men in architecture, physics and engineering. Added to this, in spite of the percentage of degrees awarded, there are far fewer female than male physicians and lawyers practising. As much as this might be due to current incumbents coming from years when the degrees obtained were more skewed to males, Pinker shows that women often start their chosen careers and subsequently leave to take up alternative options.

What is this about, then? Research by Grouzet *et al.* (2005) involved nearly 1 900 people in 15 countries taking part in a survey on intrinsic versus extrinsic goals. Intrinsic goals are defined as making a difference and belonging, whereas extrinsic goals are defined as the search for financial reward and status. The research showed that the goals are in conflict, and that people seldom pursue both. Furthermore, research indicated that women are more likely to be motivated by intrinsic goals and men by extrinsic goals. Further research indicates that these results vary from more affluent or developed countries to less affluent or developing countries.

Communication styles

We also need to consider how men and women differ in their styles of communication. Tannen's (1995) research indicates that men talk about "I" and women talk about "we". In US businesses, men's speaking style, as the majority, dominates. Women tend to be over-ridden and interrupted. Women in a business environment say "we" even when they do the work themselves. Pinker (2008) indicates that men tend to blame externally when something goes wrong, yet accept praise internally. Pinker indicates that women do the opposite, and are more inclined to attribute their success to chance and failure to their own inability.

If we consider confidence, women tend to minimise their certainty and men their doubts. This may create the impression that women lack confidence. This can be due to their tone of voice, hesitancy in speech or use of language. Some of this, especially in South Africa, might be due to speaking in a second or third language. As women are more inclined to feel they must know everything before speaking, and men are often happy to know 50 per cent and fake the rest (Pinker, 2008), women tend to ask more questions. Again, although not necessarily an indication of a lack of confidence, it could create that impression.

Often men and women in the same position end up being paid unequally. Usually, we attribute this to gender discrimination and injustice, but there may be an alternate reason. Babcock and Laschever (2003) showed in several studies that women do not negotiate for more money. Even women trained in negotiation skills do not negotiate salaries and perks well for themselves. Men tend to strongly negotiate on salary, position and authority; women are often more concerned about whether they are qualified enough to do the job.

How to use this

Self-awareness and practice

What lenses do you see through based on your background, culture and gender? Use first-, second- and third-position thinking to step into the other's shoes and to see from a new perspective. This is an NLP coaching technique. The coach helps the client to identify their lenses from three individual positions (first position/their own; second position/the other; third position/ themselves as coach seeing with a new perspective). Physically stand in first position (their own position); second position (the other's position); and third position (that of coach) in order to resolve a conflict or see the other person's point of view. Use this for yourself and your clients. Sunny and I use this technique frequently when the client has an issue or difficulty with another party and needs to hear, see and feel perspectives from all points of view. When coach and client enact it, the client actually verbalises what they think, feel and see – it helps you (or the client) to understand the assumptions that influence the lens through which you (or they) see the world, and helps to determine what needs to change in your (or their) behaviour in order to interact more effectively with others.

- How do you experience discrimination against your gender, and what are your views on the opposite sex?
- How does this influence the way you experience your clients' issues and their choices?
- Think of a time when one of your clients had an opposing view to yours; how did that affect your ability to be objective and to coach the client without judgement?
- Think of a difficult experience a client has experienced with a boss or direct report of the opposite sex? How did this affect their thinking and behaviour? What would they have done differently if the person in question was of the same sex?

Changing behaviour, fundamentally and transformationally, requires you as a coach to help yourself and the client to reflect on assumptions that cause specific behaviour, and to review the belief systems that underlie those assumptions. Identifying and transforming limiting assumptions to empowering ones can in itself lead to behaviour change.

Language and linguistic patterns

In a country with 11 official languages, it is necessary to view language as a diversity theme. Although the standard business language is English, we sometimes forget that for many of us English is not our first language. Although an Afrikaans-speaking South African, I speak English most of the day and tend to think and dream in English. I recently facilitated a group session where I noticed that a black man was frowning. I asked him if I had said something with which he disagreed. He spoke fluent and beautiful English, and his answer surprised me. He explained that he was translating my words into his own language, and that one word did not have a direct translation. He clarified that he tends to think in his own language, and when he goes home on Friday he leaves English in his car, picking it up again on Monday when back in the office. I was astonished that two people who, in spite of not having English as a first language, fluently speak it all day long yet have such different experiences. It made me aware of how easy it is to make incorrect assumptions about people's use of language.

Other than language, how we say what we say is learned behaviour and differs from one person to the other. We all, including our clients, have probably had the experience of speaking to a group of people, realising later that the interpretation of what we had said varied from person to person. Similarly, in talking to individuals, we may have experienced one person being overly sensitive to criticism or feedback, and another hardly feeling it at all. We often think that what we say is easily interpreted and understood, but that is not necessarily so. It is said that one should treat people the way you would like to be treated, but there are subtleties to this rule. Your view of how you would feel, if spoken to in a certain way, is not necessarily the same as that of the person being spoken to. In African tradition, for instance, when you lend something to a friend or neighbour, you may not ask for it back. If you want your lawnmower back, you need to ask to borrow it back from the same neighbour.

Table 1: Style of talking and possible consequences thereof		
	Style of talking	**Unintended consequences of style**
Sharing credit	Uses "we" rather than "I" to describe accomplishments. Why? Using "I" seems too self-promoting.	Speaker doesn't get credit for accomplishments and may hesitate to offer good ideas in the future.
Acting modest	Downplays their certainty, rather than minimising doubts, about future performance. Why? Confident behaviour seems too boastful.	Speaker appears to lack confidence and, therefore, competence; others reject speaker's good ideas.
Asking questions	Asks questions freely. Why? Questions generate needed knowledge.	Speaker appears ignorant to others; if organisation discourages speaker from asking questions, valuable knowledge remains buried.
Apologising	Apologises freely. Why? Apologies express concern for others.	Speaker appears to lack authority.
Giving feedback	Notes weaknesses only after first citing strengths. Why? Buffering criticism saves face for the individual receiving feedback.	Person receiving feedback concludes that areas needing improvement aren't important.
Avoiding verbal opposition	Avoids challenging others' ideas, and hedges when stating own ideas. Why? Verbal opposition signals destructive fighting.	Others conclude that speaker has weak ideas.
Managing up	Avoids talking up achievements with higher-ups. Why? Emphasising achievements to higher-ups constitutes boasting.	Managers conclude that speaker hasn't achieved much and doesn't deserve recognition or promotion.
Being indirect	Speaks indirectly rather than bluntly when telling subordinates what to do. Why? Blatantly directing others is too bossy.	Subordinates conclude that manager lacks assertiveness and clear thinking, and judge manager's directives as unimportant.
Source: Tannen (1995)		

As a socio-linguist Tannen (1995) discusses how linguistic style determines our view of people and ideas, and how our assumptions can be mistaken. She explains that there is a visible difference between the way men and women communicate. We assign meaning to linguistic behaviours, such as apologising, questioning, being direct or indirect, and in the process we can easily misjudge others. In a fast-changing business world, success often depends on recognising good ideas and implementing them. However, should an executive miss an idea because it was not voiced confidently enough, it could have repercussions for the business. Table 1 shows the rationale behind various styles of talking, and the unintended potential consequences.

As coaches, we should be aware of our own linguistic behaviour before coaching executives to recognise their own and their team's style and behaviour. Taking turns to speak is at the centre of any conversation or meeting, yet knowing when it is appropriate to speak depends on reading signals. Often, meetings deteriorate because some feel it is acceptable to interrupt or to finish a colleague's sentences. Some people have a rather long thinking pause and might feel left out if not given time to speak; alternatively they might choose not to participate at all. Kline (1999/2004) advocates a meeting process where everyone speaks once before anyone speaks twice. This is helpful if everyone is to be heard, and both of us use this methodology to great effect. I have found that when teaching groups, individuals who pause, taking longer to speak find this process very useful and contribute well. Extraverts or very vocal participants find it frustrating as they cannot speak as often as they would like to.

How to use this

Self-awareness and practice

- What is your home language or mother tongue (are the two different)?
- What is the home language or mother tongue of your client? If there is a language differential, how does this affect both of you?
- Are any of the language patterns shown in Table 1 true for you? How does this affect you in your communication with people around you, and especially with clients?

- How does your client gauge their effectiveness in communicating with colleagues, direct reports and more senior people in the organisation?
- Are any of the language patterns in Table 1 useful for your client?
- How can you help your client to be more aware of their linguistic patterns, and what can they change in order to have a greater impact or influence in the workplace?

Ask your client to keep a journal observing when their linguistic patterns are successful and when not in the workplace. Once your client is aware of the effectiveness of their communication and the cause of potential ineffectiveness, you can agree goals and an action plan to create substantial change.

Religion

Religion comes into play in South Africa as well, though not as radically as in some parts of the world where wars are fought due to religious differentiation. It is possible that with the variety of races in South Africa, and given the country's history, religion is not as critical a point of differentiation as elsewhere. Freedom of religion is entrenched in the Constitution.

Coach practitioners need an understanding of religion, without letting your own views on religion and spirituality cloud how you work with your clients. When conducting research a few years ago on the status of coaching in South Africa, I spoke to a coach who was a devout Christian. He insisted that Christianity be brought into his coaching practice with all clients. My view is that if clients are aware of this, and choose him accordingly, that is fine. If not, it is inappropriate. With most of my clients, I respect their beliefs and endeavour to gain enough understanding of their religion to coach them within their belief system.

This view is supported by Barney Pityana (2001), chairman of the South African Human Rights Council (HRC), in his foreword to *Clued-up on Culture: A Practical Guide for South Africa*. He indicates that religious freedom is found where a group observes its rituals without infringing on the rights of others. It is therefore important to understand the basics of other beliefs and cultural practices. Pityana says, "Religion cannot be confined to the performance of ritual; it is pre-eminently a lifestyle as well."

It is also important to note that religious belief is not necessarily evident, and people do not always adhere to the religion associated with their race or cultural group.

How to use this

Self-awareness and practice

- What are your religious or spiritual beliefs?
- How do these impact on your view of other religions?
- What religion, if any, does your client practice?
- If so, how important is it in their life and how does it impact on their business environment?
- How much do you understand about your client's religion? Should you learn more?
- If the client's religious beliefs fundamentally differ from yours, should you consider not taking the contract?

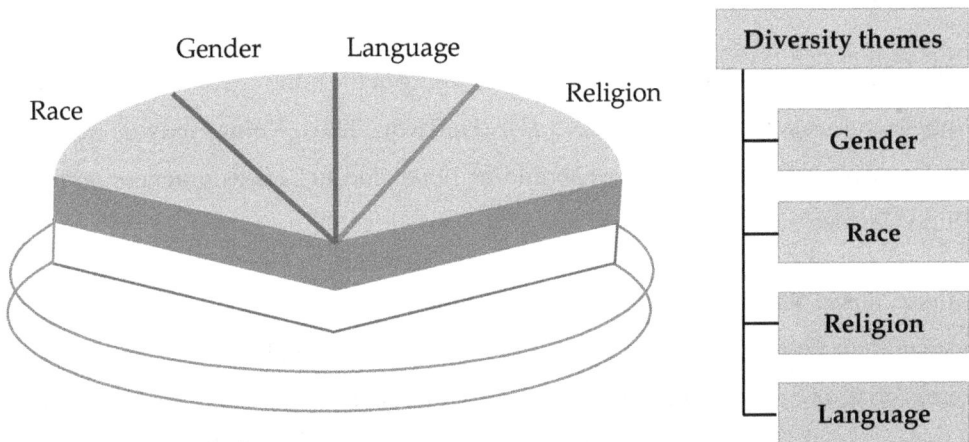

Figure 2: Which themes of diversity emerge as areas of work for you and each of your clients?

Cultural differences in the workplace

Cultural
differences

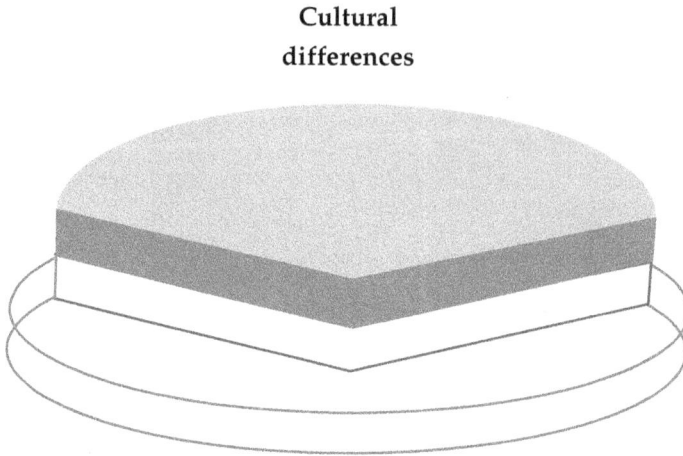

Figure 3: Cultural differences

We next consider how culture is defined, particularly within a business context, including classifications and dimensions of culture, and how these are applied to coaching.

Culture may be defined as a collective programming of the mind that shows in the values, symbols and rituals to which we hold fast (Hofstede, 2001). **Values** may be defined as people's aspirations of how things should be done, and **beliefs** as practices within the culture (Javidan and House, 2001).

Rosinski (2003) advocates understanding different cultures as necessary for a coach to broaden their understanding and be better equipped to assist the client. He talks about professional or organisational culture versus national culture, and indicates various groupings of diversity such as geography and nationality (including region, religion and ethnicity), discipline, profession and education, organisation (including industry, corporation, union and function), social life (including family, friends, social class and clubs), and gender and sexual orientation.

He compiled a Cultural Orientations Framework of seven categories, and within each of these categories are several dimensions:

- a sense of power and responsibility round the question, "Do you control nature or does nature control you?" (Rosinski, 2003:51);

- time-management approaches;

- identity and purpose;

- organisational arrangements;

- territory;

- communication patterns; and

- modes of thinking.

This work creates understanding between people who work together, and helps coaches understand the clients with whom they work, as well as the environment within which their clients operate.

Robbins (2001) attests that a flaw in most organisational behaviour research is that it is chiefly (80 per cent) conducted by Americans in the USA. Hofstede's original research included South Africa, but because the respondents were primarily English-speaking white males, the research is hardly representative of the population.

Although strongly Euro-centric, Hofstede's dimensions are internationally acclaimed as descriptive of regional, ethnic and religious cultures (Schneier, 1998). In 1998 Schneier conducted qualitative research in South Africa to determine whether these dimensions are relevant and sufficient to describe South African ethnic culture. Her research is based on the premise that an overarching imperative in cross-cultural research is the issue of meaning. She argues that quantitative calculations of dimensions may be similar or equivalent but that this does not necessarily imply their similarity or equivalence in terms of meaning. "The effective communication of meaning requires an awareness of how others view their world" (Schneier, 1998:3).

Schneier's (1998) results indicated that, although relevant, Hofstede's five dimensions are not sufficient to describe South African ethnicity. Values that are distinctly African emerged in two main areas: communalism and procedure-driven, time orientation. Communalism is described as implying an interdependence of a uniquely African kind; it stands separate from individualism and collectivism. Hofstede's reference to time in his fifth dimension links time to entrepreneurialism. He does not refer to a past, present and future orientation nor to a linear, circular or procedural perspective of time. Schneier (1998) argues that acknowledging an African procedural-traditional time orientation may play a role in focusing on the quality of an experience or intervention and its results in addition to maintaining efficiency within the traditional Western linear time orientation.

Thomas and Bendixen (2000) specifically compared Hofstede's dimensions within a South African context, examining whether this was a predictor for effective management. They used Hofstede's research questions, surveying 586 middle managers across both genders: white English-speaking and Afrikaans, Coloured, Asian, Sotho, Xhosa and Zulu. They contrasted the seven different groups with a gender split of approximately 2 to 1, male to female. The results appear in Table 2.

Table 2: South African cultural dimension scores by ethnic group						
Group	Sample size	Power distance	Individualism	Masculine	Uncertainty avoidance	Long-term orientation
Xhosa	72	-1.6	78.2	18.1	76.4	45.3
Zulu	60	-1.6	82.8	26.5	58.7	57.5
Sotho	78	-4.5	79.4	52.2	47.2	42.4
White – English-speaking	142	5.4	87.8	33.3	30.7	45.5
White – Afrikaans-speaking	144	5.6	77.3	40.1	46.3	46.5
Asian	40	-1.0	71.3	24.5	66.6	38.3
Coloured	50	-5.4	83.5	30.4	36.9	30.0
Male	397	4.5	80.3	40.2	48.3	47.4
Female	189	-5.8	82.2	21.3	47.9	39.2
Source: Thomas and Bendixen (2000:512)						

There is a wide difference regarding uncertainty avoidance between the white English-speaking group and the Xhosa group. However, the results for the Afrikaans and Sotho groups were quite similar. The rest of the results show some variation across ethnic groups, but not as much as might have been expected – which, according to Thomas and Bendixen (2000), indicates a common national culture in a business context. The overall high scores on individualism are similar to those found in the original study for the UK and the USA, the countries that had the most influence on how business is conducted in South Africa.

The study also confirms Hofstede's argument that a high score in individualism correlates with a low score on power distance. For example, the score for Malaysia on power distance was 104 and for France, 68. More relevant is the finding that management effectiveness is independent of culture and race, and that ethnically diverse management will not inhibit corporate competitive performance (Thomas and Bendixen, 2000:516). This confirms our view that the purpose of any of these studies is to assist our clients in becoming global managers.

As Percy Barnevik, the CEO of the Swedish firm Asea Brown Boveri, put it, "Global managers have exceptionally open minds. They respect how different countries do things, and they have the imagination to appreciate why they do them that way ... Global managers are made, not born" (Javidan and House, 2001:292). As coaches, we can assist in the "making" of global managers if we have open minds and have a deep understanding of our own individual worldview.

How to use this

Self-awareness and practice

- How aware are you of the cultural differences within your client's organisation?
- How do these differences influence their style of communication and how do they inhibit clear communication?
- As a coach, how can you communicate across the differences between your culture and that of your client?
- If your client operates in a multi-national organisation, how does this impact on their behaviour?
- What needs to happen to broaden understanding for the client?

> • How can you help your client to change their communication style and behaviour?
>
> **Example:** For example, Sunny is working with a female client who has a humane and very gentle orientation. The client is working within a very aggressive, male dominated multi-national. One of the areas Sunny is helping her client with, is to develop a style of interrupting to get her point across, while at the same time proposing a communication strategy behind the scenes with her line manager to change the culture of meetings. Sunny is working with the client on style of communication, linguistic patterns that do not serve the client's ability to communicate assertively, and body language that will be influential rather than submissive. She is also working with her client to help her identify the benefits and consequences of changing her style of speaking and presenting.

In any multi-cultural or multi-national organisation, it is useful to conduct a survey to understand how individuals view managing people, resolving conflict, taking decisions and solving problems differently. Once differences are identified and understood, the individual or group can aim towards creating agreed guidelines for behaviour towards colleagues and in teams.

Individualism versus collectivism

South African corporate culture could perhaps be expected to include a mix of scores on individualism versus collectivism. However, the Thomas and Bendixen (2000) study indicated a strong score on individualism for all the groups that participated.

According to Allik and McCrae (2004), Asia and Africa are predominantly collectivist and Europeans and Americans individualist. Peterson (2007) describes common values in collectivist cultures as group achievement, harmony, keeping relationships over time, contributing to the well-being of the group, and being friendly, agreeable and sympathetic. Values associated with individualist cultures are personal achievement and advancement, dominance, autonomy and self-reliance, openness to new experience, and having fun.

One of Hofstede's five dimensions (Robbins, 2001) is individualism versus collectivism. Hofstede defines **individualism** as the degree to which people act as individuals rather than members of a group, and **collectivism** as the opposite. Hofstede (1999) also defines **individualism** as something that occurs in a society where the ties between individuals are loose. Everyone looks after themselves and immediate family only. In a collectivist society, people are part of a cohesive unit from birth and this continues throughout their lifetime with unquestioning loyalty. Rosinski (2003) has a similar definition.

Hofstede (1999) also points out that, according to his research during the 1960s and 1970s, this dimension has seen the biggest change in 30 years, and there is a correlation between a shift to individualism and economic affluence. He stresses that this is not a radical shift but rather a gradual movement. Countries like Japan and South Korea have become more affluent, tending to take care of their elders less than in previous decades; however, they are by no means as individualist as Western countries. In South Africa, we have noticed the tendency in black cultures to be more collectivist, where it is assumed that elders will be taken care of. My godfather, a judge, tells the story of an old man in KwaZulu-Natal who came to see him in circuit court pleading with him to help. He had spent his money providing his children with a good education; however, once educated, they moved away and were not interested in providing for him in his old age. They said he should have provided for himself.

Javidan and House (2001) distinguish between an institutional emphasis on collectivism and in-group collectivism:

- **Institutional collectivism**: People are encouraged to belong to larger groups within society. This belonging is encouraged through incentives for such societies and groups. The society or institution decides how resources, such as the provision of child-care facilities, should be allocated. Group membership is highly valued. The group makes the important decisions, and group goals are more important than individual goals. Countries such as Greece, Italy and Argentina score low and value their individual freedom and autonomy. Self-interest is more important than the collective good. By contrast, countries such as Sweden, South Korea and Japan value group harmony and cooperation and score high in this dimension.

- **In-group collectivism**: This dimension measures the level to which people value and take pride in belonging to small groups such as family and a close circle of friends or the organisation they work for. There are strong expectations of these close-knit ties, such as being favoured for positions and rewards. It is accepted and often expected to use these ties to get doors opened. Countries such as Sweden, Denmark and New Zealand score low, and favouritism and cronyism are unacceptable.

Senghor (1965) describes African collectivism as "communalism", where individualism is not in contrast to but co-exists with communalism. I have found that my clients often grapple with these apparent dichotomies. I have several clients who take care of families or even extended families, understanding that this is expected of them. Some are drawing a line as to the extent to which they are prepared to continue to do this. A few clients believe that their organisations and/or government should take care of them; others believe that they need to do it themselves.

The distinctions between individualism, collectivism and communalism, and how these are experienced by ourselves and our clients, raise interesting questions with regard to the values underpinning the different relationships between the individual and the collective in society. In her research, Schneier (1998) presents an argument that dominant forms of European thought, such as those that gave rise to the dimensions of collectivism and individualism, are based on materialist values whilst communalism has humanism as its value base.

How to use this

Self-awareness and practice

- Do you have a tendency to be more collectivist or individualistic?
- What are your clients like: individualist or collectivist?
- How do they manage the expectation of behaving one way at work and another at home?
- How does their being either individualist or collectivist affect them and the organisations within which they operate?
- How does this influence their aspirations and goals?

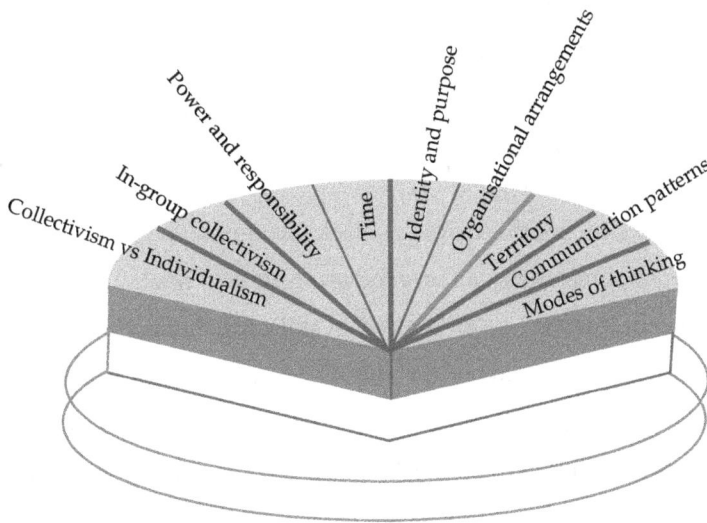

Figure 4: Cultural differences allowing for a set of cultural dimensions

Context

Peterson (2007) points out that executive coaching is about the individual, and the coach works with the individual. **Diversity**, or in his definition **culture**, plays a different role in a group setting, especially in multicultural environments. Should the coach deal with a diverse group, as in a team-coaching situation, the various cultures represented need to be taken into account. When the coach works with an individual, culture plays a different role. It becomes one of various factors that shape the personality and values of the individual – and assumptions about the culture should not "interfere with coaching the individual" (Peterson, 2007:262). Peterson cites an instance when working with a group: the Americans in the group were the most vocal, and the Japanese in the group were the least vocal. However, the individual who dominated the session was Japanese, contrary to the group norm. He states, "The deeper a coach's insights into how culture has shaped their own beliefs and values, the more sensitive they can be to how their assumptions shape their reactions and advice to the people they coach" (Peterson, 2007:262).

What is the context within which you coach? The client with whom you work might not fit the norm of their culture; but what is the norm for the organisation within which the client operates? The Japanese in the above example might have a different experience working in an American company as opposed to a Japanese company. Wilber (2000a) points out that the individual works within a system. We should consider all of the systems within which an individual works, from the family, community and organisation and how all of these influence the client's views, values and beliefs.

An important context in South Africa is Black Economic Empowerment (BEE) and its implications. Ramphele says of the exodus of skills, "South Africa is inflicting a double injury to itself. It is losing sorely needed skills in engineering, medicine and the humanities. It is also throwing away the significant investment made by taxpayers in educating these young people. We behave like a person who is limping from an injured foot who then shoots himself in the other foot to even the score" (Ramphele, 2008:86).

People who are part of the dominant culture of any organisation or country are often unaware of culture, as it is their norm. It is the minority who tend to be more acutely aware of their own culture and the way it differs from the norm which surrounds them. For example, if we take the experience of a white man versus a black female, what are the power and rank issues that arise? The white male in most organisations represents the dominant group, and represents authority and therefore sets the norms of behaviour. On the other hand, the white male is today's marginalised voice; white men could be angry about BEE and are the ones who often choose to leave the country. The experience of a black woman could be entirely different as she tries to unpack the nature of power relationships that happen between people in the workplace. For example, her experience in a predominantly white, male dominated, large corporate could be different to working in a government ministry for a democratically elected black government.

How to use this

Self-awareness and practice

- Overall, as a coach, what is your experience of context – and how do the various contextual settings affect how you view yourself and your ability to function at your best?

- Just as cultures have a dominant leadership style, so do companies. What is the dominant leadership style of the company or corporation within which your client operates and how is that different from your client's view on leadership and their dominant leadership style?
- What contrasting experiences has the client had in other companies with different teams, and more particularly with other line managers who demonstrate contrasting styles of leadership that perhaps conflict with that of your client?

What is acceptable in one context is not necessarily acceptable in another. Some organisations value aggressive and assertive behaviour, whereas others prefer a more humane orientation. Understanding that these differences are not about right or wrong, but more about assisting the client to build the capacity to discern and adapt to them, helps to build sustainability for clients developing new skills and competence.

PERSONALITY DIFFERENCES

Personality is the sum total of ways in which an individual reacts to and interacts with others. It is most often described in terms of measurable traits that a person exhibits (Robbins, 2001:92).

We have so far looked at various diversity and cultural themes. We will now look at personality differences. This is about differences among people even if they have strong similarities such as race, religion, gender and cultural context.

We look at personality profiles, learning theories, and the way we think and make decisions. Personality profiles, as well as learning and thinking styles, speak about our preferences, how and what we like to do. It has nothing to do with ability. It has long been debated whether personality is a function of nature or nurture; current thinking is that it is a combination of both, with situation as a third factor (Robbins, 2001). The relevance of the nature versus nurture debate is that genetic traits are more difficult to change than those that are environmentally driven (Mullen, 2006). Circumstances and the environment in which we function can influence how we learn and think, but we can also change and adapt it. This is of particular importance in a coaching context. I have often heard clients say that they are the way they are and cannot change. They actually can to a certain degree, should they choose to.

**Personality
differences**

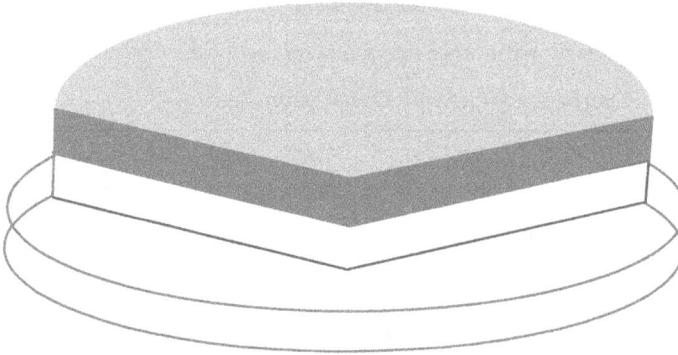

Figure 5: Personality differences

Personality profiles

There are many different personality profiles, and we will look briefly at a few. The Myers-Briggs Type Indicator® (MBTI) is a very popular personality assessment, as is the Enneagram. These two are mentioned here because they do not typecast people. They work on the assumption that, although certain characteristics dominate, we possess all of the elements that define the profile.

The Myers-Briggs Type Indicator® (MBTI)

The MBTI® has a long history and starts with the work of Carl Jung during the 1920s and 1930s. He suggested that we all have the same four instincts that drive us, and that typically one might dominate. Katherine Briggs, at about the same time, started classifying people in terms of their life style. With her daughter, Isabel Briggs Myers, she developed the MBTI® as a combination of her own work and that of Jung.

The MBTI® consists of four streams (Kroeger, Thuesen and Rutledge, 2002). It is listed as streams because we are neither one nor the other (except in very extreme cases), but tend to prefer one rather than the other. Expressed numerically, you might be extraverted 60 per cent of the time and introverted 40 per cent of the time, or any other combination:

1. The first stream looks at your **source of energy**, where the two extremes are extraverted (E) and introverted (I). Extraverts get energy from others or outside of self and talk to think; introverts lose energy to others; they get energy from inside self and think to talk. There are typically three extraverts to one introvert in the general population.

2. The second stream is **how you gather information**. People who tend to look for facts, figures and data are typically more sensing (S) in type, and those more figurative and random in approach, are more intuitive (N) in type. Again, there are typically three sensing types for every intuitive type in the general population.

3. The third stream looks at **how you make decisions**. The thinking (T) types are rational and objective, and the feeling (F) types are more subjective. The population split is equal overall, but men have a preference for thinking type and women for feeling type.

4. The fourth stream looks at **lifestyle**. Judging (J) types prefer life to be planned and decisive; perceiving (P) types prefer it to be flexible and spontaneous. This stream is the easiest to misread as the business environment prefers people to plan and to be less spontaneous. It is critical to complete the test as a preference rather than as a mode of operating. The population split is equal.[4]

A variation on the MBTI® is the Belbin® test, which is based on the work of Meredith Belbin and uses eight team roles together with the four MBTI® streams on a spider graph.

How to use the MBTI®

Most of my clients and colleagues know their MBTI® profile. It is a useful tool for self-understanding as well as developing an awareness of how others operate differently. I have had clients ask me why they are extremely tired at times and at other times not. Often, their profiles show that they are introverted. On the days they were tired, they spent lengthy amounts of time with groups; on days they were less tired, they were working alone. This is a simplistic example, as other factors might have had an influence, such as eating habits, sleeping patterns, or the type of work they were doing.

Enneagram

The Enneagram is primarily a self-awareness tool. It looks at how we behave under stress, how we can manage severe stress and cope with it better. The Enneagram is a system of nine personality types that are mostly referred to by number rather than title or label. The name derives from the Greek words "ennea" (nine) and "gram" (model). We have elements of all nine types within each of us (similarly to the MBTI®), but one is often more dominant than the others. One can also have a profile that indicates several types as a strong tendency. The purpose of the Enneagram as a growth tool is to learn to integrate all nine types.

A brief description of the nine types that show up in all of us, and as are needed in business, are:

- **One, the Reformer**, wants to change the world, often to what our view of perfection is. Those in a business environment are the custodians of ethical standards and quality control.
- **Two, the Helper**, wants to help and heal people but can also be very possessive. They serve people and anticipate their needs.
- **Three, the Achiever**, wants to be seen to be successful and can blindly pursue success and status. They bring promotional and communication skills to any business environment.
- **Four, the Individualist**, wants to be seen as an individual and can be very creative, also often somewhat moody. Fours' participation in business will give a well-designed product that caters for the possible emotional impact of the product on individuals.
- **Five, the Investigator**, wants to invent and gather knowledge and can be eccentric. Five provides innovative ideas and technical expertise in a business environment.
- **Six, the Loyalist**, in all of us wants to belong, lives for commitment and can also become anxious. Sixes in business provide teamwork and self-regulating feedback.
- **Seven, the Enthusiast**, is the highly energetic party animal who can be impulsive and scattered. In a business context, or any other environment, Sevens keep energy and enthusiasm high.

- **Eight, the Challenger**, wants to challenge and be powerful and can control and intimidate others. They provide vision and confidence in business.
- **Nine, the Peacemaker**, wants peace in the world and could become very passive. They listen to people and have the ability to bring them together.

The Enneagram is a complex system with potential for growth, integration and disintegration at all nine levels of development.

How to use this

This is a very powerful tool for development. Should you be interested in finding out more, there is a quick test and a longer one to assist with determining your type. The best way to determine your dominant type is to study all nine and to decide which type most applies to you. We have all nine types in us – and it is important to remember that the least dominant type is as important as the most dominant – it will indicate those parts of you that are being ignored. I have seen with clients that the type that emerges as the highest score is not always the dominant type. For example, a client showed up as a Six, but actually on reflection realised that he was a Nine. The usually rather complacent Nine can easily disintegrate into an anxious Six; as the client was under severe stress at the time of the test he showed up as a Six.

LEARNING AND THINKING STYLES

Working with a variety of clients, we quickly discover that we do not all think, learn and make decisions in the same way. This has an impact on how we coach and how our clients expect to be coached. Below we look at various models of how we think, learn and make decisions.

Thinking styles

Robert Sternberg (1997) contrasts styles with abilities. He defines **styles** as an indication of what people prefer to do, or the way they choose to capitalise on their abilities. This could vary over a lifespan and in different circumstances, as do music, art, books and even people you like change over time. Our life choices are often a combination of preference and ability. How we manage to exercise our options often determines success and happiness. Buckingham and Clifton (2002) refer to strengths in a similar fashion. They define a **strength** as something you like to do repeatedly and well, a combination of preference and ability. Disconcertingly, their research shows that only 20 per cent of the people surveyed felt that their strengths were utilised in their organisations on a daily basis.

Sternberg (1997) advocates that we all have a unique profile of thinking styles. He defines this as functions, forms, levels, scope and leanings of mental self-government. The profile is determined by answering a set of questions, which are scored against the norm for the relevant age, gender and education group. The profiles are listed below, and summarised in Table 3.

Table 3: Summary of the Sternberg profile of thinking styles				
Functions	**Forms**	**Levels**	**Scope**	**Leanings**
Legislative	Monarchic	Global	Internal	Liberal
Executive	Hierarchic	Local	External	Conservative
Judicial	Oligarchic			
	Anarchic			
Source: Sternberg (1997)				

- **Functions of mental self-government: legislative, executive and judicial.** This is based on how most government systems work: legislative makes the laws; executive executes the laws; judicial ensures that the laws are just and adhered to. People who are predominantly **legislative** like to create their own rules, new businesses, design innovative projects and generally invent things. They typically struggle in most education systems, and are often seen as disruptive and not very bright. Einstein is an example. **Executive** individuals want structure. They prefer to solve problems with predefined rules, will impose rules and are great implementers. The **judicial** group prefers to evaluate rules and procedures. In education, they do well when they can critique someone else's work. In business, they would rather evaluate than manage. They make good judges, systems analysts and consultants. In an educational environment, where exams are in the form of essays and innovative thinking is encouraged, legislative people do well. Where the exams are in the form of electronically scored tests, such as in the USA, executive people do well. Legislative individuals are good at starting things up, e.g. Steve Jobs and Steve Wosniak who started Apple, although they were not always as good at maintaining the company. In a team, a combination of all three works well. The legislative will come up with the idea, the executive will implement and the judicial will evaluate. We each have scores in all three, but they are ranked; this ranking can change over time and is context-driven. You could be executive in your communication style, and legislative in your management style.

- **Forms of mental self-government: monarchic, hierarchic, oligarchic and anarchic.** The forms of mental self-government speak to one's preference for dealing with more than one thing at a time. **Monarchic** individuals prefer to do one thing at a time. In a business-coaching context, where executives have to deal with many goals at any given time, the awareness of this preference is useful. **Hierarchic** people make lists of what needs to be done and prioritise the goals and objectives. They find it easier to accept complexity and are organised and systematic. They could become so absorbed in the making and prioritising of the lists that they become indecisive. **Oligarchic** people also like to deal with more than one thing at a time, the difference is that they do not prioritise. They assign equal importance to their chosen goals and objectives. They need to learn to prioritise, but are more flexible than hierarchic individuals when they need to switch priorities. **Anarchic** individuals take a seemingly random approach to problems. They regularly reject systems and anything that confines them. They have the ability to put together disparate pieces of information and solve problems creatively, but are often seen as disruptive in a business context.

- **Levels of mental self-government: global and local. Global** people prefer dealing with abstract issues and looking at the bigger picture, whereas **local** people prefer working with details and specific, concrete issues. Some people naturally do both, and in a business context it is useful to learn to traverse the two.

- **Scope of mental self-government: internal and external.** This is similar to the MBTI® definition of introverted and extraverted. **Internal** individuals turn inward and have a tendency to be task-oriented; they like to work alone. **External** individuals are more outgoing and people-oriented.

- **Leanings of mental self-government: liberal and conservative. Liberal** people prefer ambiguity, tend to go beyond rules and regulations, and are easily bored. **Conservative** individuals prefer to avoid uncertainty and ambiguity. They tend to minimise change as far as possible and prefer structure and predictability.

Typically, in a business environment, those at entry levels are promoted because they do their jobs well, doing what they are told without asking questions. This correlates with the executive style. However, most organisations say they want managers who question and reinvent. This would indicate individuals with a judicial or legislative style preference, but these are not the ones who typically get promoted. In reality, there is a good chance that people with a legislative style are seen as disruptive, and they are either not promoted, or their lives are made so intolerable that they leave the organisation. Sternberg (1985) showed that there is a negative correlation between perception of creativity and wisdom. People who question are often seen as disruptive rather than creative; behaviours that are considered to be creative are often perceived to be unwise. "This incorrect model assumes that one should learn, then think, rather than that one should think to learn and thereby learn to think" (Sternberg, 1997:7).

Examples of application

These styles are an indication of how we prefer to operate and are context-specific. In certain circumstances, some behaviours are expected and rewarded, and others not. Very often men are expected, and rewarded, for being legislative, internal and liberal whereas women are expected to be more judicial, executive and conservative. One of my clients showed the context-specific expectations very clearly. She is very bright and innovative. This was admired and rewarded in her job. She became bored after a while, as legislative people tend to do, and asked for a new challenge. She was subsequently promoted to another position in another department and country. In her new position, she was told that she was disruptive and did not fit in.

We spoke about the different contextual settings and how that affected her. She decided she would stay in the new position for a short while only as the experience suited her long-term goals. We devised a strategy for her to deal with the context in the short term, and one to deal with her longer-term plans. A different client, also legislative, worked hard to be more executive, local and conservative in style and surrounded himself with people who were hierarchical and who could assist with ensuring delivery. He achieved some success, negotiating with the organisation to allow him to start a satellite business, where he could come up with new ideas, i.e. be legislative, and more liberal and global in thinking style, which was his preference.

Learning styles

We refer to the work of David Kolb (1984) in earlier chapters, and in detail in Chapter 5. Kolb's work is seminal in experiential and adult learning, and his learning styles model is widely used. It is relevant to understand how we learn, and to understand how we are different if we are to coach clients effectively. In Chapter 5 we looked at how to use Kolb as a coaching process, and in conjunction with other four-quadrant models, we use it as an example of how diverse we are in our learning styles. Following Kolb, we briefly touch on the work of Honey and Mumford which is based on Kolb's theories.

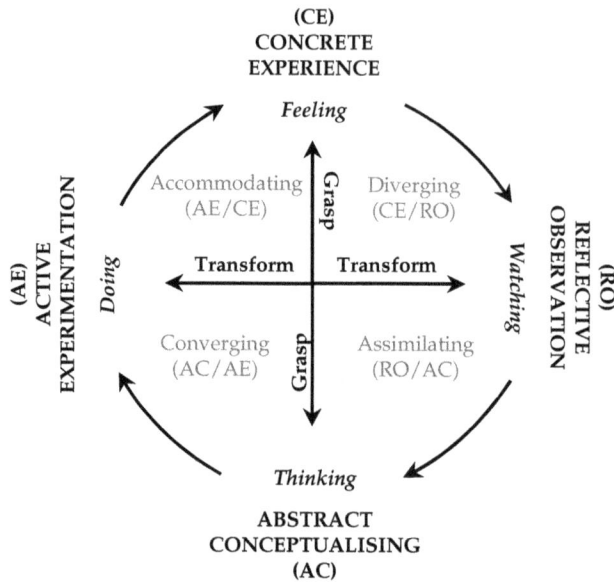

Figure 6: Kolb's learning modes and learning styles

Source: Adapted from Kolb (1984:42)

Kolb's four-stage learning cycle not only indicates individual learning styles, but also the way we effectively learn or teach. The four-stage process starts with concrete experience that is the basis for observation and reflection. Reflections and observations are ideally distilled into abstract concepts, which then produce new actions that can be actively tested creating new experiences and a continuous cycle. We learn optimally when we cycle through experiencing, reflecting, thinking and acting:

1. **Concrete experience (CE)**: Individuals with a high score are people-oriented and empathetic. They prefer an experience-based approach to learning rather than theory.

2. **Reflective observation (RO)**: A high score shows a reflective approach to learning. Individuals with a high RO score observe carefully before making judgements.

3. **Abstract conceptualisation (AC)**: People with a high score prefer logical thinking and rational evaluation. It shows an inclination towards a conceptual approach to learning.

4. **Active experimentation (AE)**: A high score indicates a proclivity towards experimentation and doing.

These four stages can also be seen as two axes: a north-south axis and an east-west axis (Figure 6). The east-west axis indicates how we approach the task or transform the experience (do or watch; act or reflect). The north-south axis indicates how we grasp or take hold of the experience (feel or think) (Kolb, 1984:40–41). From the learning cycle emerge four distinct learning styles, each being a combination of two complementary stages in the cycle. Kolb (1984:77–78) says that we internally decide to do (AE) or watch (RO), and to think (AC) or feel (CE). Our preferred learning style is the combination of our choices on the two axes. These are:

1. **Diverging (CE/RO)**: This person is often good at brainstorming. People with a high score in this quadrant tend to be imaginative and emotional. They are often found in the humanities and the arts.
2. **Assimilating (RO/AC)**: People with a high score are good at bringing disparate ideas together and creating theoretical models. They are mostly found in pure sciences and mathematics.
3. **Converging (AC/AE)**: This learning style is characteristic of engineers. Individuals with a high score tend to be good at application of ideas. They are unemotional and prefer to deal with things rather than people.
4. **Accommodating (AE/CE)**: This group is the risk-takers. They like to experience new things. They solve problems in a trial-and-error way. They can come across as pushy, and are typically found in marketing and sales.

Kolb (1984:141–145) further explained that there are three stages of development, and that our ability to integrate the four different styles improves as we mature. He defined the three stages as:

1. **Acquisition**. This is the period from birth to adolescence when we develop basic abilities as well as our cognitive structures.
2. **Specialisation**. This includes our schooling, early work and personal experiences of adulthood. At this stage, we form a learning style that is influenced by our education, social and organisational context.

3.   **Integration**. The period mid-career to later life when we learn to integrate, amongst other things, the various learning styles in work and personal life.

Preferred learning styles can be determined with the Kolb Learning Styles Inventory (LSI). It also indicates the strength of the preferred learning style. There is a difference between those who are strongly assimilating, and borderline assimilating and converging. Scientists are often strong assimilators, whereas engineers are often strong convergers. Someone who falls between the two is most likely to be good at conceptualising ideas as well as the practical application of ideas.

Example of application

Working with a group, I asked them to do the Learning Styles Inventory (LSI) as a self-assessment questionnaire. One of the participants' preferred style was diverging – the only one in a room full of accountants and analytical people. He approached me afterwards and asked, "Is this why I am so unhappy at work?" In fact, his career was chosen for him by his family. As I was working with the group and not with any individuals in the group, I suggested that he examine his unhappiness with a coach, exploring his options to either make a career change, or to change the nature of the work he was doing at the time.

Honey and Mumford

In their work with managers and executives, Honey and Mumford (1986) found that the descriptions of Kolb's learning styles were not always congruent. Even though they acknowledged their debt and gratitude to him and the influence he had on their work, they opted to create an alternative version of the learning style cycle. It is also a four-stage process with four main styles of learning. They created a Learning Style Questionnaire (LSQ) consisting of 80 questions that are statements around managerial behaviour, as opposed to the Kolb LSI that is a response to 36 words. The alternate terminology is:

Table 4: Comparison of Kolb versus Honey and Mumford terminology		
Kolb stage	**Honey and Mumford**	**Kolb learning style**
Concrete experience (CE)	Activist	Accommodating
Reflective observation (RO)	Reflector	Diverging
Abstract conceptualisation (AC)	Theorist	Assimilating
Active experimentation (AE)	Pragmatist	Converging

Honey and Mumford's (1986) learning styles are defined as follows:

- **Activist** (having an experience): These people are open-minded and enthusiastic and they will try anything once. They often throw caution to the wind and thrive on constant new challenges. They get bored quickly and can be seen as controlling all activities and hogging the limelight.
- **Reflector** (reviewing the experience): They love to observe, stand back and ponder. They are thoughtful to a fault and could take a long time to reach a conclusion. They often take a back seat in meetings and take everything into account before they act.
- **Theorist** (concluding from the experience): They often have the ability to bring opposing views and thoughts into a logical and sound theory. They can be perfectionistic, detached and analytical. Things have to make sense and be logical.
- **Pragmatist** (planning the next steps): People with a high score like to try out theories and ideas to see if they would work. They are practical and down to earth. They act quickly and do not like waiting or thinking things through too carefully.

Examples of application

Business schools generally favour logic and systems thinking. This suits the theorists. If there is a requirement for analytical reflection, the reflectors are comfortable. Role-playing will suit the activists as long as they do not have to reflect too much on the experience. The pragmatists will be mostly uncomfortable in a business school learning environment. Learning styles can also affect the efficacy of coaching. Activists may not enjoy the reflective nature of coaching and might find the process too analytical. Reflectors will enjoy the observation and reflection aspect but would not "perform" without preparation. The theorists enjoy non-directive questioning to *ad hoc* sessions, with a need for a high level of intellectual respect. The pragmatists enjoy and find coaching beneficial if they can see what the impact will be on their performance, and if they experience the coach as an authority.

Decision-making styles

Robbins (2001) refers to the work of Rowe and Boulgarides on decision-making. They indicate four different approaches to decision-making, specifically focusing on business and managerial decision-making. It is a two-by-two matrix based on two ways of thinking, rational and intuitive, and a tolerance for ambiguity with a high and low mode. This allows for the four ways of decision-making, namely directive, analytic, conceptual and behavioural:

- The **directive style** indicates a low tolerance for ambiguity and a rational way of thinking. These managers are logical and seek efficiency. They tend to make decisions without assessing alternatives. Decisions are made fast and are short-term in focus.

- The **analytic style** of decision-making has an equally rational way of thinking but a high tolerance for ambiguity. This leads to more careful decision-making and allows for adaptability with the acquisition of additional information. More alternatives are explored in the decision-making process.

- Managers with a high tolerance for ambiguity and an intuitive way of thinking are labelled as **conceptual** in their decision-making. These managers are usually very good at solving problems creatively.

- The fourth category of decision-making is when thinking is intuitive and the tolerance for ambiguity low. This style of decision-making is called **behavioural**. These managers typically work well with others, they seek acceptance and avoid conflict.

Rowe and Boulgarides have suggested that most managers have a preferred and a back-up style (Robbins, 2001). Managers who are flexible can use the style appropriate to the situation or context. Typically, the preferred style of most executives is analytic; this is linked to most business education which favours a rational style of thinking.

We looked at various ways in which we think, learn and make decisions. These modes of thinking are learned and can be changed. From a coaching perspective, it is important to understand how you think and learn as a coach and how different it might be for your client – as well as helping your client to understand and work with different styles and thinking, decision-making and learning within their team.

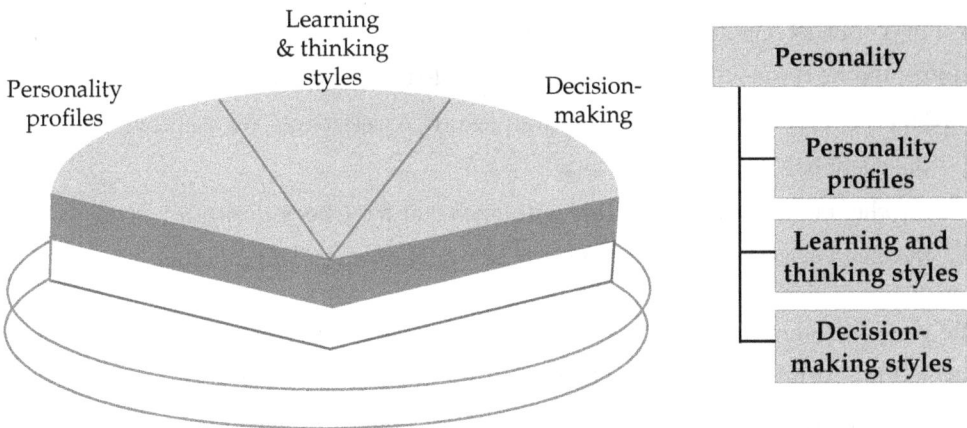

Figure 7: Personality – allowing for various personality assessments

BRINGING IT ALL TOGETHER

The great organisation must not only accommodate the fact that each employee is different, it must capitalise on these differences (Buckingham and Clifton, 2002:5).

Diversity is a universal theme. It is important in a fast-changing and ever-diminishing world for everyone – organisations, leaders, managers as well as coaches – to understand and embrace diversity. "No matter how highly skilled, well trained, or intelligent you are, if you are making wrong or culturally inappropriate assumptions, you will not be accurate in your assessment, meaningful in your understanding, or appropriate in your interactions as a leader" (Connerley and Pedersen, 2005).

We like to ask a client their life story as a start to building the relationship. Rosinski (2003) supports this when he states that in the beginning of a coaching relationship he sets aside two to three hours to hear the client's story. The goal here is to understand, not judge. Their story will bring out some of the themes we have discussed in this chapter.

It is important to note, however, that the client may not initially share much more than superficial facts. Over time, as trust is built, this should improve, leading to more information being offered at deeper levels.

It is useful to incorporate new and completed personality tests into building the relationship, using them in helping to determine the purpose, strategy and outcomes for the coaching journey. However, be aware of those assessments that can only be facilitated and debriefed by a psychologist. Peterson (2007) supports the use of personality tests, and indicates that understanding Rosinski's dimensions are similar to using the Myers-Briggs Type Indicator® (MBTI) as an example of a personality framework. Assessments are useful if:

- the client has not completed any;
- the client is very uncomfortable with ones that have been done; or
- the client is struggling with understanding themselves and their behaviour.

The various diversity themes mentioned in this chapter are a starting point, not an end destination. Although understanding diversity in all of its facets is relevant to building self-awareness, we should not underestimate its complexity. Human beings are like a five-billion-piece jigsaw puzzle. Coaching assists the client in starting a lifelong journey to discover those pieces, realising those pieces may change over time, some may fall away, and new ones be taken on.

Connerley and Pedersen (2005) suggest that multicultural awareness can be learned but not taught. They emphasise that training can provide the knowledge and skills necessary to cultivate better interaction and the growth of awareness. Their recommended framework for dealing with multicultural environments is a process that:

- cultivates awareness;
- acquires knowledge; and
- practises and applies the required skills.

They also indicate that the reasons why most training programmes fail are because of an overemphasis on one of three components while neglecting the other two. Awareness is the first level of understanding your own culture and personality, particularly how this influences your worldview. The second level is to find the information and knowledge that will help you to understand how people are different from you. The third level is to start acquiring and practising newly acquired skills and behaviour.

Context

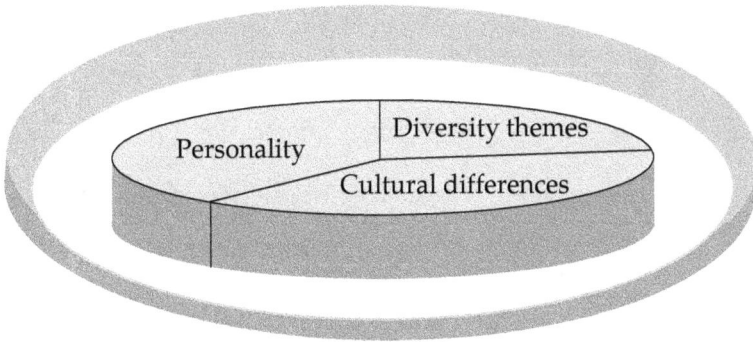

Context

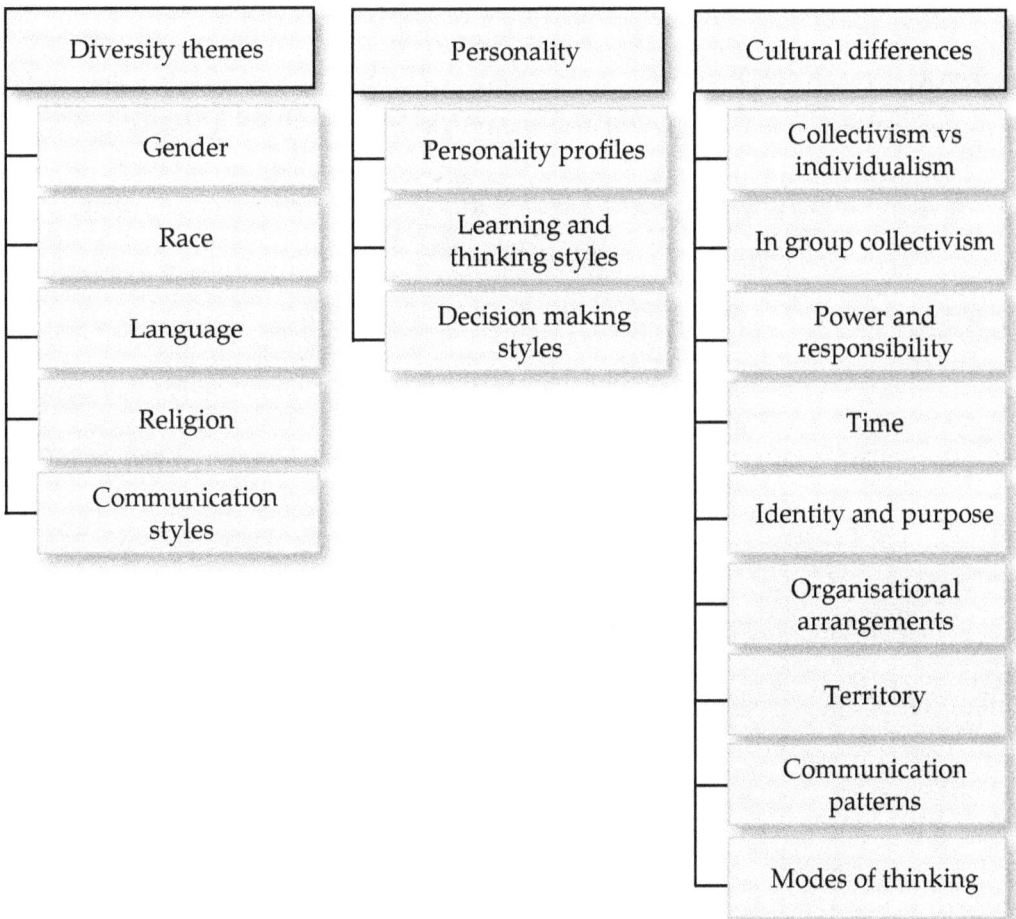

Diversity themes	Personality	Cultural differences
Gender	Personality profiles	Collectivism vs individualism
Race	Learning and thinking styles	In group collectivism
Language	Decision making styles	Power and responsibility
Religion		Time
Communication styles		Identity and purpose
		Organisational arrangements
		Territory
		Communication patterns
		Modes of thinking

Figure 8: The full circle

In this chapter we have explored various themes of diversity, personality, cultural and gender issues, learning and thinking styles. It is up to you to cultivate self-awareness, continuing your own professional development and applied practice when working with diversity and cultural issues in an organisational context. An integrated understanding of this chapter's core themes can only enhance your success as a business coach.

Regardless of the amount of cultural knowledge a coach has, the best coaches will always be those who coach with an open attitude of curiosity and interest, who meet people where they are, who accept them for what they are, and who project a genuine desire to be helpful to each person on their own terms (Peterson, 2007).

COACH'S LIBRARY

Aiken Hodge, D. (2006). *Towards coaching across divides to create alliances – an Integral approach.* Unpublished DProf dissertation. London: Middlesex University.

Babcock, L. and Laschever, S. (2003). *Women don't ask: Negotiation and the gender divide.* Princeton, NJ: Princeton University Press.

Bell, E.L.J. and Nkomo, S.M. (2001). *Our separate ways: Black and white women and the struggle for identity.* Cambridge, MA: Harvard Business School Press.

Briggs Myers, I. and Myers, P.B. (1995). *Gifts differing: Understanding personality type.* Palo Alto, CA: Davies-Black.

Buckingham, M. and Clifton, D.O. (2002). *Now, discover your strengths.* New York, NY: Simon and Schuster.

Caver, K.A. and Livers, A.B. (2002). Dear White Boss. *Harvard Business Review,* 80(11):76–81.

Connerley, M.L. and Pedersen, P.B. (2005). *Leadership in a diverse and multicultural environment.* London: Sage.

Gardner, H. (2006). *Multiple intelligences.* Cambridge, MA: Perseus.

Honey, P. and Mumford, A. (1986). *Using your learning styles.* Second edition. Maidenhead, Berkshire: Peter Honey.

Honey, P. and Mumford, A. (1992). *The manual of learning styles: Capitalizing on your learning style.* Maidenhead: Peter Honey.

Javidan, M. and House, R.J. (2001). Cultural acumen for the global manager: Lessons from Project GLOBE. *Organizational Dynamics*, 29(4):289–305.

Kets de Vries, M. (2004). Putting leaders on the couch. *Harvard Business Review*, January.

Kline, N. (1999/2004). *Time to think: Listening with the human mind.* London: Ward Lock.

Kolb, D.A. (1984). *Experiential learning: Experience as the source of learning and development.* Upper Saddle River, NJ: Prentice Hall.

Kroeger, O. and Thuesen, J.M. (1988). *Type talk: The 16 personality types that determine how we live, love and work.* New York, NY: Dell.

Kroeger, O., Thuesen, J.M. and Rutledge, H. (2002). *Type talk at work: How the 16 personality types determine your success on the job.* New York, NY: Dell.

Peterson, D.B. (2007). Executive coaching in a cross-cultural context. *Consulting Psychology Journal: Practice and Research*, December.

Pinker, S. (2008). *The sexual paradox: Men, women and the real gender gap.* New York, NY: Scribner.

Ramphele, M. (2008). *Laying ghosts to rest: Dilemmas of the transformation in South Africa.* Cape Town: Tafelberg.

Riso, D.R. and Hudson, R. (1999). *The wisdom of the Enneagram.* New York, NY: Bantam.

Rosinski, P. (2003). *Coaching across cultures: New tools for leveraging national, corporate and professional differences.* London: Nicholas Brealey.

Schneier, C.J. (1998). *Establishing dimensions of South African ethnicity.* Unpublished Masters dissertation. Johannesburg: University of the Witwatersrand.

Sternberg, R.J. (1997). *Thinking styles.* Cambridge: Cambridge University Press.

Tannen, D. (1995). The power of talk: Who gets heard and why. *Harvard Business Review,* September–October.

Thomas, A. and Bendixen, M. (2000). The management implication of ethnicity in South Africa. *Journal of International Business Studies,* 31(3):507–519.

Wilber, K. (2000a). *A theory of everything: An integral vision for business, politics, science and spirituality.* Dublin: Gateway.

Consultancies

ProCorp (www.procorp.co.za) specialises in gender and racial equity facilitation, research and development.

ENDNOTES TO CHAPTER 6

1. The television programme *Carte Blanche* broadcast a feature on DNA in September 2004 (MNet, 2008) called "Where do we come from?" – the quick answer is "from Africa".
2. The MIL Institute is based in Sweden. Their motto is "MiL Institute turns vision and values into action by designing processes of innovation and change". They design action-learning programmes (called ARL or action-reflection-learning) for companies and do coaching, at individual and team level (see www. milinstitute.se).
3. CIDA City Campus started in 2000 as a university to provide a fully accredited, practical four-year Bachelor of Business Administration qualification that emphasises entrepreneurship, business and technology. The course is offered to students from previously disadvantaged communities. Costs are kept low with leading South African experts and professionals lecturing on a *pro bono* basis, companies and individuals donating money and equipment to sponsor students, and students helping to run the campus. From donations received from companies and individuals worldwide, students are offered funding for housing, transport and food.

4. The four streams translate into sixteen types. They are ESTJ; ISTJ; ESTP; ISTP; ESFJ; ISFJ; ESFP; ISFP; ENTJ; INTJ; ENTP; INTP; ENFJ; INFJ; ENFP and INFP. For example, the ESTJs are generally referred to as administrators and organisers. They are logical, analytical, decisive, realistic, often naturally good at running activities, and hence are often the dominant group in a generic business environment. The ENTP is innovative, versatile, individualistic and often entrepreneurial. The ENTJ is called the "field marshal" and they are often natural leaders. The ISFP is the artist, often hedonistic and compulsive. The ENFJ is called the "teacher"; they are charismatic and often gifted with language. The INFP is the healer who strives for unity and is often an idealist. Each of the 16 types is profiled in the MBTI using such descriptions and categorisations.

7

Competences in Business Coaching
by Marti Janse van Rensburg

Our chief want in life is somebody who shall make us do what we can (Ralph Waldo Emerson).

Why do we need competences in business coaching? How do we know what the relevant skills and competences should be? How should these be measured?

This chapter outlines the competence frameworks developed by various coaching organisations in an effort to promote professionalism within the industry, focusing on their general approach and structure, and on how the defined competences are benchmarked. It then reviews specific skills and competences stipulated within these frameworks for particular aspects of the coaching process.

Chapter outline

- Why skills and competences?
- Competence frameworks
    - International Coach Federation (ICF)
    - Worldwide Association of Business Coaches (WABC)
    - European Mentoring and Coaching Council (EMCC)
    - Coaches and Mentors of South Africa (COMENSA)
    - In summary
- Specific competences required
    - Building the coaching relationship
    - Listening
    - Questioning
    - Self-awareness
    - Process of reflection
    - Continuous learning and development
- Developing your knowledge base
- Coach's library

WHY SKILLS AND COMPETENCES?

> ... being explicit about competences gives an identified path for progression as a coach, and so can reduce any sense amongst aspiring coaches that in the distribution of client work smoke and mirrors are the governing factor (Ahern, 2003:374).

Defined and benchmarked skills and competences serve a dual purpose: they give clarity in terms of how we might be chosen to do work, and they give the coach and the emerging coaching profession guidelines on what is expected and how to develop and improve. However, as coaching is at this stage very much a self-regulated industry, coaching skills are rarely measured or assessed using valid and reliable assessment tools (Lidbetter, 2003). In general, skills and competence are defined by coaching associations as part of a philosophy or as a means to an end or a goal.

When you are not feeling well, you might decide to go and look for a medical professional. You determine which one, depending on your symptoms. If you have a toothache, you consider going to a dentist or a generalist in oral healthcare. You assume that such professionals comply with certain criteria: that they have passed the required written and practical exams and that they adhere to a code of professional ethics. You expect that they were assessed to ensure that they have the required skills and competence to do the job before they opened up shop.

There are currently no such barriers to entry for coaching. Chapter 2 outlined how coaching emerged and progressed. For coaching to progress further, from an emerging discipline to a full-fledged profession, will require the definition of specific skills and competences as part of a theoretically sound and empirically verified body of knowledge. This process has been investigated and promoted by the Global Convention on Coaching (GCC). In the meantime, various national and international coaching organisations have drawn up competence frameworks in an attempt to self-regulate and professionalise the industry as far as possible. These frameworks are outlined in the following section.

COMPETENCE FRAMEWORKS

This section outlines the structures and general approaches of competence frameworks developed by the following international and national associations for coaches:

- International Coach Federation (ICF);
- Worldwide Association of Business Coaches (WABC);
- European Mentoring and Coaching Council (EMCC); and
- Coaches and Mentors of South Africa (COMENSA).

International Coach Federation (ICF)

The ICF (2008a) points out that its framework of core coaching competences was developed in order to:

- support greater understanding about the skills and approaches used within the coaching profession;
- support members in calibrating their level of alignment between the coach-specific training the ICF expects and the training members have experienced; and
- be used as the foundation for the ICF Credentialing process examination.

The core competences are grouped into four clusters according to those that fit together "logically". The ICF (2008a) emphasises that the groupings and individual competences are not weighted, i.e. they do not represent any kind of prioritisation but "are all core or critical for any competent coach to demonstrate".

The ICF has definitions and related behaviours for each competency, distinguishing between behaviours that should always be present and visible and those that are called for only in certain coaching situations. The 11 competences are listed below in their four groupings (with the related behaviours omitted for the sake of clarity):

A. **Setting the foundation**:
    1. Meeting ethical guidelines and professional standards.
    2. Establishing the coaching agreement.
B. **Co-creating the relationship**:
    3. Establishing trust and intimacy with the client.
    4. Coaching presence.

C. **Communicating effectively:**

    5.   Active listening.

    6.   Powerful questioning.

    7.   Direct communication.

D. **Facilitating learning and results:**

    8.   Creating awareness.

    9.   Designing actions.

    10.   Planning and goal setting.

    11.   Managing progress and accountability.

A research study tested the validity of these 11 competences. Griffiths and Campbell (2008) interviewed five ICF-certified master coaches and nine of their clients to find that some competences were well supported, and others not. They discovered some inconsistency in the competency grouping, suggesting that the competences were devised somewhat unscientifically rather than through an empirically validated process. This supports our view that these are guidelines only until further research is undertaken. As far as we are aware, this is one of two studies that endeavours to test the validity of competences. The complete ICF competence framework can be found on the Federation's website at www. coachfederation.org.

Worldwide Association of Business Coaches (WABC)

Since 1997, the WABC has worked to define the emerging profession of business coaching and to distinguish it from other types of coaching. From 2002 to 2005, in partnership with the UK-based Professional Development Foundation (PDF), the WABC conducted rigorous research into what defines a competent business coach. Their aim was to develop a robust and evidence-based framework which was congruent with the real practice of business coaches.

Stage One was an in-depth literature review of psychology, training and development and organisational development literatures from 1930 to the present day. The focus of this review was how coaching was carried out, who was doing it, how it was used within organisations, and the coaching systems which have evolved as a result. Particular attention was paid to the factors influencing the efficacy of coaching from an organisational context through to coach attributes.

Stage Two was the development of the competency framework from the analysis of this literature and its independent evaluation by experienced and senior business coaches. The WABC collaborated with an international panel of acclaimed business coaches, to undertake this work. This was not a task of setting forth requirements, but of discovering the actual working abilities of professional business coaches.

The Panel was asked to review the specific competences and rate them for level of importance, with the objective of establishing a measure of a range of achievement of competences for *mastery-level* practice in business coaching. As a result, the WABC published their first working definition of business coaching, and at the same time, a set of professional competences was formulated that describe master-level business coaching. The competences are based on the real-world tasks of master coaches in small and large businesses, governments, institutions and non-profits, that is, any organisations where business coaches practice. (The WABC have recently published a new definition of business coaching and new standards for business coaches, as a result of a three-year collaborative and global study.)

The business coaching competences are divided into three areas:
- Self-management – knowing oneself and self-mastery;
- Core coaching skill-base; and
- Business and leadership coaching capabilities.

Each area is defined with a list of competences, and each competency is illustrated by examples of the behaviour expected of a proficient master coach with at least five years' experience. WABC also includes a section on the knowledge they believe the business coach should have, which encompasses business experience, as well as knowledge of leadership and business theories. They are the only professional body I am aware of which lists diversity and multicultural issues as a competency (see Competency 7 under "Business and leadership coaching capabilities" below).

WABC (2008b) states that "Newer business coaches are not expected to demonstrate every competency listed here. Rather, the competences provide a framework against which individuals can map their training and experience. In this way, individual coaches can use the competences to gauge their progress toward master-level proficiency."

The WABC (2008b) business coaching competence framework is outlined as follows (the illustrative examples for each competence are omitted for the sake of brevity):

Self-management – knowing oneself and self-mastery

1. **Knowing yourself: self-insight and understanding:**
    (a) Having ready access to your thoughts and feelings and being aware of how they affect your behaviour.
2. **Acknowledging your strengths and development needs:**
    (a) Having a realistic perception of your strengths and development needs – knowing your strengths and limitations and showing a commitment to continuous learning and self-development.
    (b) Self-belief – believing in your self-worth and capabilities.
3. **Self-mastery: managing your thoughts, feelings and behaviours in ways that promote behaviour contributing to career and organisation success:**
    (a) Self-regulation: managing your reactions and emotions constructively.
    (b) Integrity: choosing ethical courses of action and being steadfast in your principles and beliefs.
    (c) Self-responsibility: assuming personal responsibility and accountability for your performance.
    (d) Adaptability: flexibility in handling change.
    (e) Emphasising excellence: setting for yourself and confidently pursuing, challenging goals and high standards.
    (f) Initiative: taking independent action to change the direction of events.
    (g) Creativity and innovation: being receptive to new ideas and being able to generate alternative ways to view and define problems.

Core coaching skill-base

1. **Creating the foundations for business coaching:**
    (a) Working within established ethical guidelines and professional standards.
    (b) Agreeing on a clear and effective contract for the coaching relationship.

2. **Developing the business coaching relationship:**

   (a) Establishing trust and respect.

   (b) Establishing rapport.

3. **Promoting client understanding:**

   (a) Listening to understand.

   (b) Questioning effectively.

   (c) Communicating clearly.

   (d) Facilitating depth of understanding.

4. **Facilitating personal transformation:**

   (a) Promoting action.

   (b) Focusing on goals.

   (c) Building resiliency.

   (d) Managing termination of coaching.

5. **Professional development:**

   (a) Maintaining and improving professional skills.

Business and leadership coaching capabilities

1. **Alignment:**

   (a) Understanding the business and displaying a strong grounding in business knowledge and competences.

   (b) Demonstrating proficiency in systems thinking.

   (c) Aligning coaching initiatives with the business.

2. **Leadership knowledge and credibility:**

   (a) Acting as a strong and influential role model.

   (b) Possessing thorough working knowledge of the world of the executive leader and leadership development.

   (c) Displaying highly developed communication and interpersonal competences.

3. **Coach as leader and developer of own business:**

   (a) Creating and managing business relationship networks.

   (b) Collaborating with other coaches.

   (c) Developing yourself in a business capacity.

4. **Creating and maintaining partnerships with all stakeholders in the business coaching process.**

5. **Understanding organisational behaviour and organisational development principles.**

6. **Assessment:**
    (a) Assessing the client.
    (b) Assessing the individual and organisational benefits of business coaching.

7. **Having respect for and knowledge about multicultural issues and diversity.**

The complete WABC competence framework can be found on the Association's website at www.wabccoaches.com. Their new ten standards are: responsibility and respect; professionalism and ethics; client focus; boundaries; business context; business coaching process; confidentiality; diversity; professional development; and promotion of the emerging profession.

European Mentoring and Coaching Council (EMCC)

The EMCC's (2008a) competence standards define core competences in four categories as a basis for the training of coaches and mentors, as follows:

1. **Who we are** – the incremental hierarchy of personal attributes for coaching and mentoring:
    (a) Beliefs and attitudes.
    (b) Self.

2. **Our skills and knowledge** – we will use during the coaching / mentoring process:
    (a) Communication skills.
    (b) Technical skills.
    (c) People development.
    (d) Business development.

3. **How we coach and mentor** – how we will demonstrate that we are able to apply what we have learned.

4. **How we manage the process** – what we will do as part of our coaching/mentoring practice to maintain and develop an effective and professional approach:
    (a) Managing the relationship.
    (b) Managing the contract.

The Competence Standards include examples of how the competences should be demonstrated within each of the following six levels of practice:

- Foundation 3 (equivalent to the UK's National Vocational Qualification (NVQ) level 3);
- Foundation 4 (equivalent to NVQ 4);
- Intermediate (equivalent to an undergraduate degree or NVQ 5);
- Practitioner (equivalent to a postgraduate certificate);
- Advanced Practitioner (equivalent to a postgraduate diploma); and
- Master Practitioner (equivalent to a Master's degree).

The complete EMCC Competence Standards can be found on the Council's website at www.emccouncil.org.

The EMCC's Quality Award for trainers of coaches and mentors is based on the above Competence Standards. The first accreditations were awarded in June 2006. Eric Parsloe, chief executive officer of the Oxford School of Coaching and Mentoring, said of the initiative: "Until now the market has been awash with over-simplistic communication skills programmes or pet theories presented in pseudo-technical formats. Everyone can now distinguish the genuine article" (Scott, 2007:17).

Coaches and Mentors of South Africa (COMENSA)

During 2005–2006, Coaches and Mentors of South Africa (COMENSA) developed a simple framework of standards of professional competence for coaches, which defined competences in five functional areas at four levels of expertise. The five functional areas were (COMENSA, 2006):

- questioning;
- listening;
- building rapport;
- delivering measurable results; and
- upholding ethical guidelines and professional standards.

The four levels of competence within each functional area were:

1. unacceptable;

2. entry-level;

3. intermediate; and

4. master/expert.

During 2007, COMENSA developed a revised competence framework, the draft *Membership Criteria and Standards of Competence (MCSC) Framework*, based on the EMCC's Competence Standards. COMENSA then engaged in a lengthy process of consultation with its members on this draft competence framework; it is not yet clear when the framework will be finalised and implemented. The draft *MCSC Framework* defined core competences in four categories, as follows (COMENSA, 2007):

1. **Self-awareness/Who we are** – personal attributes for coaching:

    1.1 Beliefs and attitudes.

    1.2 Self-awareness.

2. **Managing the process** – what we will do as part of our coaching practice to maintain and develop an effective and professional approach:

    2.1 Managing the relationship.

    2.2 Managing the contract.

3. **Ability to coach** – skills we will use during the coaching process:

    3.1 Communication skills.

    3.2 Technical skills.

    3.3 People development.

4. **Facilitating learning and results** – how we will demonstrate that we are able to apply what we have learned.

The draft *MCSC Framework* included examples of how the competences should be demonstrated within each of the following levels of practice:

- Minimum competence standards for all coach practitioners.

- Registered Practitioner (in addition to minimum competence standards).

- Certified Practitioner (in addition to minimum competence standards).

- Master Practitioner (in addition to minimum competence standards).

The COMENSA draft *Membership Criteria and Standards of Competence Framework* is currently under review and can be found on the Association's website at www.comensa. org.za.

In summary

All of these bodies recommend the competences of listening, questioning and managing the relationship. The WABC, and COMENSA in its revised competence framework, both identify self-awareness as a core competence. COMENSA and the EMCC do not explicitly recommend goals or outcomes. The WABC is the only body that requires business competence. The Griffiths and Campbell (2008) study indicated that a missing crucial process from the ICF competence framework (and therefore the other bodies too) is the establishment of a process of self-reflection in the client. We discussed Kolb's learning cycle in two previous chapters, and if one of the intended outcomes of coaching is learning how to learn, then the ability to reflect is critical on the part of both client and coach.

SPECIFIC COMPETENCES REQUIRED

Connerley and Pedersen (2005:70) define "competences" as "The skills, abilities, personal characteristics and other person-based factors that help distinguish between outstanding performance and average performance".

This section highlights specific competence stipulated by the ICF, WABC and COMENSA for the following aspects of the coaching process:

- building the coaching relationship;
- listening;
- questioning;
- self-awareness; and
- building self-reflection.

Building the coaching relationship

Coaching is ultimately defined by the relationship between the coach and the client, as Flaherty (1999:10) states in defining his operating principles of coaching: "Relationship is the most important one and is based on mutual trust, mutual respect and freedom of expression".

International Coach Federation (ICF)

The ICF (2008a) defines competences in building the relationship as follows:

Co-creating the relationship:

Establishing trust and intimacy with the client – ability to create a safe, supportive environment that produces ongoing mutual respect and trust:

a. Show genuine concern for the client's welfare and future.

b. Continuously demonstrate personal integrity, honesty and sincerity.

c. Establish clear agreements and keep promises.

d. Demonstrate respect for client's perceptions, learning style, personal being.

e. Provide ongoing support for and champion new behaviours and actions, including those involving risk-taking and fear of failure.

f. Ask permission to coach client in sensitive, new areas.

Worldwide Association of Business Coaches (WABC)

WABC (2008b) defines business competences in building the coaching relationship as follows:

Core coaching skill-base:

Developing the business coaching relationship:

(a) Establishing trust and respect:

- Demonstrate a genuine concern for the client's welfare and success.
- Demonstrate a strong belief in the boundless potential of others.
- Consistently work to establish trust and honest communication with the client.
- Establish clear agreements and keep promises.
- Clearly and candidly share your values, attitudes, beliefs and emotions when appropriate.
- Encourage the client to take on new and challenging tasks, while providing appropriate support.
- Create an environment of safety and security when dealing with sensitive issues.

- Create an environment of safety and security in which the client is able to share all sides of themselves (e.g. their ambitions, needs and fears).
- Be honest and truthful in difficult situations (e.g. prepared to tell the client what they need to hear but others won't say).

(b) Establishing rapport:

- Have an open and responsive presence.
- Be comfortable sharing your intuitions with the client.
- Demonstrate a willingness to take risks and to enter the unknown.
- Have a very flexible approach to coaching and be able to adapt your style to what works best for the client.
- Make appropriate use of humour to make the work more fun.
- Be able to tolerate open expression of strong emotions directed at you without becoming defensive.
- Be able to manage the client's expression of strong emotions about their situation without getting caught up in their emotions.
- Be able to work with a variety of learning styles in individuals.
- Give objective feedback in a non-judgmental manner.

Coaches and Mentors of South Africa (COMENSA)

COMENSA's (2006) original *Standards of Professional Competence* defined "building rapport" as "Establishing and maintaining trust and intimacy in the coaching/mentoring relationship and creating a safe space in which a person can courageously explore their inner and outer thinking, by mirroring, validating, empathising and truly meeting the person in their model of the world or frame of reference".

COMENSA's top two benchmark levels of competence in building rapport were defined as follows:

Level 4: This includes all the behaviours of Level 3, plus respectfully challenging the client to delve deeper to explore their less conscious intentions and desires. The coach/mentor invites and facilitates the client to apply their inner resources to difficult situations; offers statements of affirmation that convey belief in the person's potential; celebrates the client's successes; expresses own emotion about client's emotion; and allows self to be moved by the client.

Level 3: The coach/mentor is actively and intensely involved with the client. Listens for and enquires about emotions; invests energy in the conversation; matches the person's posture, gesture, language, intensity of voice; mirrors the client's state, values and beliefs; and keeps the conversation and questions focused on the client's outcomes.

COMENSA's (2007) draft *MCSC Framework* defined the following competences for building the relationship:

Managing the process – what we will do as part of our coaching practice to maintain and develop an effective and professional approach:

Managing the relationship:

Minimum standards:

- Establish trust and intimacy with the client.
- Continuously demonstrate personal integrity, honesty and sincerity.
- Establish clear agreements and keeps promises.
- Treat all people with respect and dignity.
- Demonstrate respect for client's perceptions, learning style and personal being
- Provide support and encourage new behaviours and actions.
- Employ a style that is open, flexible and competent.
- Assist client to clarify goals.
- Explore a range of options for achieving goals aligned to personal/organisational needs.
- Enable client to develop an action plan.
- Reviews progress and achievement of the plan.
- Act as an external source of motivation to support the client in achieving their goals.
- Manage conclusion of the process.

Plus:

- Managing the relationship draws on a range of techniques and methods to facilitate achievement of goals.
- Adapt to personal/organisational changes that impact on the contract agreement.

Listening

Hargrove (2003:43) discusses the fact that great coaches or teachers stand apart because they come from a place of being rather than doing, and then talks about how they listen: "They listen from a place where they see that the coachee or student is committed to being great, not just merely good or mediocre, and, as a result, they call that commitment forth".

International Coach Federation (ICF)

The ICF (2008a) defines competences in listening as follows:

Communicating effectively:

Active listening – ability to focus completely on what the client is saying and is not saying, to understand the meaning of what is said in the context of the client's desires, and to support client self-expression:

a.   Attends to the client and the client's agenda and not to the coach's agenda for the client.

b.   Hears the client's concerns, goals, values and beliefs about what is and is not possible.

c.   Distinguishes between the words, the tone of voice, and the body language.

d.   Summarises, paraphrases, reiterates, mirrors back what the client has said to ensure clarity and understanding.

e.   Encourages, accepts, explores and reinforces the client's expression of feelings, perceptions, concerns, beliefs, suggestions, etc.

f.   Integrates and builds on the client's ideas and suggestions.

g.   "Bottom-lines" or understands the essence of the client's communication and helps the client get there rather than engaging in long descriptive stories.

h.   Allows the client to vent or "clear" the situation without judgment or attachment in order to move on to next steps.

Worldwide Association of Business Coaches (WABC)

WABC (2008b) defines business competences in listening as:

Core coaching skill-base:

Promoting client understanding:

(a) Listening to understand:

- Adjust easily to the client's agenda.
- Hear the client's expectations about what is and is not possible.
- Confirm understanding by observing and interpreting non-verbal signals (e.g. body language, facial expressions, tone of voice, etc.).
- Use positive body language and non-verbal signals to demonstrate openness and undivided attention.
- Demonstrate active listening by seeking clarification, rephrasing the client's statements and summarising to check understanding.
- Encourage the client to "say more" – create a positive climate for the client to express their feelings, perceptions, concerns, suggestions, etc.
- Acknowledge the client's ideas and suggestions and build on them in discussions.
- Offer non-judgmental responses that encourage the client to explore and validate their feelings, concerns and aspirations.
- Use silence as an appropriate intervention to elicit more information.
- Listen to the client's emotional undercurrents.
- Pay attention to what the client isn't saying about issues discussed.

Coaches and Mentors of South Africa (COMENSA)

COMENSA's (2006) original *Standards of Professional Competence* defined "listening" as "Being actively present with a client, paying attention to all information presented by the client, both verbal and visual; being able to respond to and reflect the said and the unsaid".

COMENSA's top two benchmark levels of competence in listening were defined as follows:

Level 4: Conversation is characterised by long, respectful silences, followed by deeply meaningful exchanges.

Level 3: The coach/mentor clarifies the content and intent of what the client advocates, by accurately reflecting and questioning the discussion through reflecting, observing, paraphrasing and the effective use of analogies and metaphors. The coach/mentor encourages the client with verbal and non-verbal cues, e.g. nodding. The coach/mentor actively and reflectively listens more than they speak.

COMENSA's (2007) draft *MCSC Framework* defined the following competences for listening:

Ability to coach – skills we will use during the coaching process:

Communication skills:

Minimum standards:

- Explain the value of whole-body listening.
- Explain potential blocks to effective listening.
- Explain the principles of emotional intelligence (EQ) and how it is used to improve communication.
- Explain the why, what, how, when and where of feedback.
- Demonstrate how different communication styles may affect the understanding and relationship.
- Explain particular styles of coaching.

Plus:

- Explain how to match, pace, mirror and lead to help the client.
- Elicit deeper levels of communication through listening and questioning.
- Use feedback to improve interaction with the client.
- Build a long-term relationship based on trust.

Questioning

International Coach Federation (ICF)

The ICF (2008a) defines competences in questioning as follows:

Communicating effectively:

Powerful questioning – Ability to ask questions that reveal the information needed for maximum benefit to the coaching relationship and the client:

a. Asks questions that reflect active listening and an understanding of the client's perspective.

b. Asks questions that evoke discovery, insight, commitment or action (e.g. those that challenge the client's assumptions).

c. Asks open-ended questions that create greater clarity, possibility or new learning.

d. Asks questions that move the client towards what they desire, not questions that ask for the client to justify or look backwards.

Worldwide Association of Business Coaches (WABC)

The WABC (2008b) defines business competences in questioning as follows:

Core coaching skill-base:

Promoting client understanding:

Questioning effectively:

- Ask questions that reflect an understanding of the client's point of view.
- Ask challenging questions that help the client to self-discover.
- Pose open-ended questions that help the client to clarify issues.
- Ask questions that help the client to develop new perspectives and new possibilities for action and learning.
- Ask questions that evoke commitment to action.
- Ask questions that steer the client towards their desired outcomes.

Coaches and Mentors of South Africa (COMENSA)

COMENSA's (2006) original *Standards of Professional Competence* defined "questioning" as "Asking a person to turn inward for answers, resources and solutions".

COMENSA's top two benchmark levels of competence in "questioning" were defined as follows:

Level 4: Questions are intense and focused, and reflect the coach/mentor's state of intense interest and involvement in the client's process. Questions help the client transcend the obvious and find paradigm-shifting answers or perspectives.

Level 3: There is an easy flow of relevant, incisive, stimulating, challenging, open-ended questions, relevant to the topic under discussion. The client is fully engaged and participating, and verbalises new ideas and broader perspectives.

COMENSA's (2007) draft *MCSC Framework* defined the following competences for questioning:

Ability to coach – skills we will use during the coaching process:

Communication skills:

Minimum standards*:*

- Explain the principles of emotional intelligence (EQ) and how it is used to improve communication.
- Explain the principles of questioning and at least one framework.
- Demonstrate how different communication styles may affect the understanding and relationship.
- Explain particular styles of coaching.

Plus*:*

- Explain how to match, pace, mirror and lead to help the client.
- Elicit deeper levels of communication through listening and questioning.
- Build a long-term relationship based on trust.

Self-awareness

I am able to control only that of which I am aware. That of which I am unaware controls me. Awareness empowers me (Whitmore, 2002:33).

International Coach Federation (ICF)

The ICF does not define specific competences for self-awareness.

Worldwide Association of Business Coaches (WABC)

WABC (2008b) defines the following business competences for self-awareness:

Self-management – knowing oneself and self-mastery:

Knowing yourself: self-insight and understanding:

(a) Having ready access to your thoughts and feelings and being aware of how they affect your behaviour:

- Be aware of your own emotions and able to recognise what you're feeling at any given time.

- Know the reasons why you feel the way you do.
- Recognise how your feelings affect you and your work performance.
- Have a high degree of awareness of what is important to you and the contribution you want to make – your values, purpose and vision.
- Know what you want and go after it.
- Know when your self-talk is helpful.
- Know when your self-talk is unhelpful.

Self-mastery: managing your thoughts, feelings and behaviours in ways that promote behaviour contributing to career and organisation success:

(a) Self-regulation: managing your reactions and emotions constructively:

- Monitor and contain distressing emotions and regulate them so they don't keep you from doing the things you need to do.
- Maintain self-control under adverse or stressful conditions (e.g. maintain demeanour, composure and temperament).
- Manage your own behaviour to prevent or reduce feelings of stress.
- Be able to think clearly and to stay focused when under pressure.
- Accept negative feedback without becoming defensive.
- Talk yourself out of a bad mood.
- Distinguish between a client's contribution and your own contribution to your emotional reactions.

Coaches and Mentors of South Africa (COMENSA)

COMENSA's (2007) draft *MCSC Framework* defined the following competences for self-awareness:

Self-awareness/Who we are – personal attributes for coaching:

Self-awareness:

Minimum standards:

- Explains clearly their role and position of equality in the coaching relationship.
- Explains clearly the implications of the coaching relationship.
- Demonstrates self-management and self-awareness.
- Receives and accept feedback appropriately.

- Uses a formal feedback process to assist their coaching practice.
- Behaves and acts in alignment with their values and beliefs.
- Gains self-awareness from at least one personality type indicator or formal face-to-face feedback process.
- Operates and follows the COMENSA ethical guidelines and standards of conduct.
- Demonstrates empathy in a broad range of settings and with a diverse range of people in both practice and reflection.
- Demonstrates belief in competence to coach within the limits of their own experience.

Plus:

- Demonstrates application of self-management and self-awareness consistently through practice and reflection.
- Demonstrates self-belief in their ability to coach in a wide range of applications.
- Develops self-awareness using at least three feedback processes, including personality indicators and self-reflection.
- Demonstrates an ongoing process of review, reflection and revision of personal values, beliefs and attitudes to improve their coaching practice.

Process of reflection

Coaching differs from consulting in that coaching does not solve problems or give advice. It also differs in that the aim of coaching is to establish a sustainable process of experiential learning within the client. In essence, your coaching is deemed successful if you have worked yourself out of a job with your client. We use experiential learning throughout this book as a theoretical underpinning of coaching – for the client and for the coach in developing their own individual skills. If the client is to learn how to learn, they need to cultivate self-awareness through reflection on their experience, values, intrinsic drivers, the impact of these on others, the environment, and on their own future goals. This process is often implicit in the coaching relationship through the process of questions and actions that develop critical reflection and practice. Griffiths and Campbell (2008:8) confirm that:

> The ICF competencies, by focusing on coach competency, fail to articulate reflection as
> an essential coaching process ... but what emerged as an interesting phenomenon in

this study, was the tendency for clients to take on the role of questioning themselves. Through engagement with the coach in powerful questioning, gradually clients began to demonstrate the ability and tendency to self-manage this process.

The ICF study (ICF, 2008a) further confirms that coaches often assume clients are aware of their values, but within the confines of the study this appeared to be incorrect. The clients interviewed indicated they were not aware of their values, and that acquiring a process of awareness and reflection led them to become more aware of their emotions, their values and of the need to clarify their goals. Whitmore (2002) supports this and states that the goal of the coach is to build awareness, responsibility and self-belief.

Case study: Journaling

I recently met with a client with whom I had worked a few years ago. She took out a journal during our session, and paged through it, filling me in on what was happening in her life. She shared her reflections from the journal on her values, drivers and goals – and how she planned to achieve each one. She shared her thoughts on whether her designed plan was working effectively or needed adjustment. This is an example of how she has embraced self-reflection, self-coaching and a continuing development of self-awareness as a lifelong process. She referred to her own process of self-coaching as one of reading, listening to tapes, and journaling on a daily basis. She continually checks her own personal and professional plan to make adjustments and to reflect on whether she is on schedule.

The ICF (2008a) lists creating awareness as a competency, even though developing self-reflection in the client is not explicitly stated. Creating awareness is defined as the "Ability to integrate and accurately evaluate multiple sources of information, and to make interpretations that help the client to gain awareness and thereby achieve agreed-upon results". Some of the indicators are:

- Goes beyond what is said in assessing client's concerns, not getting hooked by the client's description.
- Invokes inquiry for greater understanding, awareness and clarity.
- Identifies for the client their underlying concerns, typical and fixed ways of perceiving

themselves and the world, differences between the facts and the interpretation, disparities between thoughts, feelings and action.

- Helps clients to discover for themselves the new thoughts, beliefs, perceptions, emotions, moods, etc., that strengthen their ability to take action and achieve what is important to them.
- Communicates broader perspectives to clients and inspires commitment to shift their viewpoints and find new possibilities for action.
- Helps clients to see the different, interrelated factors that affect them and their behaviours (e.g. thoughts, emotions, body, background).
- Expresses insights to clients in ways that are useful and meaningful for the client.
- Identifies major strengths versus major areas for learning and growth, and what is most important to address during coaching.
- Asks the client to distinguish between trivial and significant issues, situational versus recurring behaviours, when detecting a separation between what is being stated and what is being done.

Continuous learning and development

Coaching is not a collection of techniques to apply or dogma to adhere to, rather it's a discipline that requires freshness, innovation and relentless correction according to the outcomes being produced (Flaherty, 1999:10).

The WABC has advanced membership standards based on business experience, coaching experience and client references. Shaw and Linnecar (2007) state that a coach training programme doesn't make a good coach; instead it shows that the coach has started the process of learning about themselves and what they are doing in any given situation.

The WABC competency indicators for development include requirements for self-management. They suggest "Acknowledging your strengths and development needs, and having a realistic perception of your strengths and development needs". The important point is to know your strengths and limitations, and to commit to your own continuous learning and self-development.

GLOBAL CONVENTION ON COACHING (GCC)

At the July 2008 GCC in Dublin, the Working Group on Core Competences emphasised that coaching competences are not unique and are shared with other disciplines. The Working Group defined competence as "... an underlying characteristic of an individual (e.g. motive, trait, attitude, value, belief, knowledge, behaviour, skill) that is causally related to effective or superior performance in a role or job" and defined a formal competence model as "... a systematic list of core competencies of an effective coach, with procedural descriptions for use in the coaching process with the relevant skills" (GCC, 2008e).

The *Dublin Declaration on Coaching* (GCC, 2008e) recommends a collaborative approach among all stakeholders to identify commonalities, stressing the importance of research. They propose that all stakeholders agree an International Best Practice Competence Framework to be developed through dialogue and research process. The key question that remains, however, is "How will an international best practice framework be applied in terms of coach selection, membership, education of coaches, and codes of ethics?" (GCC, 2008e).

The key lies in your continuing self-assessment, supervision, learning and development. As a result of critically reflecting on your own practice, we suggest that you identify the core focus for your business ensuring you have competence in areas where you need to strengthen your practice. Lew Stern in *Executive Coaching: Building and Managing Your Professional Practice* (Stern, 2008: 29) suggests four areas of core competence for executive coaches:

- psychological knowledge;
- business acumen;
- organisational knowledge; and
- coaching knowledge, tasks and skills.

We strongly recommend that you focus on the following core competences which have been researched to build your capacity as a business coach:

- building the coaching relationship;

- listening and questioning;
- self-awareness and the process of self-reflection;
- continuous learning and development;
- self-management: knowing oneself and self-mastery;
- core coaching skills-base; and
- business and leadership coaching abilities.

DEVELOPING YOUR KNOWLEDGE BASE

At the Global Convention on Coaching in July 2008 in Dublin, Ireland, the Working Group for the Knowledge Base defined knowledge in the broadest sense. They included in their definition, "... the knowledge that coach and client bring to the coaching session, the emergent knowledge that is borne out of the coaching process; and the dynamic of the coaching relationship". One of their key discoveries throughout their year-long dialogue was that the knowledge base for coaches is largely driven by the needs of the client and is continually evolving.

For us as coach practitioners, this implies that we can never stop learning. We must learn to reflect critically on our own core skills and competences. We explore this in more detail in Chapter 10 where we discuss coaching research. Primarily, our responsibility is to use our own practice as a way to continue our own learning process. The secret is to balance the experiential learning that emerges in your coaching practice, with a continual building of your core competence – with capacity as a practitioner through continuing professional development. This will help you to develop elasticity and flexibility in every situation that you encounter in your coach/client sessions.

The value of this chapter to our readers is to enhance your understanding of the quality and type of existing competence frameworks. Who is the competence framework intended for, and for which type of coaching? It is also important to understand that the competence frameworks presented in this chapter have not all yet been empirically researched, and that such research is a critical next step. Given that competence frameworks underpin the accreditation programmes that the marketplace is keen to purchase, both coaches and organisations alike are encouraged to better evaluate any research which claims to support these frameworks.

The question is: "Where is the research"? The future of coaching really depends in large measure on providing evidence-based research to the end-user. With this in mind, those providing competence frameworks need to ensure that they conduct empirical research to back up their claims, which will in turn enable their frameworks to be aligned to education and credentialing programmes worldwide.

The Institute of Coaching at Harvard/McLean Medical School offers sponsorship each year in Coaching Research grants worldwide. A board decision taken in September 2008 agreed to commission research into core coaching competences as a next step in identifying criteria for practitioner excellence and to take coaching education requirements to the next level. See www.instituteofcoaching.org.

COACH'S LIBRARY

Clutterbuck, D. (2007). *Coaching the team at work*. London: Nicholas Brealey.

Flaherty, J. (1999). *Coaching: Evoking excellence in others*. Boston, MA: Butterworth-Heinemann.

Goldsmith, M., Lyons, L. and Freas, A. (eds). (2000). *Coaching for leadership: How the world's greatest coaches help leaders learn*. San Francisco, CA: Jossey-Bass/Pfeiffer.

Hargrove, R. (2003). *Masterful coaching: Inspire an "impossible future" while producing extraordinary leaders and extraordinary results*. San Francisco, CA: Jossey-Bass/Pfeiffer.

Kets de Vries, M. (2006). *The leader on the couch*. London: Wiley.

Kline, N. (1999/2004). *Time to think: Listening with the human mind*. London: Ward Lock.

Parsloe, E. and Wray, M. (2000). *Coaching and mentoring, practical methods to improve learning*. London: Kogan Page.

Shaw, P. and Linnecar, R. (2007). *Business coaching: Achieving practical results through effective engagement*. London: Capstone.

Stout-Rostron, S. (2009). *Business coaching international: Transforming individuals and organisations*. London: Karnac.

Stern, L. (2008). *Executive coaching: building and managing your professional practice*. Hoboken, NJ: Wiley.

Ting, S. and Scisco, P. (2006). *The CCL handbook of coaching: A guide for the leader coach*. San Francisco, CA: Jossey-Bass.

West, L. and Milan, M. (2001). *The reflecting glass: Professional coaching for leadership development*. New York, NY: Palgrave.

Whitmore, J. (2002). *Coaching for performance: Growing people, performance and purpose*. Third edition. London: Nicholas Brealey.

Zeus, P. and Skiffington, S. (2000). *The complete guide to coaching at work*. McGraw-Hill Australia.

8

Existential and Experiential Learning Issues

In a nutshell, what leadership coaches offer their clients is independence. True independence means being free from the domination of one's unconscious needs and desires and being courageous enough to choose one's own destiny (Kets de Vries, 2006:272).

In this chapter, we explore existential and experiential learning issues that confront the coach and client at every stage in their coaching conversation, as well as the impact of psychological research in these areas. The relationship between coach and client is crucial to the successful conclusion of whatever the coaching process is seeking to accomplish. The coach's intent is not always outcomes-based; it can also focus on **learning**, **development**, **meaning** and **transformation**. The complexity of these issues is often influenced by the three-way intervention between the organisation, the client and the coach.

Existential philosophy regards human existence as unexplainable, and emphasises freedom of choice and taking responsibility for one's acts. Within the business coaching context, the coach helps the client to articulate existential concerns such as freedom, purpose, choice and anxiety, and to identify and replace limiting paradigms with empowering paradigms, thus leading to positive change.

These existential issues are relevant to the coach too. For example, if you look at purpose, the coach might be tempted to confuse their own individual purpose with that of the client, and in the process be seduced to use their position or power to influence the client. The coach often holds "guru" status, especially in the beginning of the relationship, and it is therefore important for the business coach to be aware of their own existential issues as well as those of the client.

As in existentialism, the "relationship" comes up as an important factor in learning from experience. According to Boud, Cohen and Walker (1996:11), experience is created in the "transaction" between the individual and the environment in which they operate – in other words, it is relational. More is often lost than gained by ignoring the uniqueness of each person's history and ways of experiencing the world.

In existential terms, the meaning of individual experience is not a given; in coaching it is subject to interpretation by the individual client. In the coaching conversation, experiential learning is viewed as an active process in which the individual executive works with their own experience again and again to appreciate the meanings associated with it. In other words, the coaching client learns to actively deconstruct and reconstruct their own experience, attaching their own meaning to events, yet understanding commonly accepted interpretations of their world.

Chapter outline

- Freedom – an existential moment
- What is existentialism?
    - Being versus doing
    - Existential dilemma: meaning and purpose
    - Four ultimate existential concerns
- Existential themes at work
    - Management culture
    - The coach/client relationship
- Coaching for meaning
    - Decision-making
    - Past versus present versus future
- Human systems
    - Relationships and systems
- Using experience for learning
    - Discovering barriers to learning
- In conclusion
- Coach's library
- Endnotes to Chapter 8

FREEDOM – AN EXISTENTIAL MOMENT

"Imagine yourself in a field or a meadow at the base of a mountain. It is quiet, peaceful and safe. You're going to climb this mountain, wearing comfortable boots. When you're ready, begin to climb. Observe the scenery and the woods as you move. Feel the shade of the trees. You come to a stream. Listen to its soothing sounds. It is fresh, and you drink from it. Perhaps you freshen your face and your hands in its cool waters. You go further and, in due course, you reach the tree line where there are no more trees. As you look back over the valley, the view is unobstructed. It is a view of your everyday life: your comings and your goings; your struggles and your victories; your relationships with others and with your own everyday self.

"Now, you resume your journey. In front of you is a large abyss, spanned by a bridge. The bridge is strong and safe. You begin to cross the bridge and eventually you reach the other side. It is good to be on the mountain once again with your feet on solid ground. You climb on, up steeper and steeper rocks, going higher and higher until you reach the top. Here the view is breathtaking and the air is thinner. You feel that you are on top of the world, so rest here for a few moments. Not far from the top, you can see a small shelter made out of wood or stone. It is beckoning to you. You move towards it, and once inside you find a haven, a place of peace. To your surprise, as you are resting here, a figure enters. You are not afraid. You realise this figure is a guide, a mentor, of great wisdom. This being looks at you and knows you. You feel loved, known, understood and recognised. You may have a question that you need to ask about any area of your life. So ask it and listen to the response. Is an answer forthcoming, a gesture, or even a look? Allow yourself to hear the response, even if you hear it with your own voice. Or, perhaps, you even just hear a semblance of what the response might be.

"If anything else needs to be said, by you or your mentor, now is the time. When you're ready, your mentor hands you a gift. What is it? You acknowledge and receive it with gratitude. You begin to take your farewell, whether it be with a hug, a handshake, a look or a gentle parting. You leave the building, taking another look at the breathtaking view as you turn to walk down the mountain. With your comfortable boots you soon find yourself by the bridge. How do you feel now? You cross the bridge. Once again, you look out over the valley and behold your life.

"You have returned with your gift. Is there any way you sense that this image of your life is changing for the better? You move on down the mountain, through forest and glade, crossing the stream, till once again you find yourself in the meadow at the bottom of the mountain. For a moment you reflect on the journey you have taken. Now gently, very gently, you become conscious of being where you are in the room, in this place, listening to the sounds, conscious of your breathing, conscious of your body, and conscious of your self and your entire life right now, today. And, you know that in future, you can always return whenever needed, to that place of peace and wisdom within you."[1]

This concern with change and the client's journey through life is a core component of the coaching process, and combined with the question of "who am I", can present various dilemmas for coach and client within an organisational system. We explore several of these dilemmas in this chapter.

WHAT IS EXISTENTIALISM?

Much confusion surrounds the terms "existentialist" and "existentialism". Existential concerns have been discussed from the beginning of philosophical debate about the human condition, encompassing thinkers such as Socrates and his dialogues. The literary, philosophical and artistic response to modern cultural crises has also massively influenced existentialism. Yet existentialism remains elusive to define, and consequently today there is no cohesive school of existential therapists or coaches.

Existentialism displays a concern with individuals in crisis. The term "existence" refers to coming into being or becoming. It derives from the Latin root *ex-sistere* which means to "stand out or emerge". Existential psychology has grown out of the awareness that serious gaps exist in our way of understanding human beings. It sought to analyse the structure of human existence to "understand the reality underlying all situations of human beings in crisis" (May, 1983:44).

Basically concerned with ontology, or the science of being, existentialism is based on the underlying fact that "you and I alone must face the fact that at some unknown moment in the future we shall die" (May, 1983:51). Existential vocabulary includes terms such as

being, choice, responsibility, freedom, death, isolation, mortality, absurdity, purpose in life, limitations and **willing.**

Rollo May (1983:49) describes existentialism as the "unique and specific portrayal of the psychological predicament of contemporary Western man". Jean-Paul Sartre is the philosophical and literary figure most associated with existentialism, although he represents an extreme and is more known for expressing many of his themes through plays and novels rather than psychological analyses (May, 1983:55).

In the United States, there was an initial resistance to the existential movement for various reasons. Firstly, it was assumed that all major discoveries had been made in the fields of psychology, psychotherapy and psychiatry. Secondly, existentialism was considered to be a philosophical encroachment into psychiatry. The third area of resistance to existentialism in the USA was the most crucial, according to May (1983). He describes it as the pragmatic tendency to be preoccupied with technique and an active concern in helping and changing people.

The existential movement in the fields of psychology and psychotherapy developed in a fashion that was more, rather than less, empirical, but it also crucially acknowledged that "human beings reveal themselves in art and literature and philosophy and by profiting from the insights of the particular cultural movements which express the anxiety and conflicts of contemporary man" (May, 1983:45).

Being versus doing

Ernesto Spinelli, former existential professor of psychology at Regent's College London, noted in a lecture in Cape Town in April 2004 that:

> At the moment, we inhabit a culture which places tremendous importance on expectations. A group is growing in numbers, who are seen as "experts-in-living" and who are working with clients. We need our clients to see us as experts, but if someone asks "What is your expertise?", our tendency is to translate expertise in terms of skills, competences, specialist knowledge, certain forms of personality tests. Our primary focus is "doing" – experts do.

Existentialism challenges the notion of expertise as "doing" and reconsiders expertise from the point of view of "being". The question then becomes, "How is it that I am with other human beings, with other living beings, with living and non-living objects?"

The basic idea is this, that the way I reveal myself with other beings or the world in general exposes not only that moment of being, but gives a sense of totality – that individual's general stance towards reality. How I am with you reveals how I am, not only to you, but to myself, to others and to the world in general.

Being emphasises the activity rather than the goal. **Being in becoming** emphasises **who** the person is rather than **what** the person can accomplish. But it still emphasises the concept of development. The **doing** orientation emphasises accomplishments that are measurable by standards outside of the acting individual (Yalom, 1980:121). If we are to transform organisations – culturally, socially, emotionally and cognitively – then the ultimate goal of coaching is seeking transformation of self.

Culture plays an important role in the shaping of individual values. Florence Kluckholm, who pursued research in cultural value orientations, suggested three anthropological value orientations for the individual human: **being, being in becoming,** and **doing** (Kluckholm and Stroedbeck, 1961:15). There is constant discussion in contemporary coaching circles about which comes first, being or doing; but little mention is made about "being in becoming". This may, in fact, be the existential category where coaches most often work with their clients (McWhinney *et al.*, 1993:28).[2]

Existential dilemma: meaning and purpose

If you want to build a ship, don't drum up the men to gather wood, divide the work and give orders. Instead, teach them to yearn for the vast and endless sea (Antoine de Saint-Exupéry, 1900–1944).

Often in the business coaching environment, the client will state that one of their objectives is to determine meaning in their personal and professional life. The client may be questioning why they do what they do. The start of this personal philosophical thinking tends to originate from questions such as, "What motivates you?" and "What is important to you?". One well-known example concerns two stone masons who were asked what they were doing. One answered, "I am cutting a stone"; the other said, "I am building a cathedral". To ask your client, "What is the meaning and purpose of your work?" can be the beginning of a quest of self-discovery. A surgeon in India wanted to make cataract operations very inexpensive for the poor. Rather than tell his team that this was the ultimate aim, he explained that their real vision was to "cure blindness".

Faith or spirituality speaks to our underlying values and drivers, often being a search for something greater than we are. "Who am I and why am I here?", is ultimately a search for meaning and purpose in life. Often, individuals turn to faith or a spiritual journey with these questions. From a coaching perspective, a client may ask questions about a possible change of career, or even start to think about unfulfilled challenges. Typically, these questions evolve to "Who are they?" and "How do they be who they are?". Although coaches love to work with existential questions, such questions present a dilemma. If the organisation pays the coach's fees, and the aim of coaching is performance-related, yet the client focuses on an inner search for meaning and purpose, this may present an ethical challenge for the coach. Some clients are lucky and the organisation contracts the coach to pave the individual's road to self-discovery. This, however, is not the norm! It is useful to build this possibility into the contracting process. One way to manage this process can be to contract with clients that those individuals who undergo the coaching process sign an agreement to stay for one year from the end of the coaching intervention.

"The belief that one's life is controlled by external forces is associated with a sense of powerlessness, ineffectualness and ... can lead to low self-esteem" (Yalom, 1980:163). This is particularly relevant for clients who work within a large family-dominated organisation with a legacy to fulfil, or a large bureaucratic corporation hampered by policies and procedures. It is here that Yalom defines anxiety: "Anxiety is a signal that one perceives some threat to one's continued existence". Coaches consistently work with anxiety, although most clients tend to label this "stress" originating from external sources.

Yalom (1980:188) states that death anxiety exists at the deepest levels of being, is heavily repressed and is rarely experienced in its full sense. He says anxiety is a guide to point the way to an authentic existence, and that life cannot be lived nor faced without anxiety. Anxiety is a guide as well as an enemy and can point the way to an authentic existence.

However, Yalom also says that the real agent of change is the therapeutic relationship.

A framework for coaching (in Yalom's view) may be a synthesis of the business belief system, the coach's model with its theoretical underpinnings, plus the development of the relationship. Spinelli, in his Cape Town supervisory session in April 2004, indicated that the "relationship" is the core factor in any therapeutic, coaching, supervisory or counselling session, and perhaps even for research. My work and research have examined this and underlined, time and time again, that no matter what level the coaching intervention, it seems that the fundamental work of the coaching intervention establishes the possibility for the relationship.[3]

According to May, in the Western world, we have managed to dominate nature, but in the process we have repressed the sense of being – the ontological being. Robert Hargrove (2003) says a coach is something that you "be". He asks whether the coach is "being" or "doing" when helping clients inside the coaching conversation. Hargrove promotes the idea of "Kokoro", i.e. perfecting one's inner nature. "One must not only master the technique but also perfect the way of being consistent with the discipline, having a calm and centred inner spirit; to be able to teach people; one must perfect his/her own nature" (Hargrove, 2003:44).

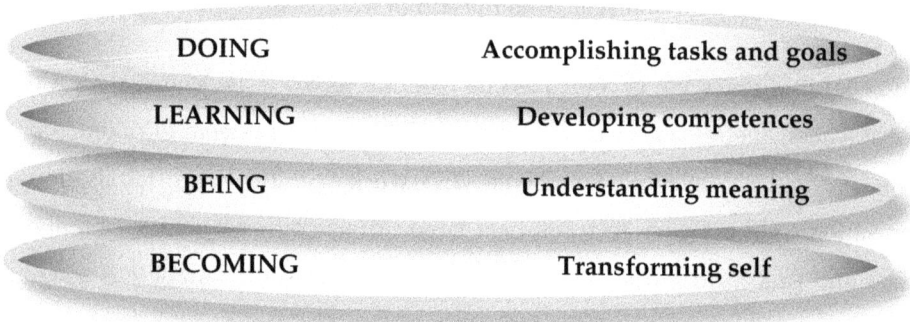

DOING	**Accomplishing tasks and goals**
LEARNING	**Developing competences**
BEING	**Understanding meaning**
BECOMING	**Transforming self**

Figure 1: Becoming – transforming self

Source: Adapted from Weiss (2004)

Hargrove (2003:48), who often brings in an existential point of view, says we have the power to choose who we are being. Choice is one of the existential concerns in the coaching process and is related to the process of setting goals and taking action. He says the coach can help the client declare new possibilities for themselves through the power of language, and that the power to choose who you need to be exists in your conversations, in your speaking and listening, and not in grappling with your history. This emphasises the learning and performance model versus a psychological model.

Within the coaching conversation, the coach is not necessarily looking for the psychological paradigm, but listening more to people's language. This resonates with my linguistic background, which predisposes the coach to analyse the context, content, structure and meaning of language when working with clients, either when shadowing them at work or in the coaching conversation.

The rabbit hole story

One of my clients wanted help to structure the way she approached her daily life and business. I helped the client to translate her actions and her way of thinking into meaningful experience. The client discovered that she thinks linguistically and kinaesthetically, but it did not help her to structure her day using words and feelings. She decided that she needed to interpret her world differently, i.e. visually, in order to have more meaningful experiences and make life work better for her.

When the coach and client constructed a learning contract at the end of a first session, the client had as her **purpose**: to learn to structure her thinking differently; as her **strategy**: to use the new way of thinking to manage her life and her business more effectively; and as **specific outcomes**: (1) to work daily with visual thinking and visual language, and (2) to journal daily from words into pictures into visual language.

Previously, the client had constructed a kinaesthetic view of the world and had ascribed meaning to it kinaesthetically and linguistically. She needed to bring in visual thinking to make more sense of her world and to be able to "see her day". The coach and client focused on her limiting assumption that she could not think visually. That changed on the day when client and coach "went down a rabbit hole" in the coaching conversation. The client discovered herself visually by describing her journey down the "rabbit hole"; she came out into the light of the natural world with a visual rather than a kinaesthetic reconstruction of her experience.

> In the light of these coaching conversations, the coach was helping the client to interpret her own reality and to see how she constructed meaning within that reality. The client achieved her goal at the end of the "rabbit hole" session – i.e. to identify her avoiding behaviours when trying to think visually (Stout-Rostron, 2006c:167).

According to Hargrove (2003), masterful coaches make an existential choice to make a difference in the life of an individual, a team or an organisation. He says that it is important to introduce powerful ideas into the client's thinking because that is what has the capability of shifting paradigms. Hargrove mentions the importance of questions. In the coaching process, the purpose of questions is to create insights, shift limiting assumptions, and help decisions to be made and goals to be set.

Interestingly, Hargrove (2003) insists that, if the relationship is to be powerful or profound, it is important for the coach to provide information that could possibly be difficult or threatening or embarrassing, but which is necessary for growth and learning. This is contrary to how we see the coach's role, i.e. as one of teasing out the thinking of the client. Rather than being the active agent, the coach's role is to make observations that are challenging, but which are neither judgemental, directive, nor interpretive (a therapist might choose to be analytical, directive or interpretive). I would suggest that, if Hargrove is recommending that the coach as "guru" provide answers, this could set up a relatively disempowering relationship that renders the client more passive in the thinking process. We prefer to focus on the empowerment of the client as an "active" agent and thinker which encourages personal responsibility.

Personal responsibility and awareness

One of our first areas of focus is awareness: helping the client to grow in awareness and to accept personal responsibility to create change for themselves. How the client takes up responsibility for change emerges from the coaching conversation.

"Locus of control" measures, at a superficial level, whether an individual accepts personal responsibility for their behaviour and life experiences, or whether the individual believes that what happens to them is unrelated to personal behaviour and is therefore beyond personal control. Individuals who accept responsibility are considered to have an "internal" locus of control, and those who reject it have an "external" locus of control (Yalom, 1980:262).

A question arises: how directive should the coach be, and what is required by coaching clients with an internal locus of control versus an external locus of control? Does your coaching process account for both? In the coaching process, the assumption of personal responsibility is a key step towards growth, achieving professional goals and creating desired individual change – personally and professionally.

Existentially, choice and change offer a way of taking responsibility and defining one's own self. Sartre also wrote, "authenticity versus self-deception is the absolute personal responsibility" (Peltier, 2001:157). "We cannot make life deliver what we want, but we can control what we think and desire; rigorous self-disciplined thought is the key" (Olson, 1962:11, cited in Peltier, 2001:158). Not specifically an intervention, but 10 guidelines are offered for the executive coach by Peltier:

- honour individuality;
- encourage choice;
- get going;
- anticipate anxiety and defensiveness;
- commit to something;
- value responsibility taking;
- manage conflict and confrontation;
- create and sustain authentic relationships;
- welcome and appreciate the absurd; and
- clients must figure things out in their own way.

Coaching guidelines could advocate: reflection, developing insight and awareness, setting goals, using language appropriately, making choices and taking action. Peltier (2001:168) says, "authentic individualism requires extensive self-examination and the willingness to live with the decisions one makes as a result". This may be in contrast with other belief systems or cultural values, such as the principle of *ubuntu* in African cultures, where it is not so much individualism that is important, but relationships within the community.

Ubuntu

The African notion of *ubuntu* can be defined as "morality, humaneness, compassion, care, understanding and empathy. It is about shared values and humanity" (Boon, 1996:31). In *ubuntu* terms, you are only who you are in relation to others. In other words, *ubuntu* is about interaction within the community. *Ubuntu* sends you as an individual on a journey where you will find out who you are when you meet the people in your life. It is about life, relationships and values, and in many ways, this is a very existentialist philosophy. Northern European individualism is a very different philosophy from *ubuntu*, which experiences existence in relation to others, and within a sense of community.

The term *ubuntu* is important in the South African context as it refers to an African view of life and worldview. *Ubuntu* powerfully suggests that man is essentially a social being and that "a person is a person through other persons" (Devenish, 2005). Justice Yvonne Mokgoro of the South African Constitutional Court says that *ubuntu* is the basis "for a morality of co-operation, compassion, community (spiritedness) and concern for the interests of the collective, for others and respect for the dignity of personhood; all the time emphasising the virtues of that dignity in social relationships and practices" (Devenish, 2005).

Ubuntu is more aligned with the second of the two famously assumed existential states of being: being-for-itself and being-for-others. *Ubuntu* requires the "right balance between individualism and collectivism and is made possible by taking seriously people's need for dignity, self-respect and regard for others. Its emphasis is not on differences, but on accommodating these" (Devenish, 2005).

Four ultimate existential concerns

Yalom (2001:xvi) defines existential psychotherapy as "a dynamic therapeutic approach that focuses on concerns rooted in existence". In its technical sense, "dynamic" is rooted in Freud's model of mental functioning, assuming that "forces in conflict within the individual generate the individual's thought, emotion, and behaviour". The importance of this definition is that "these conflicting forces exist at varying levels of awareness; indeed some are entirely unconscious". These inner conflicts are not just from the individual's struggle with suppressed instinctual strivings or from traumatic memories, but are also "from our confrontation with the 'givens' of existence" (Yalom, 2001:xvii). These, "givens" or "ultimate concerns" are the "deep structures of experience". The four most closely aligned to psychotherapy are death, freedom, isolation and meaninglessness.

Four ultimate concerns: death, freedom, isolation, meaninglessness

The first concern is **death**. The existential conflict is the "tension between the awareness of the inevitability of death and the wish to continue to be". The second concern, **freedom**, is usually considered to be a positive factor in life. Existentially, freedom refers to each individual being responsible for their own individual worldview, life design, choices and actions. The existential tension is the implication of nothingness when human beings wish for groundedness and structure. The third concern is **isolation**, which is a fundamental, unbridgeable isolation from others. We enter the world alone and exit alone. The existential conflict is the tension between our "awareness of our absolute isolation and our wish for contact, for protection, and our wish to be part of a larger whole". The fourth concern is **meaninglessness**. If we are ultimately alone in a meaningless or indifferent universe, what is the point of living? Without a preordained design for each individual human being, "each of us must construct our own meaning in life". The existential conflict is the result of another paradox; human beings who seek meaning are thrown into a universe with no meaning (Yalom, 1980:8–10).

Paradigms and the four concerns

What is relevant to us as coaches is the construct of paradigms or worldviews. Yalom (1980:26) writes that paradigms "are self-created, wafer-thin barriers against the pain of uncertainty". He talks about the importance of meaning, how important it is for the individual human being to construct meaning in their life. He says that the existential paradigm assumes that anxiety emanates from the individual's confrontation with those four ultimate concerns in existence: death, freedom, isolation and meaninglessness.

Existential dilemma: individual versus collective purpose

An interesting dilemma is the client whose family's political purpose was not aligned with the career choice that she made. She began working for an NGO, which made her family happy, as she was brought up in a family with strong socialist values. She completed her studies, moving into a helping profession where she became very dissatisfied. With great difficulty, she made the decision to fulfil her entrepreneurial talent by starting her own business, even though she knew it was against the principles of her family. She has subsequently become financially successful, showing that she has the ability and capacity to be a success in the commercial world. However, her family continues to disapprove of her newfound capability, and vociferously lets her know of their disappointment. Her dilemma is: should she continue in business or move back into the NGO to please her family? Will she be desperately unhappy if she cannot align her own vision for her life with that of her family? Does she need their approval to have meaning in her life, and how isolated will she be without it?

The question for executive coaches is how do these four ultimate concerns affect coaching? How do these ultimate concerns affect the client in the workplace? Is it more about purpose because people want to be doing a job that is meaningful? We know that human beings want meaningful work, and often the workplace is a major contributor to human purpose and significance. And where does their job and career fit into the rest of their life, and how does it impact on their sense of meaning, purpose or isolation?

May (1983) talks about the "organisation man", i.e. the corporate executives who live, eat and breathe their work, deriving their identity from their position, power and status inside the organisation and society at large. May calls this the "outer-directed man" who conforms and disperses themselves to such a degree, and participates and identifies so much with others that their own being is emptied.

Closely related to the "workaholic" executive are individuals who have always strived "for competent effective power and control ... getting ahead, achieving, accumulating material wealth, leaving works behind as imperishable monuments". These driving pressures can become a way of life that effectively conceal the questions about our ultimate concerns (Yalom, 1980:120).

Death, freedom, isolation, and meaninglessness

Yalom (1980) says that death is only one component of the human being's existential situation, and that anxiety can be understood by understanding death. According to Yalom, freedom helps us to understand the assumption of responsibility, commitment to change, decision and action; isolation illuminates the role of relationship; and meaninglessness turns our attention to the principle of engagement with ourselves and others.

The assumption of personal responsibility has a parallel with coaching. It plays a major part in any business coaching conversation: what is, and what will be, the commitment and responsibility that the executive will undertake as a step towards achieving goals. The coach is ultimately trying to help the client take responsibility for their actions, to become aware of their actions, and to be conscious of how their behaviour impacts on others. In order to look at these existential concerns as they relate to coaching, it is useful to look briefly at the research in existential psychotherapy, as well as some findings from sports coaching.

Lessons from sports coaches

What has emerged from the success of athletic coaches is the importance of dreaming and setting goals: aligning everything and going for it. Athletic coaches introduced the concept of "balance" in one's life: where does work fit into your life and dreams; how driven do you want to be? On the other hand, "positive mental health and self-esteem are greatly enhanced when a person is excellent at something" (Peltier, 2001:170).

Failure can set up a sense of loss and isolation. One fundamental underpinning of success is to be able to make mistakes and to learn from failure: the coach needs to be able to empathise with the client and to discern how the client views failure, and help the client to see where failure can be a turning point. The client then makes the decision to change, looks at how to view things differently and learns something completely new, which is put into practice. A crucial component to learn from failure is awareness.

Existential isolation

Yalom (1980:357) gives a definition of existential isolation: "Existential isolation refers to an unbridgeable gulf between one's self and any other being; the separation between the individual and the world, separation from the world". In freedom, there is existential isolation, and the paradox of relationship is the problem of isolation. "One must learn to relate to another without giving way to the desire to slip out of isolation by becoming part of the other, but one must also learn to relate to another without reducing the other to a tool" (Yalom, 1980:359).

Yalom mentions the encounter group as a means of self-expression, but suggests they are simply monologues disguised as dialogues. If the coach is not careful, we can simply be listening to a monologue (with no room for awareness, introspection and reflection) on the part of the client. This also flags the necessity for awareness in group coaching. Unless the lead coach is trained in a methodology to include all voices, and to have all voices heard, the group process will simply be that of various individuals' solo thinking.

Very often in the first hour of a coaching session, I find that I am listening to a monologue – so, eventually and when appropriate, I step into the labyrinth of the monologue with interventions such as clarifying questions. I would suggest that in coaching, the coach turns toward the client with the same "listening intensity" as is developed in psychotherapy.

A very interesting question is always: how many other people are there in a room, even if it seems it is just coach and client? Yalom suggests that all other people must be swept away before an authentic relationship between client and therapist can be developed. In coaching, it is essential to explore the system. In other words, the client's relationships with others in the workplace, as well as personal relationships, are to be discovered. Although Yalom (1980:401) says that the "encounter itself is healing" and that "a positive relationship between patient and therapist is positively related to therapy outcome", in business coaching it is somewhat different. Although the relationship between coach and client is one key relationship, there is also the relationship with the organisation.

As a consequence of coaching, the organisation will be looking for visible results. These results could be made visible in a number of ways, depending on how the outcomes are defined. In the business world, it is necessary for the client to make change visible, often in behaviour or some kind of tangible results. Often the client is developing in self-awareness, and may be grappling with various existential issues. However, unless the learning is made visible in the workplace, the organisation will wonder what it is to which they are contributing. If results are not forthcoming, there could be a physical (if not existential) isolation opening up for that executive!

The importance of relationship

The key concept of Yalom's research and writing is that the relationship heals. And he says that the "throw-ins" in psychotherapy, the off-the-record contributions, help to build that relationship. He asks, "How does a therapeutic relationship heal?" He answers it firmly and finally by saying "There is much evidence for the argument that it is the relationship that heals and that the real agent of change is the relationship" (Yalom, 1980:404).

The basis of my own research has been to establish if it is the relationship that determines the success of the coaching intervention. Although relationship is in fact one of the key parameters for success, there are other components that need to be in place for the intervention to be successful. For example (Stout-Rostron, 2008):

- learning from experience;
- understanding the role of others;
- developing EQ;
- being flexible;
- making your ethical code explicit;
- being coached yourself;
- measuring coaching results;
- creating a development plan with goals; and
- assessing qualitatively and quantitatively what has shifted during the coaching intervention – i.e. which new behaviours are visible and how has performance improved.

Sartre says that engagement is the ultimate meaning, and that one must invent one's own meaning. The difficulty is that one must invent one's own meaning and then permit oneself to fulfil that meaning. Maslow says we live in order to fulfil our potential. The Austrian psychiatrist and creator of logotherapy, Viktor Frankl, said there are three categories that help to determine life meaning:

- what one accomplishes or gives to the world in terms of one's creation;
- what one takes from the world in terms of encounters and experiences; and
- one's own stand towards suffering, and towards a state that one cannot change (Frankl, 1946).

Frankl (1946) emphasises the uniqueness of each person's individual meaning, and that engagement emerges as an answer to meaninglessness. A core concept from Yalom (1980) and Spinelli (1989) is that it is the relationship that helps the client to move on. My work shows that the development of the relationship emerges from engagement and intervention.

EXISTENTIAL THEMES AT WORK

Of course, coaching is very different from psychotherapy. Hargrove picks up an existential theme, quoting Peter Senge: "I believe we suffer every day; in every single business meeting we go to". He mentions the despair that many managers experience: "they feel they are unable to have authentic communication where they discuss the un-discussable, talk about problems openly, and overcome the game playing" (Hargrove, 2003:174).

Coach practitioners often explore the client's values, ethics, meaning of life, life's purpose, significant and challenging work, choice, will, action, responsibility, decision, relationships, building alliances, self-creation and desire for self-actualisation.

Existential dilemma: value systems clash

Another potential dilemma develops when the client feels that their underlying value system clashes with that of their organisation. This does not necessarily mean the client is involved in illegal activities.

One of Marti's friends, for example, started a new job and questioned several of the organisation's business processes, indicating that they were unethical. The answer offered to him was that the company was not involved in illegal activities; their business reaped enormous capital return, and they did not plan to change their business model.

People often have a strong sense of ethical, moral or faith-based values. When they voice their concerns inside a coaching assignment, they are reflecting on whether their value system is in conflict with the values of the organisation. The issues frustrating them may not be clear-cut, and more often than not are complex. The issues raised could be related to performance ratings, recruitment procedures, or even whether the organisation's actions are in alignment with its public claims – i.e. "are they walking their talk?"

For example, an organisation's value statement may recommend specific rules and regulations, yet the leadership team might not follow or act in accordance, even behaving unethically or inappropriately. Other examples are organisations who do not adhere to environmental laws, or who pay lip service to corporate social investment for marketing purposes. Although there have been changes in corporate governance worldwide, there is still room for "massaging the numbers" or flexible management.

Management culture

Whitmore (2002:28) defines management coaching as "the management style of a transformed culture". The key existential themes to emerge from his model are responsibility demands choice, and choice implies freedom. He says because stress has reached epidemic levels worldwide, and because people are allowed little personal control in the workplace, this has impacted heavily on self-esteem. "Self-esteem is the life force of the personality, and if that is suppressed or diminished so is the person"

(Whitmore, 2002:30). Whitmore's argument is that coaching for performance is a means to obtain optimum performance, but that it demands fundamental changes in attitude, in managerial behaviour and in organisational structure.

Existential therapy takes a different view of the specific forces, motives and fears that interact within the individual. The existential view emphasises a different type of basic conflict: the existential conflict stems from the individual's confrontation with the "givens" of existence – those ultimate concerns that are inescapably part of each individual existence in the world. The four existential "concerns" do arise in the coaching context, and, although not explored as deeply as in a therapeutic context, it is important for the coach to be sensitive to them.

The coach / client relationship

"Relationship" is a key variable determining the coach's expertise. Spinelli's (1989) analysis is that we need to move away from "doing" to an authenticity which will take the coach straight to the "heart" of the relationship between the coach and the client. This is of particular significance to coaches because no matter what model or methodology a practitioner uses, it is, according to Spinelli, "the relationship" that affects the outcome of the coaching or therapy. It is the "quality" of the relationship that is of importance.

The coaching discipline worldwide has only recently begun to research the importance of the relationship in the coaching process, although psychotherapists have been analysing the skills needed in the therapeutic environment for over 100 years. The fields of existentialism and psychotherapy are very useful to us in terms of their research into the "encounter" and the "relationship" between practitioner and client.

Whitmore's (2002:20) focus is on the question of relationship: "the relationship between the coach and coachee must be one of partnership in the endeavour of trust, of safety and of minimal pressure". To develop the relationship effectively, Peltier (2001:68) looks at the principles and concepts of the Rogerian, person-centred, relationship-oriented and experiential approach. This grew out of the existential philosophical tradition, and has an underlying humanist vision. Peltier describes it as particularly American, i.e. pragmatic, optimistic, and believing in the unlimited potential of the individual. Similar to the approach suggested by Yalom and Spinelli, Rogerian theory requires that the therapist listen with acceptance and without judgment if clients are going to be able to change.

The core skills of the client-centred approach are active listening, respecting clients and adopting their internal frame of reference. The structure of the coaching intervention needs to be framed by the ability to listen and to actively intervene only when needed. However, the coach/client relationship is based on equality. This is different to the therapist/patient relationship, which is often not considered to be an equal relationship. In a coaching relationship, one is not superior to the other; both are travellers on the client's journey – each bringing their own individual and professional expertise. A "safe thinking environment" is built through the development of the relationship, and the relationship is what can help with the onset of change.

A vital aspect of the coaching intervention is the value of positive support of coach to client. Not only does it build trust in the relationship; it may be one of the few places where the client is unconditionally supported in their personal and professional life. The three essential characteristics identified by Carl Rogers for effective therapy are unconditional positive regard, genuineness and accurate empathy (Rogers, 1961:281–283).

This is aligned with the "appreciation" component of Nancy Kline's Thinking Partnership® in her six-stage coaching process. Giving support means a willingness on the part of the coach to give, but it also models the giving of support. I see this as a very important aspect of coaching. It is also important that both coach and client change as the relationship grows. "I urge you to let your patients matter to you", wrote Yalom (2001:26–27), "to let them enter your mind, influence you, change you – and not to conceal this from them".

The throw-ins

Yalom mentions the "throw-ins" that make all the difference in successful therapy. These "throw-ins" are just as relevant in business coaching. Yalom (1980:3) believes that, when no one is looking, "the therapist throws in the 'real thing' like a chef". These throw-ins, or off-the-record extras, are not written about, studied or even explicitly taught. Therapists and coaches may not even be aware of them. Most therapists, according to Yalom, cannot explain why many patients get better. This is why, in the emerging discipline of business coaching, it is critical that practitioners begin to develop a body of knowledge through research – to begin to identify what works, and what does not work, with the organisational coaching intervention.

The critical "throw-ins" or ingredients exist outside of formal theory. They are not written about, and are qualities such as "compassion, presence, caring, extending oneself, touching the patient at a profound level, or – that most elusive one of all – wisdom" (Yalom, 1980:4).

The existential approach helps us, as coach practitioners, to ask questions about relationships, e.g. how does your client relate to themselves and to others? As we know, participation involves risk, and interacting with others to develop relationships, the core of any business, involves personal risk and vulnerability. The question of relationships, building alliances with others, is a common thread in business. The old adage, "people do business with their friends" is relevant here. This influences the individual's journey or search for personal values and purpose.

Existential life-changing dilemma

What about taking on an assignment when the client has no understanding of how the coaching may change their life? Marti once turned down a potential client, who, in his initial conversation with her, revealed that he had never experienced an equal partnership in any of his relationships. He tended to fall into the role of parent or child. In marriage, he played the role of parent. He had married a much younger woman and mentored her through her academic studies. Once she was qualified, he helped her to start her professional career – then she left him. At the time of the conversation, he was in a similar relationship.

A friend had recommended that he find a coach, but he did not have a particular aim for the assignment; he said he was happy with life as it was. Marti surprised him by saying that she would rather not enter into a coaching engagement. She explained that, although he was very comfortable with his life the way it was, it did not fit the norm of a rounded or balanced set of relationships. Working on a "relationship" because society indicated he should, would require a lot of work, which could cause major personal upheaval, and it was possible that therapy was more relevant. He agreed and they parted.

> Marti addressed her own concerns with the client, and would have referred him to another coach had he insisted. Her usual approach to any potential client who asks existential-type questions, is that the client needs to be prepared to question everything in their life and be committed to the process. A recent client, on completion of a long coaching intervention, said that although she had warned him, he hadn't really internalised what was going to happen. He also said he wouldn't have engaged for so long if it hadn't been so fundamentally life-changing for him. He often says, "You can't see past choices you don't understand".

My work has examined this and underlined, time and time again, that no matter at what level the coaching intervention, it seems that the fundamental work of the coaching intervention is to establish the possibility for the relationship. It is from this position that change is possible.

The encounter

The integration of questions with the components that help to build the relationship seems fundamental to the success of the coaching intervention. The coach helps to create the container or space for the client to feel safe, even when surrounded by twenty fellow students. When compassion, presence, caring, extending yourself, touching the client at a profound level (Yalom, 1980:4) begins to open the client up to the core issues of existence such as freedom, choice, purpose and values, only then will the coaching process begin to deepen.

So, the professional encounter can cause both joy and anxiety, but it is essentially a creative experience. According to Jung, change must occur in both client and practitioner otherwise the therapy will not be effective (May, 1983:22). May suggests that the phenomena of the encounter must be studied as "it is not possible for one person to have a feeling without the other having it to some degree also" (May, 1983:23). In some ways, there is a case here for all coaches to have a theoretical understanding of cognitive behavioural psychology as well as systems theory (including family systems theory) in order to understand some of the mechanics of "relationship" that happen within the helping professions. It is for this very reason that in South Africa the establishment of COMENSA and the development of accredited educational programmes for practitioner coaches and mentors are so crucial.[4]

Questions to develop the relationship

A recent experience has led me to re-evaluate the balance between the "use of questions" by the coach and the "relationship" between coach and client and how that develops. One of my students and I demonstrated a very simple coaching process in front of a larger group of 20 students. I, as the coach asked the student three simple questions: what's working; what's not working; and what if anything can you do differently? The purpose of the demonstration was for the other students to observe and give feedback on what worked and what didn't work between coach and client, and to identify how important the questions were.

As it turned out, how the questions were asked, and how attentive and focused the coach was on the client, and the coach's ability to "sit" with the client in her thinking space proved to be the most powerful part of the process. As coach, I interrupted the process several times to turn back to the group to discuss where we were in the process. What I have learned from working with Nancy Kline, is that as long as the coachee knows explicitly what is going to happen (i.e. that you will stop and turn to the audience periodically), the coachee goes right on thinking until you turn back to the conversation between the two of you.

In this three-question process, the coachee's core values started to be identified, with depth of understanding of self. The question process allowed a key value, "health", to pop up. As it turned out, this was the crucial value. What allowed the student (as coachee) to courageously explore this value (being held internally but never made explicit in actions, commitment or taking responsibility) was the non-judgemental focus of the coach on them and staying with them in the most difficult moments.

COACHING FOR MEANING

Man's search for meaning is the primary motivation in his life (Victor Frankl, 1946)

Reconstruction of meaning is one of the most important levels in which practitioners work with their coaching clients. In coaching today, clients raise the issue and often focus on the meaning and purpose in their professional and personal lives. Whitmore (2002:119) mentions that one of the goals of humanistic psychology is the fulfilment "of human potential through self-awareness".

Elisabeth Denton defined spiritual intelligence as "the basic desire to find ultimate meaning and purpose in one's life and to live an integrated life" (Whitmore, 2002:120). Zohar and Marshall (2001) in *Spiritual Intelligence* say that in business today people are facing a real crisis of meaning. This theme is being carried forward in most of the contemporary coaching literature. Many coaches work and integrate meaning in all four quadrants (Wilber, 1997) and work at the levels of IQ, EQ and SQ (rational, emotional and spiritual intelligence) with their clients inside the coaching relationship.

Whitmore (2002) says coaching can help people to clear away their defensive shields and self-imposed blockages, often coaching their clients through various crises of meaning in their lives. He makes a salient point that maybe it is better for some businesses to steer away from the complexities of meaning and purpose. For the coach, this has an impact in how they work with the client.

Famous parent dilemma

One particular executive is the daughter of famous parents, and feels that she never quite measures up to their expectations. Marti experienced this to a certain degree with her scientist father and fashion designer mother. Being interested in both fields, she studied science at the university where her father was well known. Whenever she gained high marks it was said, "Well, no wonder, look who her father is, he probably helped her", and when she did not do well the comment was, "Do you know who her father is? He must be so disappointed." Similarly, when Marti entered the fashion industry, she was always her "mother's daughter", and the whispers suggested that the reason she was hired, or asked to design clothes for fashion shows, or gained media publicity was because of her mother. And, her parents were not necessarily famous, simply well-known. What must it be like to be the son of Govan Mbeki, or a child of Nelson Mandela?

This is a real dilemma for children of famous parents. They often struggle to find themselves in a world where they are in the first place someone's child, and in the second themselves. Marti attended a lecture by Richard Olivier, son of Lawrence Olivier and Joan Plowright. He tells how he thought he would go into the family business – acting – and then realised that with a father who is regarded as one of the best actors in the world, it would be too difficult to be the best actor even within his own nuclear family.

Decision-making

Decisions are a skill and an art for the business executive. Decisions are a lonely act; they not only force the individual to face the limitation of possibilities, but force "one to accept personal responsibility and existential isolation" (Yalom, 1980:319). Yalom describes a decision as a boundary situation, not dissimilar to an awareness of death as a boundary situation: "To be fully aware of one's existential situation means that one becomes aware of self-creation" and "decision, insofar as it forces one to accept personal responsibility and existential isolation, threatens one's belief in the existence of an ultimate rescuer; decision is a lonely act, and it is our own act" (Yalom, 1980:319). Decision forces one to accept personal responsibility and existential isolation creates anxiety.

For an executive in a senior position, the importance of the decisions taken, based on the data collected, can often either represent a risk to the business that may catapult the executive to success, or be a comfortable decision that keeps the business on a safe track without embracing the executive's or the teams's creativity and innovative thinking. Ultimately, all decisions impact on the business; this is the existential dilemma for the executive.

The exact relationship between decision to change and insight is hard to define. "Insight" is defined by Webster (Simon and Schuster, 1983) as "an instance of apprehending the true nature of a thing, especially through intuitive understanding, or penetrating discernment". In its broadest sense, Yalom (1980:339) says that insight refers to self-discovery, an inward sighting: "Once having made a decision ... one has constituted one's world differently and is able to seize truths that one had previously hidden from oneself". Insight is a tool or a catalyst for change used by both therapists and coaches.

Past versus present versus future

Yalom argues that "psychotherapy is successful to the extent that it allows the patient to alter their future. Yet it is not the future but the past tense that dominates psychotherapy literature" (Yalom, 1980). According to Yalom, psychotherapists often believe that to provide insight the therapist must relate the present event to some past situation. The therapist may explain a patient's behaviour by examining conscious and unconscious motivations which currently affect that individual. Yalom incisively asks, "Where does the ability to change come from if we are determined by the past?"

Most therapists take the position that the client's circumstances were beyond their control when a child, but paradoxically the therapy sessions offer release from the past, yet appeal to the client to take responsibility for the future. Yalom suggests existential therapists tend to focus less on the past and more on the future than other therapists, and that, although it is important to learn to forgive oneself, many individuals take on too much responsibility and guilt for the actions and feelings of others. Finally, Yalom (1980:350) reiterates, "the real agent of change" is "the therapeutic relationship ... and the past is explored in order to facilitate and deepen the present relationship".

Coaching, different to therapy, more often explores the present in order to go into the future. This is one of the reasons that coaches focus on creating a professional development plan which defines the client's overarching purpose for the coaching, the strategy required to achieve it, developmental objectives which relate to competence and capacity building, and finally actions agreed during the coaching conversation. The past can be touched on for insight but is not probed in the same depth as in a therapeutic relationship. However, it is critical that the coach is trained to recognise when the client should be referred for therapy. Bruce Peltier (2001:xix) defines counselling as "personal" and "aimed at personal problems"; he indicates that coaching carries a more positive implication in the corporate world.

Peltier (2001:ix–xx) says that contemporary psychotherapy literature is relevant and invaluable for executive coaches because it is systems-oriented, and draws from the models of humanistic, existential, behavioural and psychodynamic psychology to help executives develop themselves and become more effective.

HUMAN SYSTEMS

In recent years, "systems thinking" has become an increasingly useful and popular approach to understand how organisations, businesses and groups of people behave, and how change comes about within those structures. "Systems thinking" teaches us about the interconnectedness of people, professions, disciplines and other "structures" within a team, organisation, business or family.

Family system therapies developed to explain individual behaviour "arising from the behaviour of the family system or of the immediate family plus other relevant people and institutions" (McWhinney *et al.*, 1993:45). Systems theory, although originally developed to work with the nuclear family, was seen to be very relevant to organisations, teams, other work groups and communities, i.e. work, social, cultural and religious.

In coaching, we are particularly concerned with "human and organisational systems" (rather than mathematical or economic structures) and the way these function and change. "Human systems" take into account the various components of human nature, i.e. thinking, feelings, and attitudes, thinking patterns and the behaviours that impact on performance within the working system.

All the components of a system have an organised, consistent relationship to one another. These components interact in a predictable, organised fashion with one another and are interdependent on one another. A complex model contains smaller subsystems that make up the larger "super-system". Within each of these subsystems, different levels of power are exercised, different skills learned, and different responsibilities are assigned. It is also possible to belong to more than one subsystem at a time, which may imply a different set of relationships, responsibilities or levels of power. An example in the business world is the tiered hierarchy of executives, managers, supervisors and employees.

When dealing with human systems one is always and ever concerned with the relationships between the people in the system. In a coaching conversation, it is the immediate relationship between coach and client; in the larger system it is the others to whom the client relates – the tiered workplace or the family or social system. Relationships include conscious and overt relationships as well as the unconscious and covert relationships between members of the system.

Within my client coaching conversations, we talk a lot about building alliances with others (colleagues, customers, suppliers) in order for them to build personal and professional credibility in the workplace, and the necessity of understanding which alliances, coalitions and triangles already exist that could be threatening to the individual executive.

People need symbols and coherent systems of belief to manage meaning and purpose in their lives. Systems help us to understand the interrelationships that articulate a cultural worldview, and as McWhinney *et al.* suggest, it is time to choose "the elements of a new world-view", or, as Thomas Kuhn expresses it, to participate in a "paradigm shift" (McWhinney *et al.*, 1993:2).

The coaching conversation is an important factor in helping business clients to develop self-awareness and an understanding of their own perceptions (or lenses) through which they view the world. First, by understanding all of the systems in which they play a part; i.e. family, team, organisation, community and society. Second, the experiential nature of the coaching conversation helps them to "shift", not just their worldview, but their behaviour. This often relates to a shift in the limiting assumptions they hold about themselves, or the systems within which they operate, and the groups with which they identify or to which they are resistant.

Relationships and systems

May (1983:17) defines "anxiety" as the "patient's fear of his own powers, and the conflicts that arise from that fear". May looks at "transference", another psychological mechanism which refers to the relationship between two people (for our purposes between client and coach).

As May describes it, the patient brings into the consulting room previous or present relationships with others (mother, father, partner, children, work colleagues, friends) and perceives the practitioner as similar to those beings; thus building their world with the practitioner in the same way. From a systems point of view, the practitioner simply becomes another part of the system within which the client exists.

This is an important concept for the business coach who often works with clients in a corporate environment. The coach needs to stay aware at all times of the system within which the client works, so that the coach does not simply become part of that system. Freud emphasises how deeply we are bound to each other: "We live in others and they in us" (May, 1983:18). The concept of transference can undermine the entire experience and "rob the client of the sense of responsibility" (May, 1983:18–19).

Systems dilemma

I encountered this recently at a group coaching supervision session in which I am not the lead supervisor. The coaches have recently started to discuss their own blind spots – and where they, within the group supervision process, are parallel tracking the system of the clients within the organisational system. The coaches realised that they were beginning to interact with each other in a way not dissimilar to the way their organisational clients were behaving, and that they needed to look at their own behaviour and thinking processes to ensure they were not simply re-enacting an already existing dysfunctional system.

USING EXPERIENCE FOR LEARNING

"Construction of experience is never-ending" because experience of life is never-ending (Boud, Cohen and Walker, 1996:12)

The basic approach in my research project and in this book is that the coaching intervention helps to build the rapport and the relationship between client and coach, which leads naturally to the success of the coaching conversation. Throughout this book, I have assumed the base of the coaching conversation to be the concrete experience of the client. The conclusion by Boud, Cohen and Walker (1996) in *Using Experience for Learning* is that experience is the foundation and the source of learning, and that learning is essentially linked to personal experience.

In studying existential philosophy, it is clear that there are certain universal themes. Experience is not simply an event that happens, it is an event with meaning, or it could be said that experience is a meaningful **encounter**. However, because experience is so "multifaceted, multi-layered and so inextricably connected with our experiences ... we must take account of, and build on, the unique perceptions and experiences of those involved, for without this we are dealing with only the most superficial aspects of learning" (Boud, Cohen and Walker, 1996:7).

In *Using Experience for Learning* (Boud, Cohen and Walker, 1996), a wide variety of writers share their research in using experience for learning, and they ask, "How do we learn from experience; how does experience impact on individual and group learning; what is the role of personal experience in learning; and do emotions have a vital role to play in intellectual learning?"

When I began my Doctoral research I thought I would search for the perfect template of coaching interventions, and very soon began to realise this was not realistic, and that, due to the unique experiences of life on the part of all clients, there would be no such thing as the perfect template. In other words, question frameworks need to be tailored to the client. Below are the five propositions that Boud, Cohen and Walker (1996) make about learning from experience.

Proposition 1: Experience is the foundation of and stimulus for learning

It is meaningless to talk about learning in isolation from experience. Learning can only occur if the experience of the individual is engaged, at least at some level, and every experience is potentially an opportunity for learning (Boud, Cohen and Walker, 1996:8). In other words, learning always relates, in one way or another, to what has gone before. This means that the effect of all experience influences all learning, which further implies a seeking of new meanings from old experience. The writers say that we do not simply see a new situation afresh, but we see it in terms of how we relate to it and how it resonates with what past experience has made us.

Proposition 2: Individuals actively construct their experience

Individuals attach their own meaning to events, and reach commonly accepted interpretations of the world. In experiential learning, experience is always subject to interpretation. This is because (in existential terms as well), the meaning of experience is not a given.

It is interesting that "relationship" comes up as an important factor in learning from experience. According to Boud, Cohen and Walker (1996), experience is created in the "transaction" between the individual and the environment in which they operate; in other words, it is relational. How learners construct their experience is what Boud, Cohen and Walker (1996:11) term the individual's "personal foundation of experience".

Proposition 3: Learning is a holistic process

The authors make a common division between **cognitive**, **affective** and **conative** learning. Cognitive learning is concerned with thinking; affective learning is concerned with values and feelings; and conative or psychomotor learning is concerned with action and doing. Learning is cognitive, affective and psychomotor; therefore learning involves feeling and emotions (affective), the intellectual and cerebral (cognitive) and action (conative).[5]

Proposition 4: Learning is socially and culturally constructed

Individuals do not exist independently of their environment, and learning does not occur in isolation from our social and cultural norms and values. While individuals construct their own experience, they do so in the context of a particular social setting and range of cultural values. Other considerations are language, social class, gender, ethnic background and our own learning from an early age. The most powerful influence from the social and cultural context on our learning occurs through language.

Proposition 5: Learning is influenced by the socio-emotional context in which it occurs

Denial of emotions leads to a denial of learning. There are two key sources of influence in learning: past experience and the role of others in the present that support our learning. Furthermore, different kinds of learning occur depending on whether the context is perceived as positive or negative. "The way in which we interpret experience is intimately connected with how we view ourselves" (Boud, Cohen and Walker, 1996:15–16). This determines how we develop confidence and self-esteem, which are necessary to learn from experience.

An existential and experiential learning dilemma

One of my financial sector clients recently discovered that he was not to be promoted into the top executive position in his organisation. His dilemma became one of "now what?" "Do I stay or do I go?" as everything he had been working towards had been aimed at taking over this particular position within his organisation. Coach and client looked at the pros and cons of all the possibilities. We used his experience in building, maintaining and running the business as the base point to answer the question: "Where do you have freedom of choice?' We identified three potential scenarios: 1) accepting the new reporting structure, in the short term, to sit on the new Board; 2) accepting the status quo of his position yet influencing the continued independence of the business unit; 3) looking elsewhere in the financial sector for a new position.

As coach and client reconstructed the client's experience, it became clear that he had many possible scenarios for action that would enable him to continue to create change and build relationships internally and externally, which was his forte. We identified what the current position gave him in terms of: freedom of movement, integration of activity within the organisation, and being able to manage his 700 people in a relationship-oriented way. His key learning that would ultimately influence his final decision was that he was not observant of politics which had influenced the choice of his new line manager. Coach and client began to reflect on the areas where the client was resistant to identifying how and when to play the game of politics within the organisation, and how he would choose to learn to do so, or not.

Discovering barriers to learning

With a focus on the client, practitioners need to identify what are the barriers for their clients in beginning to learn from their own experience. How does experience transform their perceptions? What is the relationship between experience, reflection and learning? As coaches, do we provide enough time for reflective activity? Reflection on experience leads to awareness and an ability to identify what is working, what is not working, and what needs to change.

Finally, how can you as a business coach use your coaching model to help the client reflect on and learn from their experience? Whatever else we do as reflective practitioners, it is important that we help the client to consider their entire experience as relevant and not be too surprised when critically reflecting that they make connections which previously they were unable to see.

IN CONCLUSION

In the context of the coaching conversation, when the client talks about their experience, they are creating a story. Storytelling constructs meaning in a different way than merely describing an experience. There is power in the client's use of language and in the content of their story, and the significance which comes from the interpretation and structure of the story itself.

But, if clients do not see themselves as learners, or as learning from experience, or even see their stories as reconstructions of reality, then we need to ask how we can use the coaching conversation, and especially coaching interventions, to help clients to learn, change and achieve their outcomes. Learning, and particularly learning from experience, therefore seems to be a major component of the coaching conversation.

In existential philosophy, all human beings must create meaning for their own lives. Existentialism emphasises freedom of choice and taking responsibility for one's actions. Existential issues that arise in the coaching conversation, such as "freedom", "meaning and purpose" and "choice", are aligned to anxiety. Working with the client in the coaching conversation, from this point of view, is about coming to a new way of understanding ourselves and our interaction with the world and with all of the systems of which we are a part.

Spinelli's analysis is that we need to move away from "doing" to an authenticity which will take the coach straight to the heart of the relationship between the coach and the client. This is of particular significance to coaches because no matter what model or methodology a practitioner uses, I agree with Spinelli that it is "the relationship" which affects the outcome of the coaching or therapy. However, it is the **quality** of the relationship that is of importance.

If the relationship which develops as a result of the coaching conversation is to shift or move the client from the level of "doing", to developing competence and capacity through "learning" – ultimately "becoming" and living out their full potential as a human being – this then provides us with some serious reflection for thought, research and debate as we continue to explore the dynamic of experiential learning, the development of the relationship and the existential concerns which arise as a result of the coaching.

COACH'S LIBRARY

Boon, M. (1996). *The African way*. Sandton: Zebra Press.

Boud, D., Cohen, R. and Walker, D. (eds). (1996). *Using experience for learning*. Buckingham: SRHE and Open University Press.

Devenish, G. (2005). Understanding true meaning of *Ubuntu* is essential in politics. *Cape Times*, 17 May.

Frankl, V.E. (1946). *Man's search for meaning*. London: Hodder and Stoughton.

Hargrove, R. (2003). *Masterful coaching: Inspire an "impossible future" while producing extraordinary leaders and extraordinary results*. San Francisco, CA: Jossey-Bass/ Pfeiffer.

May, R. (1983). *The discovery of being*. New York, NY: Norton.

McWhinney, W., Webber, J.B., Smith, D.M. and Novokowsky, B.J. (1993). *Creating paths of change: Managing issues and resolving problems in organisations*. Venice, CA: Enthusion.

O'Neill, M.B. (2000). *Coaching with backbone and heart: A systems approach to engaging leaders with their challenges*. San Francisco, CA: Jossey-Bass.

Peltier, B. (2001). *The psychology of executive coaching: Theory and application*. New York, NY: Brunner-Routledge.

Rogers, C.R. (2004). *A therapist's view of psychotherapy*. London: Constable and Robinson.

Whitmore, J. (2002). *Coaching for performance: Growing people, performance and purpose*. Third edition. London: Nicholas Brealey.

Wilber, K. (1997). An integral theory of consciousness. *Journal of Consciousness Studies,* 4(1):71–92.

Yalom, I.D. (1980). *Existential psychotherapy.* New York, NY: Basic Books.

Zohar, D. and Marshall, I. (2001). *Spiritual intelligence: The ultimate intelligence.* London: Bloomsbury.

ENDNOTES TO CHAPTER 8

1.   This exercise is adapted from an audio CD by Dr Michael Wetzler (2000).

2.   McWhinney *et al.* (1993:28) detail five systems theories with their structural assumptions, dominant causes, processes and metaphors: classic, dynamic, communication, field and evolutionary: The Classic Theory – ordering; The Dynamic (Mechanistic) Theory – moving; The Communications Paradigm – signalling; The Field Paradigm – knowing; and the Evolutionary Paradigm – becoming. This is the unfinished paradigm of "self-organisation". Considered to be the paradigm of adaptation and survival, this theory is related to the phenomena of persistence, change and innovation. The earliest traditions are the myths of origin, and this paradigm connects ancient myth and modern science, and questions arise about complexity versus simplicity. The larger role of this paradigm is to define an evolutionary system theory and to define a theory of complexity. This is the basis, according to McWhinney *et al.*, of a new social paradigm (McWhinney *et al.*, 1993:79–101).

3.   Yalom (1980:3–4): "I am convinced that the surreptitious 'throw-ins' made all the difference ... I believe that, when no one is looking, the therapist throws in the 'real thing'. But what are these 'throw-ins', these elusive, 'off the record' extras? They exist outside of formal theory, they are not written about, they are not explicitly taught ... Indeed, is it possible to define and teach such qualities as compassion, 'presence', caring, extending oneself, touching the patient at a profound level, or – that most elusive of all – wisdom?" Yalom (1980:5): "Existential psychotherapy is a dynamic approach to therapy which focuses on concerns that are rooted in the individual existence ... it is the relationship that heals".

4.   Coaches and Mentors of South Africa (COMENSA) is the institution set up to develop ethical codes, a supervision framework and standards of competence for coaches and mentors working in South Africa. It is affiliated internationally to the European and Mentoring Coaching Council (EMCC), and to the Worldwide Association of Business Coaches (WABC).

5.   According to Webster's Encyclopaedic Unabridged Dictionary (1989), "conative" pertains to the nature of conation, or expressing endeavour or effort. Conation is the part of mental life having to do with striving, including desire and volition.

9

Supervision, Contracting and Ethical Concerns

Coaching supervision worldwide is in its infancy, and is influenced by the role supervision plays for psychologists, who are required to be in supervision throughout their training and years of practice. This chapter examines how supervision is defined and practised internationally. COMENSA (2010:1), for example, defines the importance of supervision as follows: "Accountability, effectiveness and professionalism are core values for coaches and mentors. Supervision serves to help the coach/mentor manage high levels of complexity, have a mechanism for ensuring accountability and ethical practice and maintain continued professional development."

This chapter explores how you should go about being supervised and/or play the role of supervisor. Chapter 9 also looks at the role of ethics in business coaching, and ethical codes that have been developed in recent years through professional bodies such as the Worldwide Association of Business Coaches (WABC), European Mentoring and Coaching Council (EMCC), International Coach Federation (ICF), Chartered Institute of Personnel and Development (CIPD), and Coaches and Mentors of South Africa (COMENSA). Ethical dilemmas are as important as the professional codes themselves, and the authors explore some of the potential dilemmas that arise during a coaching intervention period. A third corporate governance issue for business coaches is the standard contract they draw up for the client. This chapter makes recommendations for key areas to consider when contracting with a client, a client organisation and a supervisor.

Throughout this book, I refer to **ethical** dilemmas that emerge during the coaching process, the need for **supervision** for all coach practitioners, and **contracting** with the client for the logistics of the coaching process. I discuss the context and guidelines for contracting, what is the importance of committing to an ethical code, and the rationale for coaching supervision. All three areas are related and for this reason are included in this chapter. Here I look at contracting, supervision, ethics and supervision models.

Chapter outline

- Contracting with the reader
- Contracting
    - Contracting the relationship
    - Contracting for change inside the bigger picture
    - Logistics: fees, legality and subcontractors
    - The scope of the contract
- Supervision
    - What is coaching supervision?
    - What are the benefits of supervision?
- Ethics
    - What ethical codes for coaching are in existence?
    - Confidentiality issues
    - What are ethical concerns?
    - The complexity of supervision and ethics
- Models of supervision
    - To practise the Seven-Eyed Model of Supervision
    - Supervision as a form of empowerment
    - Developing a professional approach
- Coach's library
- Endnotes to Chapter 9

CONTRACTING WITH THE READER

What I would like to ask of you, the reader, is that we contract together as you work through this chapter. As you read, what types of questions go through your mind, particularly as you read some of the stories and incidents that are explored? For example, what are your thoughts, your assumptions, and do you wonder how you might address the dilemma? How conscious are you of information that comes into your awareness at any given moment? Are you always aware of the ethical and professional questions that might arise during the coaching conversation, or that might be overridden by your own emotional or belief system ... or perhaps assumptions that might be operating? This aspect of high-level professional awareness may need reinforcement – this would include the self, the other, and any systems that may need to be held in your awareness.

CONTRACTING

Contracting the relationship

We contract in supervision with our coaching supervisor, and in coaching with our client. According to Spinelli, contracting is deeply challenging to our normal way of "being" in the world. We normally just "do" without agreeing the parameters of the relationship. The contract leverages the entire relationship, creating a set of conditions or framework within which the coach can work (Spinelli, 1989, cited in Stout-Rostron, 2006c:38).

Developing the habit of both formal and informal contracting is one of the first steps in beginning to understand the dynamics of formulating a coaching relationship. The coach and client agree to conditions of time, space, fees, confidentiality and goals. In contracting, the business coach agrees to a specific set of conditions. For example:

- As your coach I agree to support you in achieving the results you want. In turn, I expect you to give your best. Your success and your results will be determined by the commitment and responsibility to which we both commit ourselves.

- I will always act with integrity, honesty and openness, and will consistently take responsibility for my actions, communicating any concerns or issues I have.

- I will provide excellence in coaching, offering value and professionalism.

- I will respect the confidentiality and boundaries of our relationship at all times.

- The measure of my effectiveness as a coach will be your success and achievements.

- I agree to respect the boundaries of the contract that we structure together.

The purpose of the contract is to open up the potential for trust between coach and client. This is essential if the client is to trust their own self-exploration. As the agreement lays the foundation for the relationship, it must be adhered to in action for trust to develop.

Contracting definitions

The contract between coach and client sets out which services have been agreed and delineates all fees as well as the outcomes and deliverables that can be expected. The contract sets out ground rules for the coaching relationship so that both parties are aware of their obligations. This helps prevent future misunderstandings and provides a firm basis to deal with disagreements. The contract describes the relationship between the coach and multiple parties, such as the individual client, the client organisation, the HR unit, and line management. It is important for the contract to describe the difference between coaching and the other helping disciplines such as therapy, counselling, mentoring and training. Objectives for the individual executive and for the organisation need to be clarified, with boundaries made explicit in terms of confidentiality, fees, cancellation and termination of the contract.

Often in coaching, the contracting process is linked to the generation and fulfilment of outcomes. Contracting usually deals with the management of the process, roles played, evaluation of the process, learning and outcomes, and the exit clauses. As a function, contracting has emerged as a critical function of coaching supervision. "The contracting for therapy and coaching have similarities in their purpose, i.e. to provide safety, set boundaries, manage time, money and ethical issues, but what is contracted and to what end creates a distinction. The contracting and the relationship building are crucial to the outcomes of the coaching intervention and this is no different to that of supervision" (Pampallis Paisley, 2006:85–86).

Contracting is complex as it determines what areas, and how deeply, the coach can work with the organisation at an individual, team and systemic level. A question raised in Pampallis Paisley's (2006) research was, "How do you get change in coaching that is innovative and not superficial if you do not go deep?" This is a question for supervision, and needs to be considered in the contracting process.

Questions to ask when setting up the contract

1. What are the needs of the individual executive client versus those of the organisation?

- What is the organisation looking for?
- What are the goals for the individual client?
- Which performance improvements are desired?
- What are the organisational goals for the coaching programme?
- What are the organisational conditions and are they conducive to coaching?
- Are the line manager and senior management supportive of the process?
- Is the individual ready for coaching and is coaching appropriate?
- How do you know?

2. Coaches must be able to define their work in terms of outcomes and solutions:
   - What will be better as a result of coaching?
   - How will we know, and what difference will it make?
   - How will we measure success, effectiveness and value for money?
   - What will be the initial goals?
   - Which pre-coaching assessments are recommended?
   - Who will provide the feedback?
   - Will there be a specific action and development plan to achieve goals?
   - How is the coaching contract terminated?
   - What follow-up and monitoring will occur after the coaching has been completed?

3. Coach and client need to discuss and agree the structure of the coaching sessions:
   - How many sessions will there be?
   - How often should they take place?
   - How long will they last, depending on the individual needs and breadth and depth of the client's issues?
   - Where will the coaching sessions take place?
   - Will the sessions be face-to-face, by telephone, or a combination of both?
   - Will there be any contact by telephone or email between sessions?

Contracting for change inside the bigger picture

Bruce Peltier (2001:xxiii–xxiv) defines the coaching intervention as a four-step process:

1. **Get things started**: coaches must define their work in terms of outcomes and

solutions, confidentiality, recording relationships, dimensions of the project and contracting (i.e. time, money and methodology).

2. **Gather information and make a plan**: with executives, it is important to develop a clear plan that includes measurable outcomes (executives work best to a development plan with clear goals and end points).

3. **Implement**: it can take from three months up to two years to produce results, develop skills and achieve objectives. The implementation may include work shadowing when the coach walks alongside the executive in the workplace and observes the client in action.

4. **Lock in the changes**: the coach should arrange for ongoing improvement and support, for short-term behaviours to be translated into long-term behaviours.[1]

Common pitfalls

For the business coach, a common pitfall can be to mistakenly assume that the relationship between coach and executive happens in isolation from the dynamics of the executive's team, or outside the organisational dynamics. In other words, the coaching relationship is set within the context of the team and the organisation. It is part of the overall system within which the executive works. This has huge implications for the coach's interventions with the executive. "If the prevailing organisational culture is one of blame and fear, then perception of learning needs and opportunities is likely to be correspondingly low" (Parsloe and Wray, 2000:35). Grayson and Larson (2000:121) define the six most common pitfalls as:

- failure to commit;
- unrealistic expectations;
- defensiveness;
- passive role in the coaching process;
- playing it safe; and
- failure to involve others.

It does not help that you are potentially the best coach in the world if you cannot recognise these and navigate the relationship, i.e. say no to the coaching assignment or walk away. Noer (2000) states that there are three big derailment factors:

- lack of clarity as to who is the client;
- coaches using a single model or approach; and
- creating a dependency relationship.

In the coaching conversation, Mary Beth O'Neill advocates three core principles for the coach: (1) self-management, (2) a systems perspective and a methodology, and (3) the use of backbone and heart. She cites her four phases of coaching as using a systems lens to contract, plan, conduct live action interviews and debrief (O'Neill, 2000:xvii,10).

The bigger picture needs to be part of the contracting process. It is important for the coach to recognise the larger systems at play and the "force field" that shapes and influences all the individuals working within the system. Therefore coaches need to hold a "bifocal" view, being able to see their client in the system, as well as seeing oneself in the system (O'Neill; 2000:xv). It is important to remember that contracting determines at which level the coach will work individually and systemically.

Another important aspect of contracting is the evaluation of the contract, including termination or renewal. In any business contracting process, it is important to draw up the "marriage" and the "divorce" papers at the beginning: a bit like a prenuptial contract. It is as important to specify the boundaries and parameters of the entire coaching intervention, i.e. how the process will proceed from beginning to end, and how to terminate the process, whether at the contracted termination point or sooner if required by either party.

Defining coaching in your contract

It is useful to include a definition of coaching within your contract, specifying how coaching differs from the other helping professions. For example, "the services to be provided by coach to client are coaching as designed jointly with the client. Coaching, which is not advice, therapy, or counselling, may address specific personal or professional projects, business issues, or general conditions in the client's life or profession".

Also to be included could be the following clause which we use in our own coaching contracts:

Throughout the working relationship, the coach will engage with the client in direct conversation. The client can count on the coach to be honest and straightforward in asking questions, making interventions and facilitating the setting of goals. The client understands that the power of coaching is in the relationship between client and coach. If the client or the coach believes the coaching is not working as desired, either client or coach will communicate this.

Client questions in the contracting phase

The contracting phase of the intervention is about building the relationship, identifying the executive's goals, determining the boundaries for the coaching relationship, and setting up expectations for coach, client and the organisation. Your contract needs to make explicit to the client what will happen within the entire coaching intervention. Here are several questions clients may ask you during the contracting phase:

- How quickly can you begin to understand my position, the environment within which I work and the pressures that I need to learn to negotiate?
- What can you understand about my needs and position?
- How practical and effective will you be in helping me to achieve my goal?
- How will you help me to work more effectively within the organisation?
- How will we work together?
- What is the breadth and depth of your coaching experience?
- Share with me some of your successes and failures as a coach.
- How will you help me to become a more effective leader and manager?
- Here is one specific issue I have to deal with ... what would you advise me?
- What could possibly get in the way of our coaching relationship that I might not have thought about?

Client commitment to the coaching process

During the contracting phase, the commitment of the client to the coaching intervention is vital. For example, the client may commit themselves to:

- being frank, open and honest with the coach at all times;
- communicating with the coach specific concerns about the client/coach relationship;

- taking responsibility to communicate with the coach at all times;
- understanding that the essence and strength of the coaching conversation is in the "relationship"; and
- agreeing to be "coachable" and to consider the coach's observations on all issues.

Logistics: fees, legality and subcontractors

The written contract needs to include the coaching commencement date and the agreed period of the coaching intervention. For example, the intervention could be for 20 hours, six months or one year, renewable after an agreed period. Built into the contract will be the agreed meetings between coach, executive and line management, and the structure of the coaching fees.

The legal contract may be overseen by a sponsor, an HR division, or another third party. Whichever, for your contract, we suggest a workable and flexible system for payment of fees. It might be on a monthly, hourly, or retainer basis, or paid in several tranches throughout the agreed period of the coaching intervention.

The contract will build in the supervision sessions with line management, or with the lead coach if the individual coach is subcontracted through a lead coach. If you as coach are subcontracted by a lead coach, ensure that you sign a legal contract that protects you for payment of fees, cancellation and for indemnity purposes. Many subcontractors build into the contract that you are responsible for your own coaching consultancy boundaries. Also, if you have been subcontracted, the client organisation is not your client, but is the client of the lead contractor. Ensure that your contract includes details of how to handle future contracted work if offered to you.

It is useful to obtain samples of contracts from colleagues, coach training institutions and your professional body. Ensure that, if you supply the contract, an attorney approves that it will stand on its own as a legal document.

Managing cancellations and additional requests

Suggested clauses to include in your contract to handle cancellations and miscellaneous requests:

- We agree to provide one another with one month's notice in the event it is desired to cancel further coaching after the initial period of ...
- We agree to let each other know of any overseas or long-distance meetings or holidays at a minimum of two weeks' notice.
- The coach is available to speak on request by telephone, in addition to the normal face-to-face coaching sessions. Where the coach can, they will take the client's call. Failing that, client and coach will agree a time convenient to both.

The scope of the contract

The two most critical areas in contracting are possibly those of ethical issues and defining the scope of the overall coaching intervention. Both of these should be addressed in the coaching contract. Coaching processes often fail due to poor or insufficient contracting (Nowack and Wimer, 1997). As we have discussed above, contracting should include ethical issues such as the disclosure of personal and inappropriate information to a client's superior (Williams, 1996), and aligning the contract to corporate objectives in order to be credible (Olesen, 1996). Conflict of interest between the goals and expectations of the individual being coached, and those of the company, as well as the issues of quality standards and confidentiality can impact on trust between the individual executive and the coach (Janse van Rensburg, 2001b:24–25).

Success means contracting and goal setting. Outcomes and goals are to be discussed and reviewed at each subsequent session as agreed between coach and client. The contract needs to specify the parameters of the overall coaching period: for example, whether there will be the creation of a personal/professional development plan, and how outcomes will be measured from the beginning of the contract to the end. In terms of the coach's intervention, the underlying goal in the contracting phase is the development of the relationship.

> **First meeting with the client**
>
> I include a "coachable moment" during the first meeting with the client. This is to introduce the client straight away to the "feel" of the coaching relationship. The client usually begins to talk about their issues in your first meeting anyway, and you will have typically asked what are their overall aims for the coaching intervention. If you contract in the first session without beginning the coaching process (if only to identify the client's aim for coaching, the possible strategy of working together, and overall goals) there is a risk that the client may remain confused about how the process is to work. The client begins to understand how you work and it helps the client to decide about the reality of working with you.

Husserl's (1962/1913) concept of "intentionality" would be important in many areas of coaching – and definitely in the area of contracting, i.e. what is the intention of all parties, coach, client and organisation? This would be similar for supervision contracting.

What O'Neill (2000:93) terms "the partnership", I call the relationship. It begins when the executive actually begins to talk about the specific issues where they are currently stuck. O'Neill's (2000:94) recommended coaching intervention questions in the contracting phase are:

- Which recurring patterns are present in this situation?
- Which patterns work well and which detract from the effort?
- How are you a part of these patterns?
- How have you responded to this issue?
- What is your knee-jerk contribution?
- Can you imagine a different pattern?
- How willing are you to develop the stamina required to stop your part of the pattern that is no longer effective?
- How will this help you get to your goal?
- How can I be useful to you?

O'Neill (2000:215–219; 97) suggests interventions at specific stages in her four-step model, and in alignment with certain themes (concreteness, empathy, confrontation, respect):

A. **Concreteness** – invite the executive to be more specific about their issue.

B. **Empathy** – make an effort to show you understand the leader's concerns.

C. **Confrontation** – point out discrepancies between what the leader says and what they actually do.

D. **Respect** – believe the executive has the ability to handle their situation.

Contracting interventions

Mary Beth O'Neill (2000) recommends other possible questions for contracting. Many of the questions O'Neill adapted and used, with the permission of Rob Schachter (1997), come from "Questions when contracting with leaders", from an unpublished document (Stout-Rostron, 2006c: endnote 13–14):

- Which business challenges are you facing?
- Have you met this challenge successfully before?
- What is your best thinking about this issue?
- What are the gaps in meeting the same kind of challenge this time?
- What is keeping you from getting the results you want?
- How have you responded to this issue?
- Do you have any sense of your part in not meeting the challenge this time?
- How urgent are you?
- How much time do you have to achieve this?
- What do you find personally challenging about leading this effort, given the results you have to date?
- How do you think I could be useful to you?
- Do you have the authority to sponsor this plan, or do you need sponsorship from someone else?

Always build debriefing into the coaching contract. Here are four suggested categories to the debriefing session (Stout-Rostron, 2006c:39).

1. celebrate achievements;
2. identify key recurring patterns;
3. assess the alignment of roles; and
4. develop a personal and professional plan.

What should be in your written contract?

1. Ground rules and parameters such as confidentiality, reporting relationships, and dimensions of the project (people to be coached, timing and fees) must be established.
2. Include deliverables, explicit ways to know if and when you have accomplished your goals.
3. What will you deliver and how will you know when you have done so?
4. How will you make goals measurable and achievable?
5. Establish what will be different as a result of coaching.
6. Clarify your code of ethics and standards and the professional association of which you are a member. Clinicians use formal ethics codes and standards. As coaching is a new, emerging profession and formal structures are in the making, it is important to state to which code you are committed.
7. Negotiate explicit contracts that are fair to all parties.
8. Do you have a malpractice or liability carrier? Let them know that you are doing coaching as part of your professional practice. Check with other coaches to find out whom they are using.
9. Find out which contracts are currently in use and check the coaching literature (Whitworth, Kimsey-House and Sandahl, 1998:180).

Individual learning contracts

As well as the overall contract, which defines the parameters of the coaching relationship, you may develop learning contracts with your clients. These are "works in progress" throughout the entire coaching intervention period. Within my coaching process, at the end of a coaching session – to fully integrate the learning with goals set and commitment to action – we complete a learning contract to:

- Redefine the vision, where the client is going.
- Outline the strategy, how the client is going to achieve the vision.
- Identify the specific outcomes that need to be accomplished in the intervention period in order to work towards achieving the vision and putting the strategy into action.
- Identify the obstacles to achieving the goals identified, and the strengths that will enable the client to progress.

- Summarise what the client gained from the session in order to help underline self-reflection and continue to help the client to understand that they are responsible for their own thinking, feeling and behaviour.

The learning contract becomes the focus at the beginning of the next session with the client, and is the beginning of the client's learning or leadership development plan.

SUPERVISION

When contracting with a client, ethical issues such as confidentiality and boundary management are critical to the success of the intervention. Key areas to be clarified centre on fees, boundaries and confidentiality. For the coach practitioner in supervision, ethical issues and dilemmas often emerge as core topics for exploration. We have tried to include some of the main issues that have arisen for us, as coach practitioners, within our own practice, as well as those that have emerged with the founding and maintaining of the professional body, Coaches and Mentors of South Africa (COMENSA). There are consistent themes that have arisen in our own individual supervision, as well as issues that have emerged when supervising fellow practitioner coaches.

A likely story – with consequences

I often tell the story of an early experience in supervision. I did not clearly contract the parameters of confidentiality, or the ethical guidelines and boundaries for supervision in this instance. I was working from a set of assumptions with my supervisor, rather than a defined contract, because of a long-standing relationship with my supervisor. Even so, it demonstrates the consequences of not clearly contracting, verbally and in written form.

As a coach, I shared some of my uncertainty at how to best manage some of the difficulties I had recently faced with a client, whom I did not name. The supervisor listened, made observations, and even offered some advice about how to deal with the issue. At a later date, I was in a coaching conversation with this client, only to discover that the client knew all about the content of my conversation with my supervisor. How did that happen?

It is a small marketplace for the coaching community in South Africa, and the supervisor guessed immediately who the client was. The coach and the supervisor had not clearly contracted the boundaries of confidentiality, including the ethical consequences of divulging client information. The supervisor somehow did not realise the damage that could be done in sharing this information with the client. So what was the damage? Essentially, the trust the client had in her coach was bruised, and it would take some time for it to be restored. Furthermore, the coach was dismayed, felt betrayed, and lost faith in her supervisor. What should she have done to clarify the situation?

We all make mistakes, and so it is important to be big enough to say, "Whoops, I really messed up here" and to take responsibility for one's own errors. The coach has done so with her client. However, her relationship with her supervisor also needs to be addressed. The coach needs to be clear with her supervisor about the consequences of broken confidentiality, the ethical dilemmas broken confidentiality can present, and what the boundaries in future should be. As we continue to discuss ethics and supervision in this chapter, it may be helpful to reflect back on this story.

What is coaching supervision?

The role of the supervisor is to support the development of the coach practitioner and to assess their competence. The term "supervision" describes the process by which the work of the practitioner is overseen and guidance is sought. The process may differ in significant ways from that undertaken in other professions, such as psychotherapy and counselling. Usually, both coach practitioner and supervisor will be bound by the Code of Ethics of their professional body. The purpose of supervision is to ensure that the coach maintains the highest standards of competence; best serves the needs of the client; is professionally trained and skilled in the practice of coaching; and is committed to a programme of continuing professional development throughout the years of their practice.

Williams (1992) claims that supervision is the "cornerstone of counselling" (Ruru, 2008). Within the emerging discipline of coaching, supervision has become a requirement for membership in many professional associations. However, if supervision becomes a monitoring function, it is possible that it might overstep the bounds of intention in the global environment of this developing profession.

Purpose of clinical supervision

The importance of the "coach being coached" or in supervision cannot be over-emphasised. While supervision has been a fundamental underpinning of therapy from the beginning, it is not yet a given for the coaching industry worldwide. The importance of coaching supervision is to ensure that the coach understands what the client goes through, and more importantly, to work through their own issues so that they do not become entangled with client concerns.

Some of the main themes that have arisen from research into executive coaching supervision are (Pampallis Paisley, 2006):

- boundary management;
- whether supervision interventions needed to have a client-centred or coach-centred focus, or both;
- how to cope with the complexity of the supervisory system in which client, coach and organisation were represented – the triangulations;
- the depth to which one should go in the coaching relationship; and
- the importance of creating a space to think.

As Yalom (2001:48) says, human problems are "largely relational" and an individual's interpersonal problems will ultimately manifest themselves in the here and now of a therapy encounter. The same is true of the coaching environment. The client's interpersonal issues will soon emerge in the relationship between coach and client. The client can trigger a coach's underlying drivers, even in a small way. For example, if coach and client are undergoing divorce simultaneously, it is important that the coach is able to maintain a "meta" position throughout the coaching conversation if divorce comes into the conversation. And, similarly, in my story, the next time I am in supervision, I need to be sure that I have cleared the air with my supervisor so as to be free of feelings of doubt or mistrust.

Caplan (1970) distinguishes between **supervision** and **consultation**. Supervision is an ongoing process of inspecting the work of the individual being supervised in a hierarchical power structure; consultation is a less formal, intermittent interaction between colleagues arising out of current work-related problems (Stout-Rostron, 2006c:80). What coaching supervision refers to is more consultation arising out of the needs of the coach, individual executive and client organisation.

Kadushin (1976) describes the three main functions of supervision as educative, supportive and managerial. He describes these functions as formative (namely educational), normative (which focuses on policies, organisation and evaluation), and restorative (including a debriefing of both positive and negative feedback on practice). Hawkins and Shohet (2000) describe four categories of supervision, the fourth category being particularly relevant to coach practitioners:

1. **tutorial** – focusing on the educational function, but may include supportive and managerial aspects;
2. **training supervision** – where supervision is normative and managerial;
3. **managerial supervision** – which relates to hierarchical line management; and
4. **consultancy supervision** – for experienced practitioners.

Where does supervision originate from?

The origin of supervision within health and social care originates in psychological mental health care fields. The development of counselling has had a formative impact on the creation of a supervision model, and in occupational therapy, supervision has been in practice since the 1970s. The UK Department of Health defines clinical supervision as "a formal process of professional support and learning which enables the individual practitioner to develop knowledge and competence, assume responsibility for their own practice and enhance consumer protection and safety of care in complex clinical situations" (Jones and Jenkins, 2006:26).

The UK Chartered Society for Physiotherapy (CSP) guidelines state: "Clinical supervision can be seen as a collaborative process between two or more practitioners of the same or different professions. This process should encourage the development of professional skills and enhanced quality of patient care through implementation of an evidence-based approach to maintaining standards in practice. These standards are maintained through discussion around specific patient incidents or interventions using elements of reflection to guide the discussion" (Jones and Jenkins, 2006).

The UK perspective positions "clinical supervision within service quality and governance, and professional development and lifelong learning". The USA perspective defines clinical supervision as a specific aspect of staff development dealing with the clinical skills and competences of each staff member. The structure for clinical supervision is typically one-to-one or small groups who meet on a regular basis (Jones and Jenkins, 2006:23–24).

Why do coaches need supervision?

Due to the international growth and development of coaching and mentoring as disciplines, most professional coaching bodies now recommend an ethical code of conduct for their members; and, as part of that code, a commitment to supervision on the part of the practitioner.

The European Mentoring and Coaching Council (EMCC) states in its *Code of Ethics* that "a coach/mentor must maintain a relationship with a suitably qualified supervisor, who will regularly assess their competence and support their development" (EMCC, 2008b). The Chartered Institute of Personnel and Development (CIPD) in the UK cites guidelines for buyers of coaching and recommends that practitioners articulate what formal supervision arrangements they currently have in place (Jarvis, 2004).

COMENSA's policy on supervision is that "Supervision offers a context in which practitioners can develop professionally – to re-construct their experience, to reflect, to understand, to design their professional reality, and to develop new responses for future practice. It can be described as a collaborative, co-constructed space in which coaching/mentoring competencies are explored and developed" (COMENSA, 2010:1). The COMENSA (2009) *Revised Code of Ethics* requires that all members have regular supervision with a suitably qualified supervisor who will regularly assess their professional development and competence. COMENSA's (2010) policy on supervision details the guidelines for their practitioner members, recommending a ratio of 1:15 hours of supervision to coaching or mentoring.

Supervision is useful as it ensures that the coach works to the executive's agenda, not to the coach's agenda. The need for supervision is something that COMENSA, in alignment with other international professional coaching bodies, recommends for all coaches in their continuing professional development (CPD).

A key component of a coach's personal and professional approach to their coaching practice is to work on a regular basis with a supervising coach, counsellor or therapist. The purpose of this is three-fold: first, and crucially, to deal with any unresolved issues of their own (an ongoing process for any coach), and specifically to learn not to bring personal concerns to the coaching conversation; second, to benefit from invaluable and ongoing supervision for the individual's coaching practice; and third, the supervision process provides the coach with an invaluable tool to understand the client/practitioner process from another perspective, i.e. from the client perspective rather than from the perspective of the practitioner. It provides an excellent alternate perspective on the coaching intervention (Stout-Rostron, 2006c:14).

The structure of group supervision

An individual supervision session usually takes place in a one- or two-hour timeframe. Group supervision with anything up to ten practitioners usually lasts about three hours. The way that I structure group supervision consists of:

1. A group check-in: what is going well with the client-coach relationship? This allows the group to icebreak, and to connect with each other within the coaching and the organisational system.

2. A "round" (where everyone speaks once before anyone speaks for the second time) to flipchart key issues and challenges each practitioner wishes to address in the supervision session. A subsequent round-table discussion about the specific issues and challenges highlighted. The group could break up into pairs to discuss and bring their thoughts back to the plenary session, or the discussion could be around the key topics highlighted from the previous round.

3. A demonstration with supervisor and an individual coach to work on one of their challenges. The other practitioners observe the conversation, making notes about what is happening in the coach-supervisor dialogue, what the supervisor is doing, and their own thoughts and feelings throughout the dialogue.

4. Feedback from coach and supervisor as to any learning gained from the dialogue; followed by a discussion bringing in the other practitioner observations, recommendations and questions. Questions help the supervisor to facilitate the next round of discussion. The supervisor and the participants encourage the supervisor to be aware of their own internal processes that are evoked when listening to the contributions from the practitioner participants. The discussion brings in any parallel processes that are occurring as a result of the supervisory dialogue and the subsequent discussion. Feedback is given to the supervisor on their own performance.

5. Subsequent coaching conversations with an observer. This could be done in triads, with coach/coachee/observer. At the end, the triads bring their learning and questions back into the round format. At each supervision session, it is important to vary who adopts each of the three roles.

6. Discussion in a "round" format. Each individual shares their learning from the process, blind spots they have noticed in themselves, and any queries that may have occurred. The process allows lead coach and practitioner participants to learn from all perspectives.

What are the benefits of supervision?

There are multiple benefits for the individual practitioner in supervision, as well as for the team and the client organisation. The coach practitioners have a chance to meet, with the supervising coach ensuring that all practitioners have a sound understanding of the organisational systems at play. Coaching supervision is an important regular meeting where the coaches can connect with each other, and can begin to understand the connections between their clients. It is an important meeting where the individuals in the group facilitate learning from each other.

The needs of coaching supervision

In Pampallis Paisley's (2006:96–97) research into supervision for executive coaching, she identified a range of primary needs that emerged with a high degree of frequency. Her conclusion is that the coaching supervisor needs to empower the coach to:

- assess the level at which the client, the team, and the organisation is working;
- clarify that what the coach identifies may indicate a need to refer for therapy;
- be ethically responsible and ask for permission; and
- be aware of outcomes. Is this the best option for this subject/issue/client? Or is it the coach's need?

There is a big question about the sustainability of shifts and the likelihood of "relapse" to old behaviours if the coach only works in the client's sphere of conscious competence and an emotional component is not involved. Containment is important as the client needs to remain able to function in the world. This can become an ethical issue when coaching in an organisation, as the initial contract may have a time limit.

Supervision helps practitioners to grow their skills and competence whether they are supervised individually or in groups. The capacity of the coaches to facilitate learning for their clients is also significantly increased. Other benefits are:

- ensuring that the client organisation is getting a good return on investment (ROI) for their business;
- ensuring that a high value is placed on truly understanding clients;
- ensuring that the coach is as likely to enhance and develop self-awareness as the client; and
- the creation of a safe space to explore the heart of the practitioner's coaching practice.

There are some disadvantages to group supervision, and practitioners need to be particularly careful when managing client confidentiality. The advantages are the observations that the group can make when observing each other. The 1:1 supervision encompasses more intimate learning on the part of the individual coach with the time to go into depth about the client situation and one's own individual issues or concerns as a coach. It is almost inevitable that the coach can become enmeshed in some of the organisation's systemic dynamics. It is helpful to have an observant supervisor who can help the coach to step into a bigger picture position, looking at the client-coach-system dynamics from a fresh perspective.

For the moment, there are no international guidelines to measure the positive impact for clients and coach practitioners. This may be considered for future research.[2] Finally, coaching supervision will observe the developmental stages of the practitioners within their group forum. This type of supervision is more collegial and consultative, encouraging the practice of self-supervision. The lead coach or supervisor also needs to take note of their own developmental stages in the profession as they gain in expertise.

Managing the complexity of supervision

Supervision requires a tremendous amount of self- and organisational awareness to meet the levels of complexity within which senior executives are working. This is to enable the depth of questioning and guidance that is needed in managing multiple levels and contexts.

The complexity of supervision is also noted when working with a diverse group of participants who embody a range of levels of awareness and competence. They will be in different stages of personal and professional development, and will exhibit a range of learning styles and interpersonal skills. This presents an enormous challenge for the supervisor.

Pampallis Paisley (2006) considered the nature of working within different contexts in her supervision research, while working with a group of coaches from widely diverse backgrounds. She says:

> All may be utilising different models and frameworks, and have varying levels of competences, training and consciousness, which impacts on what is brought into the supervisory room. Unlike therapeutic supervision for example, where an object relations therapist would work with a supervisor who is skilled in object relations theory and practice, this in-depth but narrow band – or what I call "vertical depth of field" of specialisation may not be the domain of the coaching supervisor.

There may be specialist areas that would require a mentoring process. With regards to the supervision of coaches working with leadership in complex organisations, coaching supervisors would need to have a broader focus, or what I call a "horizontal depth of field". It follows then that the supervision of coaching is in itself a complex discipline – one that requires levels of understanding and a comprehensive framework of knowledge and skills which cover both the horizontal planes and vertical depths that coaching encompasses (Pampallis Paisley, 2006:108–110).

How to find a supervisor

As COMENSA members are increasingly taking part in the development of their profession, the Portfolio Committee for Supervision is beginning to provide training for coach supervisors. Also, other coach training organisations such as Coach Development UK are offering professional group supervision and supervision training for coach supervision practitioners. Your criteria when hiring a supervisor will include someone who:

- has knowledge of ethical, legal and regulatory aspects of the helping professions;
- is able to form a peer/collegial relationship as a supervising consultant;
- is sensitive to diversity issues of culture, ethnicity, gender, age, socio-economic and educational background;
- has knowledge of current research in the coaching supervision field;
- has competence and expertise as an executive/business coach; and
- has training in supervision.

Different types of supervision

In organisations and coach training institutions today, there are several ways to access supervision. There is one-on-one supervision, peer supervision, team supervision and group supervision. Many coach training institutes set up a peer supervision process for senior and junior graduates to work together in the supervision process, either individual, peer or group. We define the four specific types of supervision as educational, administrative, supportive and managerial.

Typically, in the South African marketplace, **educational** supervision is to assess the skills and needs and to facilitate the learning for practitioner coaches. **Administrative** supervision is to monitor the workload of the coaches within the group or the organisation, ensuring that the purpose, vision and goals of the organisation are met. **Supportive** supervision is to provide an environment for practitioners where their emotional needs are met, and where they are able to build skills and competence, whether in a one-on-one or group forum. **Managerial** supervision is to ensure that individual client, coach and line manager meet regularly to ensure that the client is on track to meet the objectives set out for the coaching intervention.

What happens when supervision doesn't work?

In supervision, there are similarities with poor coaching practice. If conflicts arise in supervision sessions, it is often due to the lack of skill on the part of the supervisor and facilitator. It is important for there to be open, transparent dialogue about what is working, and what is not working for supervisors and practitioners in any session. For example, I have experienced poor supervision when the supervisor, or even one of the practitioners, has been operating from a lack of awareness of their blind spots. Also, if the practitioner begins to "advocate" for the supremacy of their "client" versus another "client", it is often a demonstration of the practitioner having become part of the systemic dynamics of the organisation. The parallel processes and complexity of supervision require skill and self-awareness on the part of the supervisor and practitioners alike. The parallel processes are frequently where the greatest learning lies.

ETHICS

Ethics can be defined as "a set of moral principles". Ethics are most often recognised as the rules of conduct in respect of a particular group or culture, or the moral principles of an individual. Ethics is known as the branch of philosophy dealing with values which relate to human conduct (Simon and Schuster, 1983).

What ethical codes for coaching are in existence?

All professional bodies define the values, standards of competence and ethical benchmarks to which their members are held accountable. The purpose of COMENSA's (2009:1) *Revised Code of Ethics* is to "set the ethical standards for South Africa in the fields of coaching and mentoring".[3] It is agreed amongst members that this is an "organic" code which will evolve over the years as the discipline of coaching continues to emerge and gain recognition as a profession. The draft COMENSA (2007) *Membership Criteria and Standards of Competence Framework* recommended that all members commit to the ethical code as a foundation for their coaching practice. The COMENSA (2009:2–5) *Revised Code of Ethics* defines its key guiding principles as the fundamental values of inclusivity, dignity, competence, context, boundary management, integrity, professionalism, and breaches of the code.

The Worldwide Association of Business Coaches (WABC) (2008a) requires of members to adhere to their *Code of Business Coaching Ethics and Integrity*. The code tries to address the diverse range of business interactions faced all over the world by members, and has established a process to handle ethical dilemmas and issues.[4]

The European Mentoring and Coaching Council (EMCC) has been established to promote best practice and to ensure that the highest possible standards are maintained in the coach-mentor/client relationship. This is requested by the EMCC's Complaints and Disciplinary procedures. The EMCC *Ethical Code* defines five key ethical areas: competence, context, boundary management, integrity and professionalism (EMCC, 2008b).[5]

The International Federation of Coaching (ICF) defines their Standards of Ethical Conduct explicitly as professional conduct at large; professional conduct with clients, confidentiality/privacy; conflicts of interest (ICF, 2008b). All members acknowledge and agree to honour the ICF Pledge of Ethics.[6]

COMENSA's Code of Ethics

Two fundamental principles in setting up COMENSA (Coaches and Mentors of South Africa) have been:

(1) "inclusivity" – i.e. including rather than excluding coaches and mentors (the lessons learned from the divisive nature of South Africa's apartheid past informed its commitment to inclusivity); and

(2) democratic participation (every decision is taken by consensus or voting between members in the three regional chapters). The underlying purpose has been to create ethics and standards for coaches and mentors in South Africa, and to develop coaching as a credible institution.

One of the features of this project has been the COMENSA public forums (to determine ethics and criteria for membership), which have started the complex process of creating an ethical code for South Africa and criteria for membership of the institution. A major decision on the part of the members has been that COMENSA should not be an accrediting body, but rather a forum for continuing professional development. In order to uphold the highest standards of behaviour in the coaching profession, COMENSA committed itself to a consultative process to develop its ethics code involving the coach practitioners, the corporate buyers of coaching and the coach training institutions.

To whom does a coach owe loyalty?

In business coaching, the question often arises, "To whom does the coach owe loyalty?" To the individual client, or to the organisation who is paying the coach's fee? In fact, it is to both, which can sometimes create an ethical dilemma. For instance, what if your client asks you to coach them out of the organisation and into a new job? The question then arises, what are you bound to in your contract with the client organisation in terms of client confidentiality and boundary management?

A coach must be able to understand the point of view of the organisation with whom they have a coaching contract, and must find a way to synthesise the two interests: cooperative and competitive. Peltier (2001:222) appropriately quotes Robert Solomon (1997): "the search for excellence, whatever it may be, begins with ethics". Peltier explains that executive coaches have to navigate two types of cultures: the business culture, which is a proprietary culture based on market enterprise; and the individual client culture, which cultivates the ethics of care, where looking after the client's best interests engenders a cooperative culture.

In clinical practice, clinicians look after their client's interest. These interests are the hub of the contract, and the arrangement is a **cooperative** one. However, in business there is a proprietary culture based upon a **competitive** market philosophy. Both providers and buyers of coaching compete for the best deal they can get, and each party expects the other party to behave competitively. One party does not expect the other to look out for them or their interests. Coaches need to navigate these two cultures. One is a business culture, where profit is the motive, and the other is the ethics of care for individual clients. A coach needs to understand the point of view of the organisation and find a way to integrate the cooperative and the competitive points of view. This can often present a coach with dilemmas that challenge their ability to be loyal to both the organisation and the individual client.

In terms of client intervention, Peltier (2001:224) suggests three overall steps:

1. Develop clear written contracts – with clarity from the beginning of the relationship about confidentiality and boundary issues.
2. Whistle-blow when colleagues behave poorly or are found to be incompetent.
3. Know your limits and practice within those limits with supervision.

Peltier's main message is to focus on the single thing that one does best as a business coach, creating sustainable competitive advantage and being exceptional. His second step, to whistle blow, is something most coaches would be reluctant to do, not wanting to damage their image or a colleague's in the marketplace. However, without legislated ethical guidelines (unlike psychotherapists), coaches need to establish their behavioural norms through their working practices and commitment to their professional body's ethical code. Furthermore, if there is a definite dilemma regarding a colleague, the first step is **always** to speak to the person in question; second to speak to the lead supervisor confidentially; finally if unresolved to speak to the Ethics Committee of your professional association in complete confidence. However, any communication must be done having informed the colleague in question.

Human behaviour is always complex. In my supervision story earlier in this chapter, the coach only discovered the broken confidentiality in a subsequent coaching session with her client. She needed to first clear the situation with her client, then to clear the air with her supervisor. In this case, it did not need to be brought to anyone else's attention. One of the key difficulties with an emerging profession is that there are not necessarily precise guidelines for ethical behaviour, which is what all the international coaching bodies are gradually trying to build into their coaching guidelines for members.

Who is the client?

Coaches often forget to consider who the actual client is. Is it the organisation that hires and pays the coach's fees to help with a business need? Or, is it the individual who is seeking to grow, develop and move forward in their career? The question is essentially answered when the executive personally pays the coach's fee. However, what happens when the company pays the bill? To whom does the coach owe loyalty?

Ethical dilemma

What happens if the client decides to focus on skills that the organisation clearly does not condone, or skills that the client wishes to use in a future job or career? It is important to clarify the parameters of capacity building in your contract so that you do not find yourself in this situation.

What happens when a client is angry, contemplating legal action against the organisation, or is plotting their next move to a new organisation? How can the coach work with this client? What information needs to be shared with the organisation? When does it become unethical for the coach to continue to work with the individual client?

In this situation, once again, it is important to have stipulated in your contracting process, how you will handle a conflict of interest between the individual client and the organisation. In this instance, you have several choices. You can advise your client to speak with the appropriate superiors within their organisation, or you can advise your client that you and the client should possibly meet with the line manager, HR or OD, and that you will facilitate the discussion.

Or, if those two scenarios are unacceptable to the client, you can withdraw from the contract letting the client know you can no longer work with them as they are unwilling to address

---

the issue in a manner appropriate to the situation. If it is stipulated in your contract that you are facing an inappropriate conflict of interest between client and organisation, only then would we advise taking it to the appropriate superiors in the organisation. However, it is important that, if you are unsure of what to do, your first port of call may be to discuss it with your supervising coach.

Confidentiality issues

Another issue is that of confidentiality. It is often said that the rules for content confidentiality are up for grabs when it comes to coaching. To what extent is the relationship between coach and client confidential? In clinical practice, the counselling relationship and the content of that relationship are confidential. The only relationship that is legally protected in terms of confidentiality is that between lawyer and client, and we are aware of at least one case where a psychologist was subpoenaed to testify in court.

Many organisations insist that coach and client work in an organisational meeting space for their sessions. Often coach and client work in public spaces such as hotel foyers, coffee shops, and organisational canteens. What is the impact on privacy and confidentiality in these situations? How do you introduce your client when someone you know enters and interrupts your meeting? Have you agreed in advance how you will introduce each other when you meet other individuals you already know? How will interruptions influence the coaching conversation?

Coaches and clients must establish, in their contract and working arrangement, how they will manage the boundaries of confidentiality. For example, some clients are happy to introduce you as their coach; others will not introduce you at all, and others will introduce you as a colleague. Furthermore, the coaching relationship is not as strict as the therapeutic relationship. For example, coaches can be invited to product launches, media presentations, business and social events with their clients. It is important to address the boundaries of these events with your clients. How will you be introduced and what behaviour and feedback is expected from you?

Honouring the client's agenda

Marti had a client a few years ago who was uncomfortable with being in the limelight and wanted to be coached on dealing with all the social and networking requirements of her new role. She invited Marti to join her at one of these events to observe her behaviour. Coach and client agreed that the coach would be introduced as a supplier, not as a coach. Marti played the role and to her surprise found herself introduced as "my coach". The client had changed her mind and was very comfortable with people knowing she had a coach. What is important is that only the client could make this choice, not the coach.

Part of a coach's code of ethics is to honour confidentiality in the coaching conversation. There will be a contracted agreement between client and coach about what is communicated to superiors in the working environment. This confidentiality must be agreed to and honoured at all times. The client entrusts the coach with confidences, and must feel safe to do so.

Confidentiality dilemma

A question around confidentiality issues that needs to be addressed is to what extent does the coach owe the organisation a confidential relationship, and take responsibility for the confidential boundaries defined in that relationship?

Coaches are consistently presented with confidential information about the company, its systems, processes, challenges and mistakes. For example, say you are working with a client organisation about which there is much controversy in the marketplace and in the media. An example could be an organisation responsible for media and communications, or for the supply of energy.

How do you handle information that, if passed on to the media, could expose your client's organisation? What happens if you mention this piece of information in passing to a colleague, breaking the bounds of confidentiality, and this colleague, without thinking, then shares it with a journalist friend who reports it in the media, thus exposing your client's organisation? What is your ethical responsibility in this instance? Should you confess your part? What bounds of confidentiality have you trespassed?

Firstly, in this instance, you have broken the bounds of confidentiality and are therefore in breach of contract with your client. Secondly, the person you spoke to who subsequently passed it on to the media, is in breach of confidentiality with you. However, there are no legal guidelines as coaching is only an emerging discipline. So, you have a problem. What should you do?

You may choose to speak honestly to your client, or your client organisation, to let them know it came from you. Furthermore, you will need to clear it with your colleague who passed it on. If there has been any damage done to the client organisation, you may face the consequences of your client losing trust in your services. It is for this reason that having indemnity insurance is critical in case the organisation takes up legal proceedings against you. The moral of the story is to keep all confidences to yourself at all times. Remember that it is hard for most human beings to resist gossip.

What are ethical concerns?

Think about some of the ethical concerns that you have encountered as a coach. Examples may include fraud, broken confidentiality, three-party dilemmas, having a sexual relationship with your client, or seemingly coaching someone out of a job. For example, what do you need to have in place in your contract to ensure that, if your client is involved in some kind of criminal activity, such as embezzling funds, theft or fraud of any kind, you are protected if the client confesses to their organisation and their organisation chooses to inform the legal authorities? If this is the case, and you knew about the illegal activity and did not report it to the organisation in question, the need for indemnity insurance may become an issue.

Other concerns centre on malpractice for coach practitioners. For example, what if a client organisation sues you for failure on your part as a coaching professional to render services as contracted?[7] How important is it to have insurance indemnity protection in a similar manner to clinical psychologists? Do you have an arbitration clause in your contract about what the procedures are if conflict or misunderstandings arise?

These seem like abstract issues that may not concern you at present. But, as coaching continues to grow as a discipline, there will be claims against practitioners who do not fulfil contracts as promised. As an emerging profession, there is currently no legislated protection for practitioners. This is one of the reasons for setting up professional bodies such as COMENSA, EMCC, ICF and WABC. These organisations do not necessarily provide indemnity insurance as they consider that to be the responsibility of the individual practitioners. However, they can help practitioners to think about which types of protection are needed for them to practice with confidence and security. This is one of the key benefits of creating ethical guidelines, in parallel with an ethics complaint process.

How can you manage your ethical dilemmas?

Which ethical dilemmas have arisen for you in your practice? It is useful in your supervision sessions to discuss, on a regular basis, any ethical issues that arise. Here are several dilemmas a coach can face:

1. **It is recognised that there are circumstances where the coach may have two "clients", the individual being coached and the organisation who may have commissioned the coaching.** How do you handle the giving of information to the senior manager and the organisation? What needs to be in a written contract, and what do you need to verbally agree with your individual client? We tend to ensure that the written contract specifies the bounds of confidentiality between all parties, with agreed terms for reporting back to the organisation. However, we also verbally contract with the individual client to ensure we are in agreement about how each of the coaching conversations will be held, and how we will handle written reports to the organisation. We believe that any written communication to the third party needs to be seen and agreed to by the individual client before it is passed on to the relevant senior authority.

2. **What if you coach your client out of a job, and they leave the organisation when under your coaching?** This may be a result of the client specifically asking you to coach them into a new job. Or, it may be that in developing self-awareness the client realises that the job in which they are currently positioned is no longer suitable to their intrinsic drivers, values and career aspirations. What is your responsibility to the organisation? Should you inform them? I experienced this recently. One of the senior executives I was coaching grew in self-awareness and decided to move out of

his current position in the organisation. There was no opportunity for him to do so within his current organisation for at least a year, and he was bored. The discussion came up in the coaching conversations, and client and coach discussed the ethical difficulty under which this placed both coach and client. We agreed we would continue to work on his developing self-awareness and possibilities for growth – but the coach would not help him to leave the organisation. The coach suggested that the client discuss his thinking with his line manager; he chose not to.

By contrast, Marti had a client where the client's boss, and therefore the representative of the company paying for the coaching, indicated that the client needed to figure out what they wanted – and if that meant that the client would leave the organisation then that would be acceptable.

3. **Should you coach all the members of one team including the team leader or line manager?** This question often arises in supervision. Is it ethical in terms of boundary management for you to coach a team leader and one or more of their direct reports? What needs to be put in place in your contract to manage confidentiality? You will be in a very privileged position of knowledge, and you may lose the trust of one or more individual clients by simply carrying an individual's closely guarded secrets in terms of aspirations, personal conflicts, self-doubts and self-esteem issues. Both Marti and I have experienced lead coaches divulging information about team members to the entire team. In one instance, this has led to the client organisation refusing to hire external coaches in the future.

4. **How do you honour confidentiality when coaching a senior manager and their boss?** Is it ethical, and if not why not? How can you manage the boundaries of confidentiality? A typical scenario is that you are in the process of coaching a senior executive in an organisation, and they recommend to their line manager that you would be suitable to coach them too. What are the issues of confidentiality that must be managed, and how do you go about it? Would it be useful to meet with both of them to discuss and agree the parameters, and what will, and will not, be disclosed to the organisation as a result of the coaching? Usually, we agree that all conversations remain confidential, and the only results shared are those of the professional development plan, i.e. vision, strategy, overall goals, obstacles to success and outcomes achieved. How can you ensure that individual clients are

satisfied that their confidentiality will be respected and all boundaries honoured?

5. **Do you have a policy about meeting with the individual executive and line manager together?** Have you contracted this in written form so that it is open and transparent to the organisation (i.e. HR, OD or line management)? Most importantly, how do you manage the issue of confidentiality if you meet the line manager without the individual client? And, how do you manage confidentiality when the line manager, coach and individual client all meet together for the regular intermittent session? In our work, we often agree to meet several times during the contracted intervention period to align overall objectives on the part of individual client, line manager and the organisation. How should you facilitate that session, and what are the parameters of what you can disclose to the line manager? We usually plan the session with the individual client, asking the client for their objectives of the meeting, and what is appropriate to be shared during the session. Once all three parties are together, the individual client facilitates the session, and brings into the conversation the overall objectives of the line manager for that session. What is important to be discussed, and what are the organisation's expectations of both the coach and individual client for the duration of the coaching intervention?

6. **Ethical questions regarding a sexual relationship with a client.** In the field of psychology worldwide, this is strictly legislated against. However, in the fields of coaching and mentoring it is not necessarily defined as a part of ethical boundary management. It is important to understand what the professional conduct guidelines are for the professional body of which you are a member, and to be sure you understand the ethical conduct review process if it arises as an issue. It is essential to find out what the client's organisational policy is for colleagues/consultants working together, and many organisations have specified that it is or is not policy. The questions that arise are due to the consequences of such a relationship occurring. What are the implications for the success of the coach/client relationship, and how do the intimate boundaries created in a sexual encounter impact on the professional boundaries of coach/client? As a coach is always looking out for the client, a key question would be what the consequences for the individual would be if such a relationship occurs.

7. **Interference from the leading executive in the coaching intervention.** This is an

interesting situation. An executive can readily see the benefits of coaching, and introduces coaching into their department. On perceiving the impact that they could achieve on bottom-line results, this leader instructs the coaching supervisor to direct the team of coaches to work on specific business outcomes. However, this type of goal setting was not made explicit or agreed at the outset of the coaching intervention, or during the contracting process. The question is how coaches should manage the pressure of organisational demands from the sponsoring executive and yet confidentially hold the individual client's needs.

The complexity of supervision and ethics

It is critical that the coach develops self-awareness with the ability to self-regulate. Awareness of the ethical situations that arise is a first step; the second step is to manage them. Without self-awareness, integrity and the ability to manage complexity, ethical decisions may prove difficult or even remain in the unconscious. Personal lives, careers and organisations are often at stake and there is a high moral responsibility in this interpersonal journey. Bonds of trust, openness, fragility and honesty are developed at high levels and these need to remain honoured and deeply respected.

Supervision serves both the coach and their client, while also providing a place for learning. Supervision is a complex process, and in addition to the demanding aspect of this discipline, it needs to be in the hands of an experienced practitioner (Bluckert, 2008). The supervisor may be supervising a team of coaches, and as such would have to be able to hold multiple perspectives and processes in consciousness, and would therefore require a framework that would support this complexity.

Part of the complexity in executive coaching is its multiple triangular relationships. In business, coaches often work with an individual client, as well as other members of a board or team. This raises boundary and ethical questions as well as issues around managing psychological and systemic processes.

The organisation itself becomes a third party (the first triangle) – which forms a very powerful third force that can pull a coach into an enactment. The supervisory relationship is yet another triangle (the second triangle) that has to be negotiated, but one that can be extremely useful in highlighting parallel processes, i.e. what happens in the supervision relationship may mirror a pattern that is prevalent in the organisation or other individual relationships (Pampallis Paisley, 2006:26–27).

Supervisors contain and hold the stories told by the coach, the executive and the organisation. Adherence to the highest levels of existing professional codes is paramount.

Developing a professional body for practitioners

One of the wider issues that became apparent during my doctoral research project (2002–2006), was the vital matter of ethics. When I commenced my doctorate, there was no accepted professional body in South Africa to represent or regulate the emerging disciplines of coaching and mentoring. This clearly led to the possibility, especially with a relatively new profession, of the abuse of standards and exploitation by opportunistic practitioners.

A core group of committed practitioners spearheaded and founded a professional body to discuss the creation of standards of competence, ethical guidelines and a recommended supervision framework, along with suggestions for the continuing professional development (CPD) of all practitioners. COMENSA has recognised the need to develop at the same pace as the disciplines of coaching and mentoring in South Africa. However, the body is creating organic frameworks for practice as needs arise, while remaining in alignment with international standards.

In other developing and underdeveloped countries there is a call for the founding of a professional body, for networking purposes and for creating a committed body of practitioners who can work together collaboratively to build the profession. In South Africa, COMENSA sought help from the European Mentoring and Coaching Council (EMCC) and the Worldwide Association of Business Coaches (WABC). Both continue to respond very generously. However, if a relatively developed country such as South Africa needed such help, COMENSA may have a role to play assisting sister professional bodies as they grow. The Global Convention on Coaching (now the Global Community of Coaches or GCC) has acknowledged that, in the interest of the reputation of the coaching profession internationally, established bodies need to work together more proactively to promote the values and ethics of the coaching profession.[8]

Because COMENSA was mentored throughout their process, it may be helpful for the organisation to think about how to play a mentoring role to assist other African countries, where coaches may be operating in a similar vacuum and might benefit from their experience and expertise.

GCC Working Group on Developing a Code of Ethics

From July 2007 to July 2008, the role of the Global Convention on Coaching (GCC) was one of worldwide collaboration to bring the best thinking of coach practitioners and researchers together. At the end of the week-long convention in July 2008, the Working Group on Ethics published a statement. They stated that in their year-long dialogue it had become evident that a strong Code of Ethics is of paramount importance, and they believe that a Code of Ethics underpins the emergence of coaching as a profession – i.e., its status, education and development, and core competences. They stated that they believed a strong Code would help to sustain the profession, and that it is evident that such a Code needs accountability mechanisms.

Their aspiration was that there will ultimately be a Universal Code of Ethics with regional tribunals made up of stakeholder representatives. The Code will be made up of the common features across the six available codes we have today (International Coach Federation, European Mentoring and Coaching Council, Worldwide Association of Business Coaches, Association for Coaching, Coaches and Mentors of South Africa, and European Coaching Institute). The Working Group on Ethics invited further contribution from parties not represented at the convention, making it clear that local codes will have their own accountability mechanisms. They envisioned it will be accompanied by a set of practical guidelines and tools to support ethical decision-making and practice (GCC, 2008b).

Extending the social range of coaching

The GCC has made an effort to take into account the cultural worldviews of the various nations which have taken part in the global dialogue. This is important in South Africa where the principles of empowerment and transformation influence the particular social and historical conditions of the country. Many practitioners' clients reflect the diverse facets of the South African community. As currently practiced, however, coaching is usually a top-level management or corporate activity. In the specific historical realities of South Africa, this often still means that previously privileged executives are the ones who chiefly benefit from the great riches that coaching has to offer. The irony is that many who would equally benefit are working in the same corporations, but are "previously disadvantaged" (i.e. black or mixed-race men and women who suffered under apartheid), and do not qualify for coaching within their organisations, as they are not yet employed in sufficiently senior executive positions. With coaching, they might be.

Extending the reach of coaching

One of my female senior executive clients, Miriam, would not normally have had the luxury of a coaching experience had we not agreed to a collaborative *pro bono* coaching relationship. Miriam's work in developing "previously disadvantaged" women highlights, for me, the fact that not only was my client a prime candidate for executive coaching, but other managers in her non-governmental organisation (NGO) would have gained immeasurably from such an experience. Sadly, the view of coaching is often that of an expensive "luxury" far beyond the financial parameters of the institution. This is an ethical dilemma in South Africa, which has been raised within COMENSA, but has yet to be resolved. Most practitioner coaches are keen to ensure that the coaching profession in South Africa does not appear "elitist" and exclusive. This dilemma may or may not apply, to a greater or lesser extent, in other countries, but could be something worth considering by other professional bodies.

The requirement for diversity could impact on the education of coach and mentor practitioners, looking at their gender and background. In the interests of being fully representative – particularly in South Africa – it is important that all facets of society be encouraged to join the coaching profession, to make it truly reflective of the community within which it works. For example, COMENSA has already begun to consider these important social issues. Steps are being taken by several COMENSA member coach training institutions to provide a system of learning and mentoring for coaches from disadvantaged backgrounds to ensure that the emerging profession becomes inclusive rather than exclusive. The creation and maintenance of this body is an important initiative which will have a long-lasting impact and influence on coaching and mentoring in South Africa.

The variety of perspectives and cultures in South Africa, in particular, calls for a high level of sensitivity and awareness from coaches. One place to develop and refine this consciousness is in supervision.

MODELS OF SUPERVISION

There are many different models of supervision, but one of the most common models used today is the Seven-Eyed Model of Supervision. This framework is used in the supervision of coach and mentor practitioners, and in other helping professions. The model was developed by Peter Hawkins and Robin Shohet (2000). The seven modes of supervision are (Mike the Mentor, 2008a):

1. **The Client System**: The focus is on the coachee situation; the problem the coachee wants help with, how they represent the issues and the choices that they are making.

2. **The Coach's Interventions**: The focus is on the interventions the coach made, how and why they made them, and what else they might have done.

3. **The Relationship between the Coach and the Client**: The focus is on neither the coach nor the client but on the conscious and unconscious interactions between the two of them so that the coach develops a better understanding of the dynamics of the coaching relationship.

4. **The Coach**: The focus is on the coach's own experience as an instrument for registering what is happening beneath the coachee system.

5. **The Parallel Process**: The focus is on what the coach has absorbed from the client system and how it may be playing out in the relationship between the coach and supervisor.

6. **The Coaching Supervisor's Self-reflection**: The focus is the supervisor's "here and now" experience with the coach and how this can be used to shed light on the coach/client relationship.

7. **The Wider Context**: The focus is on the wider organisational, social, cultural, ethical, and contractual context within which the supervision is taking place.

The seven modes of supervision are illustrated in Figure 1.

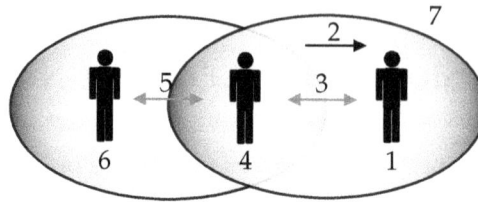

Figure 1: The Seven-Eyed Model of Supervision

Source: Mike the Mentor (2008a)

To Practise the Seven-Eyed Model of Supervision[9]

1. **Focus on the coach/client situation**. The practitioner identifies their problem or challenge, focusing on what actually happened in their sessions with clients, how the clients presented themselves, what was discussed, and any connections between issues.

2. **Explore the coach's interventions with the client.** The supervisor focuses on the interventions made, the coach's rationale, and helps in developing alternative strategies for interventions, and examines consequences now and for the future.

3. **Explore the relationship between coach and client.** The supervisor focuses on the dynamic between coach and client, at both a conscious and unconscious level. This step in the process can assist the coach to understand the deeper, underlying processes which could affect the outcome of the coach/client intervention. The aim of this mode is to help the coach gain greater insight and understanding of the dynamics of their relationships with clients.

4. **Focus on the coach practitioner's experience**. The aim of this step is to increase the capacity of the coach to engage with clients effectively. This offers the opportunity to develop self-awareness, deepening the learning about how to deal with conscious and less conscious assumptions and behaviours.

5. **Focus on the supervision relationship**. This is a parallel process to the coach/client relationship. This part of the discussion offers valuable perspective as to the dynamics

present between coach/client that is played out in the supervisor/practitioner relationship. This process focuses on what is happening in the relationship between the supervisor and the coach and explores how it is playing out or paralleling the coach/client relationship.

6. **The supervisor self-reflects**. The supervisor observes and notes what they are experiencing in the supervision sessions. The aim of this step is for the supervisor to use their responses to provide another source of information to the coach. This is a very similar process to clinical psychology supervision.

7. **Focus on the bigger picture or wider context**. The supervisor and practitioner/s reflect on the wider client and organisational context. This brings in the ethical, cultural, systemic, organisational and social aspects of the coaching intervention. The aim of Step 7 is to observe and understand the wider context to build capacity on the part of the practitioner.

Individual supervision

My model of individual and group supervision (Figure 2) is a précised version of the Seven-Eyed Model summarised above (although I also place it on a background of four quadrants with reflection on the UL; practice on the UR; and Observation split between LL and LR). Working with an individual practitioner, I will ask the practitioner for their reflections on the challenges currently facing them. Supervisor and coachee/s prioritise the issues to discuss, and work on one at a time. The supervisor leads the session in a coaching manner, by facilitating thinking on the part of the practitioner rather than thinking for them. However, the supervisor may share their observations and experience. The supervisor is helping the practitioner reflect on the content of a coaching session, as well as on their own internal dialogue and their response to the client. The supervisor will ask the practitioner to explain their processes and other interventions that might be useful or appropriate. The practitioner is adopting a meta position, looking at the coaching session in question from first, second and third positions; in NLP terms, this would be third-position thinking. In psychotherapeutic terms, the practitioner would be identifying any transference from the client. In third-position thinking, the practitioner can see themselves in miniature as if looking down from a corner of the ceiling. This reflective practice helps to develop self-awareness.

In the practice part of the session, the practitioner may coach the supervisor, with feedback from the supervisor at the end. At the end of this, the supervisor and practitioner move back into a reflective space to develop self-awareness, and identify what went well in terms of content, process and any parallel processes that might have been happening. It is important here for the supervisor to be aware of their own internal process; the supervisor is modelling coaching and self-awareness with the practitioner.

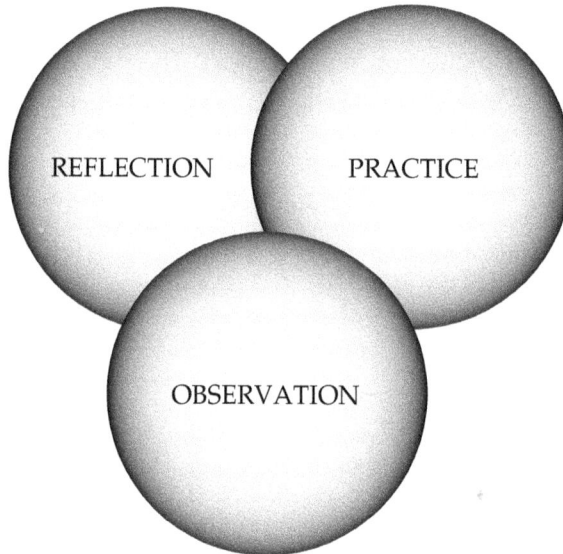

Figure 2: Sunny's supervision model

In terms of observation, the practitioner notices the learning gained overall from the session and any changes needed to their overall practice. Any steps for action or reflection are noted and the next session booked. Observation is about the wider context. How does the learning from this session impact on the overall coaching intervention with the client, and the overall coaching style of the practitioner? The supervisor needs to help the practitioner refer back to the context in which the coach, supervisor and client organisation are working together, as well as the wider context of the practitioner's developing competence and capacity within their profession.

Group supervision

Reflection

With group supervision the facilitator begins a "round" asking a set of questions and hearing from each individual. Sample questions could be, "What's working for you in your coaching practice?" and "Which issues or dilemmas do you wish to work on today?" The facilitator elicits all challenges and issues and then breaks the group into pairs/triads. The pairs/triads select several issues to reflect on, creating strategies or recommendations for managing each issue. The group meets again in plenary and the facilitator takes thoughts and recommendations from each pair/triad. The issues that can be addressed in a reflective discussion are either answered here, or saved until the end of the supervision session.

Practice

The group prioritises the issues and challenges that have been raised in the reflective session. A few practitioners volunteer to take part in a supervision demo. The lead coach, or supervisor, supervises a coaching conversation with the volunteer practitioner and coachee. The rest of the group gather round in a circle and observe, quietly taking notes. If necessary, the lead supervisor takes time out to speak to the group as part of the teaching.

Observation

At the end of the supervision demo, the facilitator solicits thoughts, observations and questions from the volunteer coach and coachee and the group, and facilitates a discussion on the questions raised. The group shares their learning from the session overall in a final round. If there has been no demo, but simply plenary rounds and thinking pairs/triads, the facilitator facilitates a discussion of learning gained from the session.

Supervision as a form of empowerment

In supervision, there is the cultural context of the organisation and society as a whole to be aware of. Traditional models of supervision have been developed in Western consumer cultures, and more particularly in academic environments. These environments do not necessarily share the same assumptions as the developing profession of coaching or the developing culture of a country such as South Africa. We have discussed culture and diversity at length in Chapter 6 and the supervisor needs to be aware of the capacity and limitations of the practitioners under their supervision.

Coaching and mentoring are fundamentally about empowering people, resulting in their ability to think through their challenges and issues successfully. This point is particularly crucial in the South African context. In the past, politically dominant groups did the thinking for the non-dominant groups, and the negative impact of this should not be underestimated. In a very real sense, therefore, the role of supervision is to help empower the coach practitioner to think through all the perspectives that can impact on client issues and dilemmas. Supervision can be seen as both an empowerment tool as well as a commitment to best practice.

Developing a professional approach

The need to educate coaching supervisors, practitioners and managers in understanding the need for supervision is critical. The supervision relationship is a complex one, and the benefits from supervision are exponential for practitioners and client organisations. Developing an inter-professional approach is a sound one. Coaching can learn from the other helping professions until more research is undertaken – not just in the South African marketplace, but worldwide. Whichever supervision model is worked with in the coaching context, it is important to develop a number of highly skilled supervisors who can help practitioners to work with greater knowledge, depth, skills and competence.

Contracting, supervision and ethical conduct are not new concepts. They have been practised in the helping professions for decades. However, they are not yet regulated and require understanding at all stages of development for practitioners. We have looked at each of the roles and functions of these three key areas and, although there are as yet no internationally agreed guidelines on the regulation of supervision, ethics and contracting, all of the professional bodies worldwide in alignment with the Global Coaching Community (GCC) are assessing and establishing what frameworks need to be in place for their member practitioners. Ultimately, these processes will benefit and protect coach and client. The development of professional supervision, contracting and ethical codes is emerging as a vital function within the discipline of coaching.

COACH'S LIBRARY

Coaches and Mentors of South Africa (COMENSA). (2010). *Coach/Mentor Supervision Policy*. Available at: www.comensa.org.za.

Coaches and Mentors of South Africa (COMENSA). (2009). *Revised Code of Ethics*. Draft policy. Available at: www.comensa.org.za.

European Mentoring and Coaching Council (EMCC) email: info@emcccouncil.org; web: www.emcccouncil.org.

Grayson, D. and Larson, K. (2000). How to make the most of the coaching relationship. In M. Goldsmith, L. Lyons and A. Freas (eds). *Coaching for leadership: How the world's greatest coaches help leaders learn*. San Francisco, CA: Jossey-Bass/Pfeiffer.

Hawkins, P. and Shohet, R. (2000). *Supervision in the helping professions*. Buckingham, United Kingdom: Open University Press.

ICF (2008b). *ICF ethical guidelines*. Available at: www.coachfederation.org/ICF/For+Current+ Members/Ethical+Guidelines/.

Jarvis, J. (2004). *Coaching and buying coaching services: A guide*. London: CIPD.

Jones, R. and Jenkins, F. (eds). (2006). *Developing the allied health professions*. Oxford: Radcliffe.

Kadushin, A. (1976). *Supervision in social work*. New York, NY: Columbia University Press.

Noer, D. (2000). The big three derailment factors in a coaching relationship. In M. Goldsmith, L. Lyons and A Freas (eds). *Coaching for leadership: How the world's greatest coaches help leaders learn*. San Francisco, CA: Jossey-Bass/Pfeiffer.

Peltier, B. (2001). *The psychology of executive coaching: Theory and application*. New York, NY: Brunner-Routledge.

Steere, J. (1984). *Ethics in clinical psychology*. Cape Town: Oxford University Press.

Worldwide Association of Business Coaches (WABC). (2008a). *Code of Conduct*. Available at: www.wabccoaches.com.

Whitworth, L., Kimsey-House, H. and Sandahl, P. (1998). *Co-active coaching: New skills for coaching people toward success in work and life*. Palo Alto, CA: Davies-Black.

ENDNOTES TO CHAPTER 9

1. This author has changed "gains" to "behaviours".

2. Current doctoral research available in South Africa was produced by Dr Paddy Pampallis Paisley, and is available from Middlesex University London. An abstract can be accessed from the COMENSA website at www.comensa.org.za.

3. COMENSA's (2009) *Revised Code of Ethics* is available on the website: www.comensa.org.za.

4. The WABC Code of Business Coaching Ethics and Integrity includes their Business Coaching Philosophy, Principles and Safe Harbor Consultation and Adjudication Process. The WABC recommend their code as the most advanced for coaching practitioners today (www.wabccoaches.com).

5. European Mentoring and Coaching Council (EMCC) email: info@emcccouncil.org; web: www.emccouncil.org.

6. The ICF's (2008b) *ICF Ethical Guidelines* are available on their website: www.coachfederation.org/ICF/For+Current+Members/ Ethical+Guidelines/.

7. Malpractice is defined as "failure of a professional person to render proper services through reprehensible ignorance of negligence or through criminal intent, esp. when injury or loss follows; or any improper negligent practice; misconduct or misuse". Indemnity is protection or security against damage or loss, or compensation for damage or loss sustained (Webster's Encyclopedic Unabridged Dictionary of the English Language, 1989).

8. The Global Convention on Coaching (GCC) was established to create a collaborative framework of stakeholders in coaching. The aim was to professionalise the industry. Nine working groups were established by the GCC's Steering Committee to discuss critical issues related to the professionalisation of coaching. All nine groups produced "white papers" across a 12-month working period (July 2007–July 2008) on the current realities and possible future scenarios of each area. These papers were presented in Dublin from 7–11 July 2008 at the GCC Convention. A tenth group, Coaching and Society was added just prior to the July 2008 convention. Regional conferences are now held on an annual basis around the world.

9. The Double Matrix or Eight-Eyed Supervisor Model: This is an adaptation of Hawkins and Shohet's seven-eyed supervision process model from the counselling and psychotherapy professions (Jones and Jenkins, 2006:30):

    i.   reflection on the content of the therapy session;

    ii. exploration of the strategies and interventions used by the therapist;

    iii. exploration of the therapy process and relationship;

    iv. focus on the therapy process as it is reflected in the supervision process;

    v.   focus on the supervisee's transference;

    vi. focus on the here-and-now process as a mirror or parallel of the there-and-then process;

    vii. focus on the supervisor's counter transference; and

    viii. focus on the wider context.

10

Developing a Body of Knowledge – Coaching Research

One of the emerging disciplines in coaching is research. Another way to describe it is "ongoing critical appraisal" of your own coaching practice. In this chapter, we discuss the current global thinking in terms of coaching research, stressing the importance of writing up your findings as you work within the business environment. This requires more than just being coached yourself and participation in supervision.

The work of the Working Group on a Research Agenda at the Global Convention on Coaching (GCC) in Dublin, July 2008, defined research as "the life blood of practice. It feeds our continuing development and brings fresh perspectives to our work. It can be the place to visit in our dilemmas and in our successes. In valuing research we are valuing our work, as one is the exploration of the other. Engagement in that exploration sustains our practice and fuels our own development" (GCC, 2008d).

Chapter outline

- What is research?
  - What motivates research?
  - What research is available?
  - Building your knowledge base
- Developing a new model of research
- An emerging profession
- The need for collaboration
- Coach's library
- Endnotes to Chapter 10

WHAT IS RESEARCH?

Research can be defined, in the traditional sense, as an academic investigation into the origins and developments of a given subject. However, it is not just academic research that is needed at this critical stage of the emerging profession of coaching. We are looking to encourage practitioner research, defining it as "specific critical reflection and evaluation" of your given practice.

The GCC defines research as "a 'search' for new knowledge and understanding, which can be undertaken in many different ways and from many perspectives. It becomes a continuum which includes individual critical reflective practice and goes through to distinct projects undertaken as teams" (GCC, 2008d).

A very new approach is to consider all practitioner coaches as potential contributors to the emerging body of knowledge in the local and global coaching community. This requires three specific sets of skills on the part of practitioners: a critical reading of research, an application of research to practice, and the capacity and ability to generate research. This should not in any way reduce the need or the requirement for quality. A body of knowledge has to be sustainable. At present, as is acknowledged by the GCC, academics and practitioners are responsible for both good and bad research.

What motivates research?

Organisations buying coaching services today are well informed about the business coaching process and the value of coaching for their executives and their business overall. They are asking for measurable results, as well as the evidence base that underpins coaching, and the qualifications and experience of the coaches they employ. Many large organisations have begun assessment interviews to develop a bespoke bank of external coaches, and are looking to educate their internal coaches in quality coach training programmes with the appropriate credentials.

Although it is believed that coaching provides a positive intervention in building executive and management capability, there is very little empirical research into how the coaching relationship builds executive aptitude and impacts business positively. One reason for this lack of empirical research is that it has proved difficult to use longitudinal designs and control groups when evaluating coaching interventions. Rigorous evaluation historically is through randomised controlled trials (Grant and Cavanagh, 2007a). A second reason is that coaching is not yet a defined profession with regulated requirements for professional coaches.

Two other difficulties are that research often needs substantial funding and is not necessarily the domain of the newly "skilled" coach practitioner. The Working Group on a Research Agenda for the Global Convention on Coaching (GCC) has recommended that all coach training programmes internationally offer a basic module in research methodology and application. Other possibilities to build a body of knowledge are either for the supervision process to create a foundation for research into practice, or for a coach practitioner to work in conjunction with an academic student who is looking for a project. This idea is sound, particularly if your practice forms part of a coaching services business involved in large coaching interventions, and if you are interested in providing some kind of qualitative or quantitative benchmarking for your clients.

It has been previously assumed that coaches are scientist-practitioners, conducting research that ultimately informs and enhances their own practice. Another term applied to coach practitioners who critically appraise their own practice is that of the "scholar practitioner", i.e. someone who is a student of their own practice. However, research is expensive, and most coach practitioners are neither critically reflective of their own practice, nor do they research the outcomes of their coaching interventions. Research is needed to show a range of results: from the coaching process, to the skills and competence of the coach, the results of coach supervision, how organisations benefit from supervision, and the overall outcomes of coaching for the individual executive and the business.

Another possibility is to work collaboratively with other coach practitioners. This could be called a "partnership" model in which both full-time researchers and full-time practitioners work together, bringing their respective strengths to the research process (Green, cited in GCC, 2008c). However, partnership needs management. I recently spoke to a South African doctoral student at the University of South Africa (UNISA) who hopes to investigate core coaching competences being used by South African coaches. However, he has found it difficult to access coaches who are prepared to take part in such a research project. Although we cannot all spend time facilitating enquiry or research into our practice, it is crucial that we either facilitate or participate in building a body of knowledge for our discipline through critical reflection on our own coaching processes.

What research is available?

A major question today: what is the value of existing coaching research – particularly as there is no one existing database of research? Although a substantial body of coaching literature has emerged in the last few years, there are only a few academic coaching journals currently published, including a new Harvard coaching journal, *Coaching: An International Journal of Theory, Research and Practice*. The *International Journal of Evidence-Based Coaching and Mentoring* was established in August 2003, and the *International Coaching Psychology Review* in April 2006.

Fillery-Travis and Lane (2006b) argue that those who wish to research whether coaching works are in fact asking the wrong question. Their argument is that we first need to determine how coaching is being used and within which framework and only then can we analyse what is working. According to Baek-Kyoo (2005), "executive coaching has become increasingly popular despite limited empirical evidence about its impact and wide disagreement about necessary or desired professional qualifications".

In the last few years, there have been a number of business coaching, non-executive coaching, and life coaching studies. We list a variety of sources at the end of this chapter, including the compilation of research papers gathered by the GCC Research Agenda Working Group during their 2007/8 dialogue and current research through the Institute of Coaching at Harvard/McLean Medical School.

Building your knowledge base

A major reason to encourage practitioners to critically reflect and appraise their own practice, either in supervision, in partnership with other practitioner coaches or through academic research, is due to the need to build the knowledge base for coaching. A current definition of the knowledge base for coaching is that of competent practice, where competence drives the discipline and the knowledge base grows through the application of defined competences. In Chapter 7, we explored the competences required by various professional coaching bodies, and the GCC has recommended that a foundation of core competence be researched and accepted internationally in the near future.

However, if in future coaching is to emerge as a profession, key requirements include "identifiable and distinct skills; education and training to acquire proficiency; recognition outside the community as a profession; a code of ethics; public service by coaches; a formalised organisation; evaluation of credentials and self-regulation; an established community of practitioners for networking and exchange of ideas; public recognition that coaching is a profession", and finally: "a coaching practice grounded in theoretical and factual research and knowledge" (Bennett, 2006:241–2).

In coaching, the knowledge base is multi-disciplinary, yet the field is undefined.[1] At the moment, it is driven by market forces, the momentum of its practitioners, and the different learning contexts for practitioners and commercial innovation. There is a growing interest in evidence-based and peer-reviewed coaching journals. This includes demands from clients to measure the return on coaching investment (ROI), with tangible proof of rigour and credibility in coaching as a developmental tool for business. More and more books are being written about coaching, and coach education programmes have a growing foundation in universities. The downside is that practitioners need money for research projects, and are not necessarily skilled in the rigour and techniques of research.

There is a gulf between practitioners with and without academic know-how who have the rigour to initiate practitioner research or to facilitate evidence-based work. Even so, what does the accumulation of evidence mean for the coaches themselves? Will they actually apply the findings of current research to their own practice, and crucially, how can they apply new findings if they themselves are not rigorously and critically reflecting on their own practice?

The majority of coaches are not necessarily trained in psychological science whose foundation of practice is its established knowledge base (Grant and Cavanagh, 2007a:241). Instead, coach practitioners tend to be trained in proprietary models with an unproven evidence base. Hence, the growing divide between psychologists and coaches not trained in psychological practice. In parallel with the Human Potential Movement (HPM) of the 1960s and 70s, there is a strain of "anti-intellectualism" within the coaching community globally that reflects a strong desire among some "to liberate themselves from the bonds of socio-political systems that stifled individuality including science" (Spence, 2007b:259).

As a result, and particularly in South Africa, many coach practitioners do not see the value in researching evidence or outcomes from their practice. The consequence of this move could be towards a fashionable human development industry which is resistant to any mandatory professional training or accreditation. This may eventually result in the loss of freedom, so greatly sought after, due to inevitable future regulation and market demands. One of the emerging themes of the GCC was the need for coaching to regulate itself before someone else does, creating guidelines in ethics, supervision, core competences, and a research agenda in order to move coaching practice towards a robust, self-regulated, evidence-based, multi-cultural discipline.

DEVELOPING A NEW MODEL OF RESEARCH

One of our recommendations is for coach practitioners to think about how they reflect on their practice, assessing and evaluating their skills and competence through supervision. One of the discussion points at the GCC was the potential for supervision to be a place for research and critical enquiry into practice. We recommend that coach practitioners begin to write up and publish case studies on their findings, but from a reflective and critical place of appraisal. The thinking that emerged from the GCC recommends that value be given to practitioner enquiry into practice as well as the high value given to academic and psychological research.

One possibility for non-academic coaching research could be from a supervision point of view. According to COMENSA, "Supervision offers a context in which practitioners can develop professionally – to re-construct their experience, to reflect, to understand, to design their professional reality, and to develop new responses for future practice." (COMENSA, 2010:1).

Today, there is no widely recognised "non-academic" model of research for coach practitioners, which means doing a little "research" yourself to find e-zines, professional magazines, journals, and other media which will publish your findings. This is not about positioning or promoting your practice commercially. It is more about writing up discoveries, dilemmas and complexities to contribute to the growing body of knowledge for business coaching. The partnership model, working with a scholar or academic who will help you to research and write up your findings, is worth considering.

However, these suggestions may continue to be difficult until a new model for practitioner research is designed and tested. The author, in alignment with the GCC, recommends the development of a new model for coaching research that is "multi-disciplinary, multi-methodological and multi-cultural" (GCC, 2008d).

AN EMERGING PROFESSION

Throughout this book, we have spoken about what is required for coaching to be recognised as a regulated discipline or profession. Grant and Cavanagh (2006:3) have indicated that one requirement is that it should be done through peer-reviewed and accepted research. Spence concluded that the accepted foundation of a profession includes a requirement for members to have formal academic qualifications, that they adhere to an enforceable code of ethics, that licensed practice is only granted to qualified members, that members comply with applicable state-sanctioned regulation, underpinned by a common body of knowledge and skills (Spence, 2007b:261).

There is at present a gap between the criteria needed to develop a profession, and the current reality of coaching internationally. This gap presents a challenge to professional coaching bodies for several reasons. First, there is uncertainty about the role played by psychology in the development of the coaching profession. Spence (2007b:263) suggests, "psychologists have a unique role to play in securing the future of coaching and helping to establish it as a respected and credible sub-discipline of psychology". This point of view will never be popular with many practising coaches, and needs to be resolved in the current climate. What is greatly needed is for coaching-related research to be carried out "in order better to understand and refine the coaching process and hence coaching outcomes" (Linley, 2006:1).

THE INSTITUTE OF COACHING AT
HARVARD/MCLEAN MEDICAL SCHOOL

In September 2008, a group of 40 internationally recognised coaching researchers, professionals and other coaching stakeholders came together in a historic meeting at Harvard. The International Coaching Research Forum (ICRF) had very specific aims. First of all, to promote the field of coaching research worldwide by creating 100 coaching research proposals that could be disseminated to all coaching practitioners, academics and organisations; secondly, to foster coaching research on a global scale to collaboratively advance this emerging profession.

While by no means inclusive, the ICRF participants met together with a third goal: to build coaching research networks which would support coaching research at all levels. These individuals, who are considered to be at the forefront of academic coaching research and professional coaching practice, came from seven different countries. Collectively they publish books and peer-reviewed journal articles on coaching and coaching-related topics; teach at academic and practitioner level; and work to facilitate positive change coaching professional clients and their teams.

A final aim was to communicate the message that practitioner and academic research is one of the primary ways to advance coaching as an evidence-based discipline, and to signpost that coaching is a powerful incentive to create positive change for both individuals and society. The document produced at the forum is available on the website of the Institute of Coaching at Harvard/McLean Medical School (www.instituteofcoaching.org) and on the ICRF site (www.coachingresearchforum.org).

You can access the 100 coaching-related research proposals which the forum hopes will prompt new coaching research at all levels of practitioner and academic coaching worldwide. The ICRF was sponsored by The Foundation of Coaching, and the subsequent Institute of Coaching at Harvard/McLean Medical School. The Institute of Coaching is committed to sponsoring executive and life coaching research through their grant process to encourage the advancement of the field.

Key themes that emerged at the ICRF which are as important to coaching research are in: coaching specialities; modalities and process; outcomes and methodology; business coaching, politics, ethics and governance; training, development, and knowledge base; theoretical frameworks; definitions of coaching; coaching skills and core competences; coaching and society; and core diversity issues. One of the key questions to emerge from the ICRF for further consideration was how to most effectively mobilise and coordinate coaching research resources within each country and internationally.

The Institute of Coaching at Harvard/McLean Medical School will also engage with other bodies including the GCC as it promotes research in important areas such as coach training, education and development; theoretical frameworks; selection of potential coaches; coaching sustainability; health and wellness; executive leadership coaching; and methodologies for coaching research.

THE NEED FOR COLLABORATION

In this chapter, we have sought to broaden the definition of research, and have identified possible contributing roles for coach practitioners, academic researchers and coaching psychologists. To cultivate the sustainability of practice through a growing body of knowledge, we believe that collaboration provides a dynamic and realistic way forward, meeting the needs of all coaching stakeholders.

A growing knowledge base is critical for the mature establishment of coaching. We believe that every practitioner has the responsibility to research their own practice. Unusually, the GCC recommends that practitioner and academic research be considered of equal value, and that education in research be included in all coach education programmes at an appropriate developmental level. We believe that research is the vital component to grow the coaching profession. If it was a core competence for practitioner education, it would ensure the sustainability of coaching, whether or not coaching emerges as a defined profession.

COACH'S LIBRARY

Baek-Kyoo, B. (2005). Executive coaching: a conceptual framework from an integrative review of practice and research. *Human Resource Development Review*, 4:462–488.

Carter, A., Wolfe, H. and Kerrin, M. (2005). Employers and coaching evaluation. *International Journal of Coaching in Organizations*, 3(4):63–72.

Dagley, G. (2006). Human resources professionals' perceptions of executive coaching: Efficacy benefits and return on investment. *International Coaching Psychology Review*, 1(2):34–45.

Feldman, D.C. and Lankau, M.J. (2005). Executive coaching: A review and agenda for future research. *Journal of Management*, 31(6):829–848.

Fillery-Travis, A. and Lane, D. (2006b). Does coaching work, or are we asking the wrong question? *International Coaching Psychology Review*, 1:23–36.

Laske, O.E. (2004). Can evidence-based coaching increase ROI? *International Journal of Evidence-Based Coaching and Mentoring*, 2(2):41–53.

Lawton-Smith, C. and Cox, E. (2007). Coaching: Is it just a new name for training? *International Journal of Evidence-Based Coaching and Mentoring*, Special issue.

Mackie, D. (2007). Evaluating the effectiveness of executive coaching: Where are we now and where do we need to be? *Australian Psychologist*, 42(4):310–318.

Stout-Rostron, S. (2011). How is coaching impacting systemic and cultural change within organisations? *International Journal of Coaching in Organisations*.

Thach, E.C. (2002). The impact of executive coaching and 360 feedback on leadership effectiveness. *Leadership and Organization Development Journal*, 23(4):205–214.

Papers consulted by the GCC Research Working Group

Bennett, J.L. (2006). An agenda for coaching-related research: A challenge for researchers. *Coaching Psychology Journal: Practice and Research*, 58:(4):240–249.

Cox, E. (2007). *Collaborative dialogue on the research agenda for coaching.* Proceedings of a meeting of the Oxford Brookes Coaching and Mentoring Society on 14 December 2007. Mimeo.

Fillery-Travis, A. (2007). *Where's the evidence? First steps into the literature.* Mimeo.

Fillery-Travis, A. (2008). *Current state of knowledge production in the United Kingdom.* Mimeo.

Fillery-Travis, A. and Lane, D. (2006a). How to develop your research interests, in S. Palmer and R. Bor (eds). *The practitioner's handbook: A guide for counsellors, psychotherapists and counselling psychologists.* London: Sage.

Grant, A.M. (2003a). The impact of life coaching on goal attainment, metacognition and mental health. *Social Behaviour and Personality*, 31:253–264.

Grant, A.M. (2003b). *Keeping up with the cheese! Research as a foundation for professional coaching of the future*. Keynote presentation to the International Coach Federation Conference Symposium on Research and Coaching, Denver, CO, November.

Grant, A.M. and Cavanagh, M.J. (2007a). Evidence-based coaching: Flourishing or languishing? *Australian Psychologist*, 42(4):239–254.

Lane, D.A. and Corrie, S. (2006). *The modern scientist-practitioner: A guide to practice in psychology*. Hove: Routledge.

Linley, P.A. (2006). Coaching research: Who? What? Where? When? Why? *International Journal of Evidence-Based Coaching and Mentoring*, 4(2).

Salkovskis, P.M. (2002). Empirically grounded clinical interventions: Cognitive-behavioural therapy progresses through a multi-dimensional approach to clinical science. *Behavioural and Cognitive Psychotherapy*, 30:3–9.

Spence, G.B. (2007). Further development of evidence-based coaching: Lessons from the rise and fall of the human potential movement. *Australian Psychologist*, 42(4):255–265.

Whitmore, J. (2007a). *Corporate coaching and much more*. Mimeo.

Whitmore, J. (2007b). *Where are we coming from? Where are we going?* Mimeo.

ENDNOTES TO CHAPTER 10

1. From the final paper published by the Knowledge Base for Coaching group at the GCC; the paper lists a few examples of theoretical bases that coaches are informed by:
   - learning theory (Kolb, Bloom, Bandura, Boud, Mumford);
   - change (Hudson, Batson, Kotter, Scott and Jaffee);
   - developmental (Kegan, Dubrowsky, Kohlberg);
   - ego (Loevinger, Cook);
   - communication (Wittgenstein, Watzlavick);
   - systemic thinking (Lewin, Senge);
   - social psychology (Izen);

- organisational development (Ulrich, Smallwood, Schein, Beckhard, Burke);

- process work (Mindell);

- action learning (Revans, Board, Weinstock);

- culture (Schein);

- self-directed learning (Boyatzis);

- leadership (Bennis, Jaques, Blanchard, Greenleaf);

- existential theory and philosophy (Yalom, Spinelli);

- chaos theory (Poincaré, Wheatley);

- cognitive behavioural psychology (Beck, Ellis, Bandura, Skinner, Thorndike, Seligman);

- emotional intelligence (Pert, Goleman); and

- spiritual intelligence (Zohar).

11

Integration and Synthesis

How can you move to the next level in your practice? If we talk about adult stages of development, coaching as an emerging profession is currently journeying from adolescence into its adult phase. A danger is that it becomes a fashion to call oneself a coach, or to be a coach in training. In other words, rather than a respected profession, coaching becomes a passing trend.

I see coaching today in terms of its life curve, both in South Africa and globally, as more in adolescence than in maturity, with "hormones racing up and down". Right now, coaching needs direction and the continual building of a knowledge base in order to begin to define its move towards professional practice.

Chapter outline

- Continuous reflection, learning and practice
    - The complexity of the coaching process
    - Coaching from a systems perspective
- Developing competence
    - Knowledge, wisdom and experience

CONTINUOUS REFLECTION, LEARNING AND PRACTICE

I have based this book on my research, teaching and business practice, emphasising the need for continuous reflection and learning. The purpose of the book has been to integrate wisdom and practice with recommendations and suggestions for practitioner coaches, HR and OD professionals, and managerial leaders who want to fine-tune their business coaching skills.

Throughout the book, I have endeavoured to provide a broad understanding of the business coaching process. I have looked at the origins and current reality of coaching, the influence of psychology, adult and experiential learning, and existential and diversity theories as the theoretical and developmental underpinnings of coaching.

Coaching embraces a process of experiential and continuous learning for client and coach. Although I have explored how to use various question frameworks and models, these are not by any means all that is available to the business coach. In examining diversity issues that clients and coach experience, we have identified linguistic, cultural, ethnic and gender issues that require flexibility and the development of new competences on the part of the coach. We have endeavoured to share with you a broad range of business coaching approaches that will help you to identify gaps in your knowledge, but also to integrate new learning into your own practice.

The complexity of the coaching process

We have analysed the complexities of the coaching conversation – the basic tool of the business and executive coach. We think that business coaching has a huge contribution to make to leadership competence inside organisations, and we have tried to take an in-depth, dynamic and integrative look at the coaching process, question frameworks, how to use current coaching models, examining current coach/client concerns such as ethics, contracting, supervision and the "relationship" between coach and client. The book's focus has been on the hub of the coaching conversation: learning from experience, which we believe is crucial for individual and organisational transformation.

The importance of experiential learning is that it emphasises a client's individual, subjective experience. In existential terms, the meaning of experience is not a given, it is subject to interpretation. Coach and client use the business coaching conversation to actively reconstruct the client's experience, with a focus on setting goals that are aligned to the client's internal drivers, by which we mean their intrinsic values, beliefs and feelings. However, it is important that there is some kind of synthesis with the values of the organisation within which they work.

Jaques and Clement (1991:xiv–xv) advocate that managerial leaders acquire qualities of cognitive complexity, appropriate knowledge and skills, and wisdom about people. Coaching is an egalitarian relationship, even if the focus is that of the coach on the client.

Both individuals bring their experience, expertise and wisdom to the relationship. In coaching, the coach will adapt their style according to their model, but most important is the development of the relationship through the client/coach interactions.

Coaching from a systems perspective

Coaching models help us to understand the coaching intervention from a systems perspective, and to understand the need for "structure" in the interaction between coach and client. Models help us to develop flexibility as coach practitioners. They offer structure and an outline for both the coaching conversation and the overall coaching journey.

Specific frameworks of questions are useful for the business coach, either as a way to get started with a new client, or simply as a tool to be used as part of their own coaching model. Common experiences which shape the culture of a society may impact on which frameworks are more useful to you than others.

South Africa is an extremely complex, multi-cultural society, yet within organisations there will be commonly shared values, beliefs and assumptions about leadership, management, responsibility, experience and language. Question frameworks are simply tools for you to structure the coaching conversation. Gradually, as you begin to refine your own coaching model, it will become clear which question frameworks are the most useful to you.

In this book, we have explored a range of diversity themes: from personality traits to gender, race, ethnicity, language and linguistic patterns, as well as religion and styles of communication. In the business environment, the coach needs to become aware of, and to manage, their own responses to questions of diversity before they can begin to coach a client on similar issues. We have focused on raising the business coach's awareness to crucial diversity issues, both within themselves and within their individual and organisational clients.

DEVELOPING COMPETENCE

Defined and benchmarked skills and competences serve a dual purpose. They give clarity in terms of how we are selected for an intervention, and they give the coach guidelines on what is expected and how to continually develop and improve. However, as coaching is at this stage very much an unregulated industry, skills and competence are simply defined by coaching associations as part of a philosophy or as a means to membership of their association.

We aim to help you identify your own level of skill and competence, recognising your own strengths as well as targeting areas for development. We explained in detail the required skills and competences defined for business coaches by professional bodies, highlighting specific competences on which you should focus within your continuing professional development (CPD).

Although contracting, supervision and ethical conduct have been practised in the helping professions for decades, they are not yet regulated for coach practitioners. We have looked at each of the roles and functions of these three key areas, as ultimately these processes will benefit and protect coach and client. The development of professional supervision, contracting and ethical codes is emerging as a vital function within the discipline of coaching.

A very new competence under appraisal in the Global Coaching Community (GCC), and as a result of the ICRF, the Institute of Coaching at Harvard/McLean Medical School, and the new Professional and Practice-Focused Research Special Interest Group at Middlesex University London, is that all practitioner coaches are potential contributors to an emerging and sustainable body of knowledge. This requires very specific skills from practitioners, including the ability to read and apply research as well as to generate critical enquiry into practice.

Knowledge, wisdom and experience

We see the business coaching process as one that helps business executives and leaders to develop a clear understanding of their roles and responsibilities. Business coaching, like sports coaching, is about high performance, but ultimately embodies sustained behavioural change and breakthrough performance.

Today, coaches need to understand human behaviour and human complexity. Within the business coaching context, the coach helps the client to articulate existential concerns such as freedom, purpose, choice and anxiety, and to identify and replace limiting paradigms with empowering paradigms, thus leading to positive change. Although existential philosophy regards human existence as unexplainable, it crucially stresses freedom of choice and taking responsibility for one's acts.

In a sense, we have been building your knowledge base, looking at how to transform your skill and competence into wisdom and experience as you work with individual executives and teams. Covey (1990) advocated that individuals need to change first if organisational transformation is to be sustainable. He inspired the dream that trust be built within an organisation, insisting that leadership begins with the individual. It is the same in business coaching – the work starts first with the individual coach to enable them to work with their executive clients.

Reflection and learning from experience must be applied by the coach in their own work. We attempt to model best practice, while at the same time helping the client to self-reflect and learn from experience. We hope this book will be of lasting value to you: take what you have learned here and turn it into practice. As coaches, we should always aim to practise what we preach: striving for excellence.

Bibliography

Ahern, G. (2003). Designing and implementing coaching/mentoring competences: A case study. *Counselling Psychology Quarterly*, 16(4):373–383.

Aiken Hodge, D. (2006). *Towards coaching across divides to create alliances – an Integral approach*. Unpublished DProf dissertation. London: Middlesex University.

Allik, J. and McCrae, R. (2004). Toward a geography of personality traits: Patterns of profiles across 36 cultures. *Journal of Cross-Cultural Psychology*, 35:13–28.

American Management Association (AMA) (2008). *Coaching: A global study of successful practices*. New York, NY: AMA.

Ancona, D. and Bresman, H. (2007). *X-teams: How to build teams that lead, innovate and succeed*. Cambridge, MA: Harvard Business School.

Argyris, C. and Schön, D. (1974). *Theory in practice: Increasing professional effectiveness*. San Francisco, CA: Jossey-Bass.

Babcock, L. and Laschever, S. (2003). *Women don't ask: Negotiation and the gender divide*. Princeton, NJ: Princeton University Press.

Baek-Kyoo, B. (2005). Executive coaching: A conceptual framework from an integrative review of practice and research. *Human Resource Development Review*, 4:462–488.

Bandler, R. (1985). *Using your brain – for a change: Neuro-linguistic programming*. Edited by C. Andreas and S. Andreas. Boulder, CO: Real People Press.

Bandler, R. and Grinder, J. (1992). *Reframing and the transformation of meaning*. Moab, UT: Real People Press.

Barinaga, M. (1994). Surprises across the cultural divide. *Science*, 263(5152):1468–1469.

Bar-On, R. (1997). *The emotional quotient inventory (EQ-i): A test of emotional intelligence*. Toronto: Multi-Health Systems.

Beck, D.E. and Cowan, C.C. (1996). *Spiral dynamics, mastering values, leadership, and change*. London: Blackwell.

Bell, E.L.J. and Nkomo, S.M. (2001). *Our separate ways: Black and white women and the struggle for identity*. Cambridge, MA: Harvard Business School Press.

Bennett, J.L. (2006). An agenda for coaching-related research: A challenge for researchers. *Coaching Psychology Journal: Practice and Research*, 8(4):240–249.

Bluckert, P. (2008). *Coaching supervision*. Available at: www.pbcoaching.com

Boon, M. (1996). *The African way*. Sandton: Zebra Press.

Boud, D. and Walker, D. (1990). Making the most of experience. *Studies in Continuing Education*. 12(2):61–80.

Boud, D., Cohen, R. and Walker, D. (eds). (1996). *Using experience for learning*. Buckingham: SRHE and Open University Press.

Braaten, J. (1991). *Habermas's critical theory of society*. New York, NY: State University of New York.

Bradberry, T. and Greaves, J. (2005a). *The emotional intelligence quick book*. New York, NY: Simon and Schuster.

Bradberry, T. and Greaves, J. (2005b). Heartless bosses. *Harvard Business Review*, December.

Briggs Myers, I. and Myers, P.B. (1995). *Gifts differing: Understanding personality type*. Palo Alto, CA: Davies-Black.

Buckingham, M. and Clifton, D.O. (2002). *Now, discover your strengths*. London: Simon and Schuster.

Burger, A.P (ed.). (1996). *Ubuntu: Cradles of peace and development*. Pretoria: Kagiso.

Caplan, S. (1970). *The theory and practise of mental health consultation*. New York, NY: Basic Books.

Carter, A., Wolfe, H. and Kerrin, M. (2005). Employers and coaching evaluation. *International Journal of Coaching in Organizations*, 3(4):63–72.

Carter, E.A.K. and McGoldrick, M. (eds). (1990). *The changing family life cycle: A framework for family therapy*. Second edition. Boston, MA: Allyn and Bacon.

Caver, K.A. and Livers, A.B. (2002). Dear White Boss. *Harvard Business Review*, 80(11):76–81.

Chalkbored.com (2008). Available at: www.chalkbored.com/lessons/chemistry.

Children's Institute (2008). University of Cape Town. Available at: www.childrencount. ci.org.za.

Clutterbuck, D. (2007). *Coaching the team at work*. London: Nicholas Brealey.

Coaches and Mentors of South Africa (COMENSA). (2006). *Standards of professional competence*. Draft policy. Available at: www.comensa.org.za.

Coaches and Mentors of South Africa (COMENSA). (2009). *Revised Code of Ethics*. Available at: www.comensa.org.za.

Coaches and Mentors of South Africa (COMENSA). (2010). *Coach/Mentor Supervision Policy*. Available at: www.comensa.org.za.

Coaches and Mentors of South Africa (COMENSA). (2007). *Membership criteria and standards of competence framework*. Draft framework. Cape Town: COMENSA.

Connerley, M.L. and Pedersen, P.B. (2005). *Leadership in a diverse and multicultural environment*. London: Sage.

Cormier, L. and Bernard, J. (1982). Ethical and legal responsibilities of clinical supervisors. *Personnel and Guidance Journal*, 60:486–491.

Covey, S.R. (1989). *Seven habits of highly effective people*. London: Simon and Schuster.

Covey, S.R. (1990). *Principle-centred leadership*. London: Simon and Schuster.

Cox, E. (2007). *Collaborative dialogue on the research agenda for coaching*. Proceedings of a meeting of the Oxford Brookes Coaching and Mentoring Society on 14 December 2007. Mimeo.

Criticos, C. (1996). Experiential learning and social transformation for a post-apartheid learning future, in Boud, D., Cohen, R. and Walker, D. (eds). *Using experience for learning*. Buckingham: SRHE and Open University Press.

Crocket, K. (1999). Supervision: a site of authority production. *New Zealand Journal of Counselling*, 20(1):75–83.

Cummings, T.G. and Worley, C.G. (2004). *Organization development and change*. Eighth edition. Mason, OH: South-Western College Publishing.

Dagley, G. (2006). Human resources professionals' perceptions of executive coaching: Efficacy benefits and return on investment. *International Coaching Psychology Review*, 1(2):34–45.

DeLozier, J. and Grinder, J. (1987). *Turtles all the way down: Prerequisites to personal genius*. Santa Cruz, CA: Grinder, DeLozier & Associates.

Devenish, G. (2005). Understanding true meaning of Ubuntu is essential in politics. *Cape Times*, 17 May.

Dialog on Leadership (2007). Available at: www.dialogonleadership.org/Wilber.

Dilts, R. (2003). *From coach to awakener*. Capitola, CA: Meta.

Ditzler, J. (1994). *Your best year yet: The 10 questions that will change your life forever*. New York, NY: Warner.

Downey, M. (2003). *Effective coaching, lessons from the coach's coach*. Second edition. New York, NY: Texere.

Drefus, S. and Drefus, H. (1980). *A five-stage model of the mental activities involved in directed skill acquisition*. Berkley, CA: University of California.

Dye, H. and Borders, L. (1990). Counselling supervisors: Standards of preparation and practice. *Journal of Counselling and Development*, 69(1):27–29.

Eggers, J.H. and Clark, D. (2000). Executive coaching that wins. *Ivey Business Journal*, 65(1):66–70.

Elion, B. and Strieman M. (2001). *Clued-up on culture: A practical guide for all South Africans.* Second edition. Cape Town: Juta Gariep.

European Mentoring and Coaching Council (EMCC). (2008a). *EQA – The European Quality Award*. Available at: www.emccouncil.org/eu/public/european_quality_award/index.html.

European Mentoring and Coaching Council (EMCC). (2008b). *Code of ethics*. Available at: www.emccouncil.org/fileadmin/documents/EMCC_Code_of_Ethics.pdf.

Faull, J. (2008). We can harness outrage over violence to rejuvenate democracy, bring change. *Cape Times*, 5 June.

Feldman, D.C. and Lankau, M.J. (2005). Executive coaching: A review and agenda for future research. *Journal of Management*, 31(6):829–848.

Fillery-Travis, A. (2007). *Where's the evidence? First steps into the literature*. Mimeo.

Fillery-Travis, A. (2008). *Current state of knowledge production in the UK*. Mimeo.

Fillery-Travis, A. and Lane, D. (2006a). How to develop your research interests. In S. Palmer and R. Bor (eds). *The practitioner's handbook: A guide for counsellors, psychotherapists and counselling psychologists*. London: Sage.

Fillery-Travis, A. and Lane, D. (2006b). Does coaching work, or are we asking the wrong question? *International Coaching Psychology Review*, 1:23–36.

Flaherty, J. (1999). *Coaching: Evoking excellence in others*. Boston, MA: Butterworth-Heinemann.

Flaherty, J. (2005). *Coaching: Evoking excellence in others*. Oxford: Elsevier Butterworth-Heinemann.

Flaherty, J. (2008). *Detail of: Habermas' domains of competency*. Available at: coaching.gc.ca/documents/ coaching_essential_competences_for_leaders_e.asp

Foy, N. (1994). *Empowering people at work*. Aldershot, Hampshire: Gower.

Frankl, V.E. (1946). *Man's search for meaning*. London: Hodder and Stoughton.

Freire, P. (1973). *Education for critical consciousness*. New York, NY: Continuum.

Freud, S. (1974). *Introductory lectures on psychoanalysis*. Harmondsworth: Penguin.

Gallwey, W.T. (1974). *The inner game of tennis: The classic guide to the mental side of peak performance*. New York, NY: Random House.

Gallwey, W.T. (2000). *The inner game of work: Focus, learning, pleasure and mobility in the workplace*. New York. NY: Random House.

Gardner, H. (1983). *Frames of mind*. New York, NY: Basic Books.

Gardner, H. (2006). *Multiple intelligences*. Cambridge, MA: Perseus.

Gardiner, D. (1989). *The autonomy of supervision*. Milton Keynes: SRHE/Open University Press.

Garratt, B. (2001). *The learning organization: Developing democracy at work*. New York, NY: HarperCollins.

Garvey, R., Megginson, D. and Stokes, P. (2008). *Coaching and mentoring: theory and practice*. London: Sage.

GCC Steering Committee. (2007). *Global Convention on Coaching: Visioning the future together*. Media release. Global Convention on Coaching.

Global Convention on Coaching (GCC). (2008a). *Current reality*. Draft paper of the Working Group on Mapping the Field. Available at: www.coachingconvention.org.

Global Convention on Coaching (GCC). (2008b). *Final paper of the Working Group on Ethics*. Global Convention on Coaching. Dublin, July. Available at: www.coachingconvention.org.

Global Convention on Coaching (GCC). (2008c). *White paper of the Working Group on a Research Agenda for Development of the Field*. Global Convention on Coaching. Dublin, July. Available at: www.coachingconvention.org.

Global Convention on Coaching (GCC). (2008d). *Final paper of the Working Group on a Research Agenda for Development of the Field*. Global Convention on Coaching. Dublin, July. Available at: www.coachingconvention.org.

Global Convention on Coaching (GCC). (2008e). *Dublin declaration on coaching*. Global Convention on Coaching. Dublin, August. Available at www.coachingconvention. org.

Goldfried, M.R. and Wolfe, B.E. (1966). Psychotherapy practice and research: Repairing a strained alliance. *American Psychologist*, 51:1007–16.

Goldsmith, M., Lyons, L. and Freas, A. (eds). (2000). *Coaching for leadership: How the world's greatest coaches help leaders learn*. San Francisco, CA: Jossey-Bass/Pfeiffer.

Goleman, D. (1996). *Emotional intelligence*. London: Bloomsbury.

Goleman, D. (1998). *Working with emotional intelligence*. New York, NY: Bantam Books.

Goleman, D. (2002). *The new leaders: Transforming the art of leadership into the science of results*. London: Little, Brown.

Goleman, D., Boyatzis, R. and McKee, A. (2002). *The new leaders*. London: Little, Brown.

Gorle, H.R. (2002). *Grief theories: Elizabeth Kubler-Ross*. Available at: www.bereavement. org/e_kubler-ross.htm.

Grant, A.M. (2000). Coaching psychology comes of age. *PsychNews*, 4(4):12–14.

Grant, A.M. (2003a). The impact of life coaching on goal attainment, metacognition and mental health. *Social Behavior and Personality*, 31(3):253–264.

Grant, A.M. (2003b). *Keeping up with the cheese! Research as a foundation for professional coaching of the future*. Keynote presentation to the International Coach Federation Conference Symposium on Research and Coaching, Denver, CO, November.

Grant, A.M. and Cavanagh, M.J. (2006). *Toward a profession of coaching: Sixty-five years of progress and challenges for the future*. Sydney: Coaching Psychology Unit, School of Psychology, University of Sydney.

Grant, A.M. and Cavanagh, M.J. (2007a). Evidence-based coaching: flourishing or languishing? *Australian Psychologist*, 42(4):239–254.

Grant, A.M. and Cavanagh, M.J. (2007b). The goal-focused coaching skills questionnaire: preliminary findings. *Social Behavior and Personality*, 35(6):751–760.

Grayson, D. and Larson, K. (2000). How to make the most of the coaching relationship. In Goldsmith, M., Lyons, L. and Freas, A. (eds). *Coaching for leadership: How the world's greatest coaches help leaders learn*. San Francisco, CA: Jossey-Bass/Pfeiffer.

Griffiths, K.E. and Campbell, M.A. (2008). Regulating the regulators: paving the way for international, evidence-based coaching standards. *International Journal of Evidence-Based Coaching and Mentoring*, 6(1):19–31.

Grouzet, F.M.E., Kasser, T., Ahuvia, A., Fernandez-Dols, J.M., Kim, Y., Lau, S., Ryan, R.M., Saunders, S., Schmuck, P. and Sheldon, K. (2005). The structure of goal contents across 15 cultures. *Journal of Personality and Social Psychology*, 89:800–816.

Hakim, C. (2000). *Work-lifestyle choices in the 21st century*. New York, NY: Oxford University Press.

Hall, L.M. and Duval, M. (2003). *Coaching conversations for translational change*. Clifton, CO: Neuro-Semantics Publications.

Hamlyn, J. (2005). *Theoretical overview of coaching*. Sandton: The People Business.

Hampden-Turner, C. and Trompenaars, F. (2000). *Building cross-cultural competence: How to create wealth from conflicting values*. New Haven, CT: Yale University Press.

Hargrove, R. (2003). *Masterful coaching: Inspire an "impossible future" while producing extraordinary leaders and extraordinary results*. San Francisco, CA: Jossey-Bass/Pfeiffer.

HarperCollins. (2005). *Collins dictionary and thesaurus*. Second edition. New York, NY: HarperCollins.

Harri-Augstein, S. and Thomas, L.F. (1991). *Learning conversations, self-organised learning: The way to personal and organisational growth*. London: Routledge.

Harvey, V. and Struzziero, J. (2000). *Effective supervision in school psychology*. Bethesda, MD: National Association of School Psychologists.

Hawkins, P. (2008). Available at: www.bathconsultancygroup.com.

Hawkins, P. and Shohet, R. (2000). *Supervision in the helping professions*. Buckingham, UK: Open University Press.

Haynes, R., Cory, C. and Moulton, P. (2003). *Professional supervision in the helping professions: A practical guide*. Pacific Grove, CA: Brookes-Cole.

Heath, A. and Tharp, L. (1991). *What therapists say about supervision*. Paper presented at the American Association of Marriage and Family Therapy Annual Conference, Dallas, TX.

Heath, P. and Shohet, R. (1991). Approaches to the supervision of counsellors, in W. Dryden and B. Thorne (eds). *Training and supervision for counselling in action*. London: Sage.

Hedricks, C.A. and Weinstein, H.P. (2001). *The personality profile of a corporate leader*. Republished conference paper of the American Psychological Association, Princeton, NJ: CALIPER.

Herrmann, N. (1996). *The whole brain business book*. New York, NY: McGraw-Hill.

Herskovits, M.J. (1955). *Cultural anthropology*. New York, NY: Knopf.

Hofstede, G. (1997). *Cultures and organizations: Software of the mind*. New York, NY: McGraw-Hill.

Hofstede, G. (1999). Problems remain, but theories will change: the universal and the specific in 21st-century global management. *Organizational Dynamics*, 28(1):34–44.

Hofstede, G. (2001). *Culture's consequences: comparing values, behaviors, institutions, and organizations across nations*. Second edition. Thousand Oaks, CA: Sage.

Hofstede, G. (2005). Foreword. In M.L. Connerley and P.B. Pedersen. *Leadership in a diverse and multicultural environment*. Thousand Oaks, CA: Sage.

Honey, P. and Mumford, A. (1986). *Using your learning styles.* Second edition. Maidenhead: Peter Honey.

Honey, P. and Mumford, A. (1992). *The manual of learning styles.* Maidenhead: Peter Honey.

Houston, J. (1982). *The possible human.* Los Angeles, CA: Jeremy Tarcher.

Hudson, F.M. (1998). *The handbook of coaching: A resource guide to effective coaching with individuals and organizations.* Santa Barbara, CA: Hudson Institute.

Hudson, F.M. (1999). *The handbook of coaching: A comprehensive resource guide for managers, executives, consultants, and human resource professionals.* San Francisco, CA: Jossey-Bass.

Hudson, L. (1991). *Frames of mind.* London: Penguin.

Husserl, E. (1962/1913). *Ideas: a general introduction to pure phenomenology,* (tr. 1931). Vol. I. New York, NY: Collier Books.

Ibarra, H. (2003). *Working identity: Unconventional strategies for reinventing your career.* Cambridge, MA: Harvard Business School Press.

Insights. (2008). Available at: www.insights.co.uk.

International Coach Federation (ICF). (2008a). *Coaching core competencies.* Available at: www.coachfederation.org/ICF/For+Current+Members/Credentialing/ Why+a+Credential/Competencies/.

International Coach Federation (ICF). (2008b). *ICF ethical guidelines.* Available at: www. coachfederation.org/ICF/For+Current+Members/Ethical+Guidelines/.

Jackson, P. and Delehanty, H. (1995). *Sacred hoops.* New York, NY: Hyperion.

Jackson, B.G. (1999). The goose that laid the golden egg? A rhetorical critique of Stephen Covey and the effectiveness movement. *Journal of Management Studies,* 36(3):353–377.

Jacobi, J. (1942/1973). *The psychology of C.G. Jung.* New Haven, CT: Yale University Press.

Jacobs, M. (ed.). (1996). *In search of supervision.* Buckingham, UK: Open University Press.

Janse van Rensburg, M. (2001a). *Executive coaching and the principles of African humanism and ubuntu*. Gordon Institute of Business Science, Pretoria: University of Pretoria.

Janse van Rensburg, M. (2001b). *Executive coaching: A natural extension of the principles of ubuntu and African humanism*. Research report for Master of Business Administration. Gordon Institute of Business Science, Pretoria: University of Pretoria.

Jaques, E. and Clement, S.D. (1991). *Effective leadership: A practical guide to managing complexity*. Oxford: Blackwell.

Jarvis, J. (2004). *Coaching and buying coaching services: A guide*. London: CIPD.

Javidan, M. and House, R.J. (2001). Cultural acumen for the global manager: lessons from Project GLOBE. *Organizational Dynamics*, 29(4):289–305.

Johnson, W.B. and Ridley, C.R. (2004). *The elements of mentoring*. New York, NY: Palgrave Macmillan.

Johwa, W. (2008). Stiff penalty for resisting job equity proposed. *Business Day*, 20 October.

Jones, R. and Jenkins, F. (eds). (2006). *Developing the allied health professions*. Oxford: Radcliffe.

Jung, C. (1977). Psychological types. In *Collected Works of C.G. Jung*. Volume 6. Bollingen Series XX, Princeton, NJ: Princeton University Press.

Kadushin, A. (1976). *Supervision in social work*. New York, NY, Columbia University Press.

Kaessmann, H. and Pääbo, S. (2002). The genetical history of humans and the great apes. *Journal of Internal Medicine*, 251(1):1-18.

Kanter, R.M., Stein, B.A. and Jick, T.D. (1992). *The challenge of organizational change*. New York, NY: Free Press/Macmillan.

Kets de Vries, M. (2004). Putting leaders on the couch. *Harvard Business Review*, January.

Kets de Vries, M. (2006). *The leader on the couch*. London: Wiley.

Kilburg. R. (2002). *Executive coaching: Developing managerial wisdom in a world of chaos.* Washington, DC: American Psychological Association.

Kline, N. (1999/2004). *Time to think: Listening with the human mind.* London: Ward Lock.

Kline, N. (2004). Keynote Address. In *Coaching in a Thinking Environment.* Wallingford: Time to Think.

Kline, N. (2005). *The Thinking Partnership programme: Consultant's guide.* Wallingford: Time to Think.

Kline, P. and Saunders, B. (1993). *Ten steps to a learning organization.* Arlington, VA: Great Ocean.

Kluckholm, F. and Stroedbeck, F. (1961). *Variations in value orientations.* New York, NY: Harper and Row.

Knight, S. (1995). *NLP at work.* London: Nicholas Brealey.

Kolb, D.A. (1984). *Experiential learning: Experience as the source of learning and development.* Upper Saddle River, NJ: Prentice Hall.

Kolb, D.A, Rubin, I.M. and McIntyre, J.M. (2001). *Organizational psychology: An experiential approach to organizational behavior.* Seventh edition. Upper Saddle River, NJ: Prentice-Hall.

Kroeger, O. and Thuesen, J.M. (1988). *Type talk: The 16 personality types that determine how we live, love and work.* New York, NY: Dell.

Kroeger, O., Thuesen, J.M. and Rutledge, H. (2002). *Type talk at work: How the 16 personality types determine your success on the job.* New York, NY: Dell.

Kuhn, T. (1962). *The structure of scientific revolutions.* Chicago, IL: University of Chicago Press.

Landsberg, M. (1997). *The Tao of coaching.* London: HarperCollins.

Landy, F.J. (2005). Some historical and scientific issues related to research on emotional intelligence. *Journal of Organizational Behavior*, 26:411–424.

Lane, D.A. and Corrie, S. (2006). *The modern scientist-practitioner: A guide to practice in psychology.* Hove: Routledge.

Langer, E. (1989). *Mindfulness.* Reading, MA: Addison-Wesley.

Langer, E. (1997). *The power of mindful learning.* Reading, MA: Addison-Wesley.

Laske, O.E. (2004). Can evidence-based coaching increase ROI? *International Journal of Evidence-Based Coaching and Mentoring,* 2(2):41–53.

Lawton-Smith, C. and Cox, E. (2007). Coaching: is it just a new name for training? *International Journal of Evidence-Based Coaching and Mentoring,* Special Issue.

Leong, F. (1994). Emergence of the cultural dimension: the roles and impact of culture on counseling supervision. *Counselor Education and Supervision,* 34(2):114–116.

Lidbetter, K. (2003). For good measure. *People Management,* 9(1):46.

Linley, P.A. (2006). Coaching research: Who? What? Where? When? Why? *International Journal of Evidence-Based Coaching and Mentoring,* 4(2).

Locke, E.A. (2005). Why emotional intelligence is an invalid concept. *Journal of Organizational Behavior,* 26:425–431.

Mackie, D. (2007). Evaluating the effectiveness of executive coaching: where are we now and where do we need to be? *Australian Psychologist,* 42(4):310–318.

Mahoney, M. (1991). *Human change processes.* New York, NY: Basic Books.

Manhire, B. (2000). Ode on a Grecian urn. Interview on Kim Hill Show. Wellington: Radio New Zealand, 5 May.

Manthei, R. (1997). *Counselling: The skills of finding solutions to problems.* Auckland: Longman.

May, R. (1983). *The discovery of being.* New York, NY: Norton.

Mayer, J.D. and Salovey, P. (1997). What is emotional intelligence? In P. Salovey and D. Sluyter (eds). *Emotional development and emotional intelligence: Educational applications.* New York, NY: Basic Books.

McDaniels, C. (1976). *Leisure and career development at mid-life*. Blacksburg, VA: Virginia Polytechnic Institute and State University.

McDermott, I. and Jago, W. (2001). *The NLP coach: A comprehensive guide to personal well-being and professional success*. London: Piatkus.

McLoughlin, M. (ed.). (2006). *Sharing the passion: Conversations with coaches*. Cape Town: Advanced Human Technologies.

McLoughlin, M. and Stout-Rostron, S. (2002). *NLP coach training skills*. Unpublished programme.

McNab, P. (2005). *Towards an integral vision: Using NLP and Ken Wilber's AQAL model to enhance communication*. Crewe: Trafford.

McWhinney, W., Webber, J.B., Smith, D.M. and Novokowsky, B.J. (1993). *Creating paths of change: Managing issues and resolving problems in organisations*. Venice, CA: Enthusion.

Mead, D. (1990). *Effective supervision: A task-oriented model for the developing professions*. New York, NY: Bruner/Mazel.

Mike the Mentor. (2008a). *Classic models: The 7-eyed supervision model*. Available at: www.mikethementor.co.uk.

Mike the Mentor. (2008b). *Classic models: The CLEAR model*. Available at: www.mikethementor.co.uk.

MNet. (2008). Where do we come from? *Carte Blanche* Science and Technology feature broadcast September 2004. Available at: www.mnet.co.za/Mnet/Shows/carteblanche.

Morris, B. and Tarpley, N.A. (2000). So you're a player. Do you need a coach? *Fortune*, 21 February, 141(4):144.

Mullen, J.D. (2006). Nature, nurture and individual change. *Behavior and Philosophy*, 34:1–17.

Noer, D. (2000). The big three derailment factors in a coaching relationship. In M. Goldsmith, L. Lyons and A. Freas (eds.). *Coaching for leadership: How the world's greatest coaches help leaders learn*. San Francisco, CA: Jossey-Bass/Pfeiffer.

Nowack, K.M. and Wimer, S. (1997). Coaching for human performance. *Training and Development*, 51(10):28–32.

Nuffield Council on Bioethics. (2008). Available at: www.nuffieldbioethics.org.

O'Connor, J. and Lages, A. (2004). *Coaching with NLP*. London: HarperCollins.

O'Connor, J. and Seymour, J. (1990). *Introducing NLP*. London: Aquarian/Thorsons.

O'Neill, M.B. (2000). *Coaching with backbone and heart: A systems approach to engaging leaders with their challenges*. San Francisco, CA: Jossey-Bass.

Olesen, M. (1996). Coaching today's executives. *Training and Development*, March, 50(3):22.

Olson, K.R. (2007). Why do geographic differences exist in the worldwide distribution of extraversion and openness to experience? The history of human migration as an explanation. *Individual Differences Research*, 5(4):275–288.

Pampallis Paisley, P. (2006). *Towards a theory of supervision for executive coaching – An integral vision*. Unpublished DProf dissertation. London: Middlesex University.

Parsloe, E. and Wray, M. (2000). *Coaching and mentoring, practical methods to improve learning*. London: Kogan Page.

Payne, W.L. (1983/1986). A study of emotion: developing emotional intelligence, self integration, relating to fear, pain and desire. *Dissertation Abstracts International*, 47:203A.

Pearson, K. (1996). Debate: this time "supervision": who needs it? *NZAC Newsletter*, 16(4):14–15.

Peltier, B. (2001). *The psychology of executive coaching: Theory and application*. New York, NY: Brunner-Routledge.

Peters, T. and Austin, N. (1985). Coaching is an essential reading for all coaches. In *A passion for excellence – The leadership difference*. New York, NY: Warner.

Peterson, D.B. (2007). Executive coaching in a cross-cultural context. *Consulting Psychology Journal: Practice and Research*, December.

Peterson, D. and Little, B. (2008). Growth market. *Coaching at Work*, 3(1):44–47.

Pink, T. (2004). *Free will: A very short introduction*. Oxford: Oxford University Press.

Pinker, S. (2008). *The sexual paradox: Men, women and the real gender gap*. New York, NY: Scribner.

Pityana, B. (2001). Foreword. In B. Elion and M. Strieman. *Clued-up on culture: A practical guide for all South Africans*. Second edition. Cape Town: Juta Gariep.

Proctor, B. (1994). Supervision: Competence, confidence, accountability. *British Journal of Guidance and Supervision*, 22(3):309–318.

Ramphele, M. (2008). *Laying ghosts to rest: Dilemmas of the transformation in South Africa*. Cape Town: Tafelberg.

Revans, R.W. (1983). *The ABC of action learning*. Bromley: Chartwell Bratt.

Riso, D.R. and Hudson, R. (1999). *The wisdom of the Enneagram*. New York, NY: Bantam.

Robbins, S.P. (2001). *Organizational behavior*. Englewood Cliffs, NJ: Prentice-Hall.

Rogers, C.R. (1961/2004). *On becoming a person: A therapist's view of psychotherapy*. London: Constable and Robinson.

Rosinski, P. (2003). *Coaching across cultures: New tools for leveraging national, corporate and professional differences*. London: Nicholas Brealey.

Ruru, T. (2008). *Consultive support – Supervision for NLP practitioners*. Available at: www. transformations.net.nz/trancescript/consultive-support.html.

Salkovskis, P.M. (2002). Empirically grounded clinical interventions: cognitive-behavioural therapy progresses through a multi-dimensional approach to clinical science. *Behavioural and Cognitive Psychotherapy*, 30:3–9.

Salovey, P. and Mayer, J.D. (1990). Emotional intelligence. *Imagination, Cognition and Personality*, 9:185–211.

Scharmer, C.O. (2007). Addressing the blind spot of our time: An executive summary of the new book by Otto Scharmer, *Theory U: Leading from the future as it emerges: The social technology of presencing"*. Available at: www.theoryu.com.

Scott, A. (2007). In confidence. Available at: www.peoplemanagement.co.uk.

Senge, P. (1990). *The fifth discipline: The art and practice of the learning organization.* New York, NY: Doubleday.

Senge, P., Scharmer, C.O., Jaworski, J. and Flowers, B.S. (2005). *Presence: Exploring profound change in people, organizations and society.* London: Nicholas Brealey.

Senghor, L. (1965). *On African socialism.* New York, NY: Stanford.

Shaw, P. and Linnecar, R. (2007). *Business coaching: Achieving practical results through effective engagement.* London: Capstone.

Spence, G.B. (2007a). GAS-powered coaching: Goal attainment scaling and its use in coaching research and practice. *International Coaching Psychology Review,* July, 2(2):155–167.

Spence, G.B. (2007b). Further development of evidence-based coaching: Lessons from the rise and fall of the human potential movement. *Australian Psychologist,* 42(4):255–265.

Spence, G.B. and Grant, A.M. (2007). Professional and peer life coaching and the enhancement of goal striving and well-being: An exploratory study. *The Journal of Positive Psychology,* July, 2(3):185–194.

Simon and Schuster (1983). *Webster's new twentieth century dictionary.* Unabridged. Second edition. New York, NY: Simon and Schuster.

Spinelli, E. (1989). *The interpreted world: An introduction to phenomenological psychology.* London: Sage.

Steere, J. (1984). *Ethics in clinical psychology.* Cape Town: Oxford University Press.

Stern, L. (2008). *Executive coaching: Building and managing your professional practice.* Hoboken, NJ: Wiley.

Sternberg, R.J. (1985). Implicit theories of intelligence, creativity, and wisdom. *Journal of Personality and Social Psychology*, 49:607–627.

Sternberg, R.J. (1997). *Thinking styles*. Cambridge: Cambridge University Press.

Stevens, A. (1994). *Jung: A very short introduction*. Oxford: Oxford University Press.

Storr, A. (1989). *Freud: A very short introduction*. Oxford: Oxford University Press.

Stout-Rostron, S. (2002). *Accelerating performance: Powerful new techniques to develop people*. London: Kogan Page.

Stout-Rostron, S. (2006a). The history of coaching. In M. McLoughlin (ed.). *Sharing the passion: Conversations with coaches*. Cape Town: Advanced Human Technologies.

Stout-Rostron, S. (2006b). Business Coaching in South Africa. *WABC e-zine*, 2(2):7–10. Available at: www.wabccoaches.com

Stout-Rostron, S. (2006c). *Interventions in the coaching conversation: Thinking, feeling and behaviour*. Published DProf dissertation. London: Middlesex University.

Stout-Rostron, S. (2008). Can coaching produce sustainable behavioural change? *WABC e-zine*, 4(1):23–25. Available at: www.wabccoaches.com

Stout-Rostron, S. (2011). How is coaching impacting systemic and cultural change within organisations? *International Journal of Coaching in Organisations*.

Sue-Chan, C. and Latham, G.P. (2004). The relative effectiveness of external, peer and self-coaches. *Applied Psychology: An International Review*, 53(2):260–278.

Swartz, L. (1998). *Culture and mental health: A Southern African view*. Oxford: Oxford University Press.

Tannen, D. (1995). The power of talk: who gets heard and why. *Harvard Business Review*, September–October.

Thach, E.C. (2002). The impact of executive coaching and 360 feedback on leadership effectiveness. *Leadership and Organization Development Journal*, 23(4):205–214.

Thomas, A. and Bendixen, M. (2000). The management implication of ethnicity in South Africa. *Journal of International Business Studies*. 31(3):507–519.

Thorndike, R.K. (1920). Intelligence and its uses. *Harper's Magazine*, 140:227–335.

Ting, S. and Scisco, P. (2006). *The CCL handbook of coaching: A guide for the leader coach*. San Francisco, CA: Jossey-Bass.

Todd, T.C. and Storm, C.L. (1997). *The complete systemic supervisor*. Boston, MA: Allyn and Bacon.

Triandis, H.C. (1975). Cultural training, cognitive complexity and interpersonal attitudes. In R. Brislin, S. Bochner. and W. Lonner (eds). *Cross-cultural perspectives on learning*. New York, NY: Wiley.

Underhill, B.O., McAnally, K. and Koriath, J. (2007). *Executive coaching for results*. San Francisco, CA: Berrett-Koehler.

Useem, J. (2005). Jim Collins on tough calls. *Fortune*, June 27:49–52.

Usher, C. and Borders, L. (1993). Practising counselors' preferences for supervisory style and supervisory emphasis. *Counselor Education and Supervision*, 33(2):66–79.

Watzlawick, P. (1978). *The language of change*. New York, NY: Basic Books.

Weiss, P. (2004). The three levels of coaching. Paper from *An appropriate response*. Available at: www.appropriateresponse.com.

Weiten, W. (2000). *Psychology themes and variations: Brief version*. Fourth edition. Pacific Grove, CA: Wadsworth-Brooks/Cole.

West, L. and Milan, M. (2001). *The reflecting glass: Professional coaching for leadership development*. New York, NY: Palgrave.

Wetzler, M. (2000). *Mountain mist*. Audio CD produced for the Bristol Cancer Help Centre, UK. Durbanville: Creative Processes.

Whitmore, J. (2002). *Coaching for performance: Growing people, performance and purpose*. Third edition. London: Nicholas Brealey.

Whitmore, J. (2007a). *Corporate coaching and much more.* Mimeo.

Whitmore, J. (2007b). *Where are we coming from? Where are we going?* Mimeo.

Whitworth, L., Kimsey-House, H. and Sandahl, P. (1998). *Co-active coaching: New skills for coaching people toward success in work and life.* Palo Alto, CA: Davies-Black.

Wilber, K. (1996). *A brief history of everything.* Dublin: Colourbooks.

Wilber, K. (1997). An integral theory of consciousness. *Journal of Consciousness Studies,* 4(1):71–92.

Wilber, K. (2000a). *A theory of everything: An integral vision for business, politics, science and spirituality.* Dublin: Gateway.

Wilber, K. (2000b). *Integral Psychology: Consciousness, Spirit, Psychology, Therapy.* Boston, MA: Shambhala.

Wilber, K. (2001). *A brief history of everything and a history of everything.* Dublin: Gateway.

Wilber, K. (2006). *Integral spirituality.* Boston, MA: Integral Books.

Williams, M.J. (1996). Are you ready for an executive coach? *Harvard Management Update,* October.

Witherspoon, R. (2000). Starting smart: clarifying coaching goals and roles. In M. Goldsmith, L. Lyons and A. Freas (eds). *Coaching for leadership: How the world's greatest coaches help leaders learn.* San Francisco, CA: Jossey-Bass/Pfeiffer.

Witherspoon, R. and White, R.P. (1996). Executive coaching: what's in it for you? *Training and Development,* March, 50(3):14.

Worldwide Association of Business Coaches (WABC). (2008a). *Code of business coaching ethics and integrity.* Available at: www.wabccoaches.com.

Worldwide Association of Business Coaches (WABC). (2008b). *Business coaching definition and competences.* Available at: www.wabccoaches.com/includes/popups/ definition_and_competencies.html.

Yalom, I.D. (1980). *Existential psychotherapy.* New York, NY: Basic Books.

Yalom, I.D. (1989). *Love's executioner and other tales of psychotherapy*. London: Penguin Books.

Yalom, I.D. (1995). *The theory and practice of group psychotherapy*. New York, NY: Basic Books.

Yalom, I.D. (2001). *The gift of therapy: Reflections on being a therapist*. London: Piatkus.

Zeus, P. and Skiffington, S. (2000). *The complete guide to coaching at work*. North Ryde, NSW: McGraw-Hill Australia.

Zohar, D. and Marshall, I. (2001). *Spiritual intelligence: The ultimate intelligence*. London: Bloomsbury.

Index

47, 49, 52, 66, 77, 82, 83, 94, 99, 100, 101, 110, 111, 112, 116, 117, 145, 148, 151, 161, 164, 167, 169, 174, 177, 181, 190, 200, 215, 218, 219, 225, 228, 234, 235, 239, 240, 245, 250, 253, 257, 262-264, 280, 281, 282, 295, 299, 303, 304, 323
- balance - 2, 4, 19, 28, 30, 35, 59, 65, 72, 98, 108, 125-127, 158, 222, 236, 239, 246, 248
- blind spots - 22, 94, 108, 254, 280, 284
- commitment - 51, 65, 68, 82, 99, 130, 131, 151, 178, 202, 211, 214, 219, 220, 235, 239, 247, 248, 261, 263, 266, 268, 273, 275, 278, 285, 287, 304
- defensiveness - 22, 67, 235, 266
- encounter - 44, 77, 240, 244, 247, 294
- feelings - 2, 25, 28, 29, 31, 32, 35, 40, 42, 44, 45, 49-51, 58, 59, 60, 65, 70, 74, 75, 77, 78, 83, 90, 94, 95, 97-102, 105, 106, 111-115, 117-125, 128-131, 135, 138, 140, 149, 152-154, 159-161, 163, 177, 184, 185, 198, 202, 211, 212, 215, 216, 219, 227, 233, 242, 243, 247, 249, 251, 252, 256, 271, 274, 276, 279, 290, 322
- life story - 31, 102, 189
- listening - see *listening*.
- objectives - see *objectives*.
- observation, observations - 22, 36, 41, 45, 51, 56, 57, 65, 85, 85, 92, 94, 96, 102, 107, 119, 120, 121, 123, 124, 126, 134, 184, 187, 188, 234, 269, 274, 280, 281, 301, 302, 303
- outcome - 6, 7, 14, 23, 40, 56, 73, 74, 77-79, 91, 99, 116, 134, 135, 190, 207, 210, 214, 219, 225, 233, 240, 241, 244, 258, 264, 265, 266, 270, 273, 281, 293, 295, 300, 311, 314, 315, 316
- questioning - 7, 16, 56, 61, 76, 163, 188, 197, 200, 203, 205, 207, 213-215, 218, 221, 230, 282
- reflection - 6, 24, 40, 42, 45, 73, 75, 82, 83, 93, 94, 95, 118, 119, 120, 121, 122, 123, 124, 125, 126, 127, 128, 131, 136, 137, 140, 141, 145, 150, 151, 160, 179, 184, 185, 187, 188, 194, 197, 207, 212, 213, 214, 217, 218, 220, 235, 240, 243, 257, 258, 259, 275, 277, 278, 301, 302, 303, 307, 310, 312, 321, 325
- responsibility - 6, 9, 19, 24, 27, 29, 40, 53, 57, 63, 65, 66, 71, 72, 77, 96, 99, 110, 116, 140, 158,

167, 173, 191, 202, 218, 221, 225, 229, 234, 235, 237, 239, 242, 243, 248, 250-253, 258, 263, 269, 274, 275, 277, 281, 290, 292, 295, 323-325
- restatement - 23, 42
- self-awareness - 2, 22, 23, 39, 41, 46, 47, 50, 53, 58, 66, 70, 71, 88, 92, 106, 112, 114, 117, 127, 128, 138, 145, 147-149, 156, 160, 163-165, 169, 172, 174, 178, 190, 192, 202, 206, 207, 215-218, 221, 225, 234, 235, 239-241, 248, 250, 253, 281, 282, 284, 292, 293, 295, 300-302, 323
- self-defensive - 23
- self-directed - 40, 45, 93, 100, 118, 319
- self-motivation - 27
- self-reflection - 32, 99, 207, 217, 218, 221, 274, 299, 301, 325
- signature presence - 53, 69, 70
- silence - 42, 45, 138, 140, 212
- summarising - 23, 42, 75, 99, 116, 135, 136, 144, 180, 211, 212, 274, 301
- thinking process - 63, 67, 234
- throw-ins - 241, 245, 247, 260
- transference - 22, 253, 301, 307
- transition - 24, 30, 34, 50, 136

coaching research:
- academic - 314, 316
- building your knowledge base - 309, 312, 325
- collaboration - 10, 28, 36, 46, 297, 309, 317
- critical reflective practice - 310
- empirical research - 21, 198, 200, 221, 222, 310, 312
- evidence-based - 21, 200, 222, 277, 312, 313, 314, 316, 318, 319
- measurable results - 34, 205, 310
- measurement, measuring results - 3, 4
- multi-cultural - 24, 57, 170, 314, 315, 323
- multi-disciplinary - 313, 315
- multi-methodological - 31
- peer-reviewed - 21, 313, 315, 316
- practitioner research - xi, 1, 3, 10, 21, 28, 33, 164, 167, 172, 194, 221, 222, 232, 241, 244-246, 254, 255, 264, 276, 281, 282, 296, 297, 304, 306, 309-317, 321, 324